Expecting a Miracle
ANY DAY WILL DO!

BOOK 1: A BRUTAL JOURNEY OF FAITH

BRENDA JOY DAVIS

Expecting a Miracle!
ANY Day Will Do!
Book 1: A Brutal Journey of Faith

Copyright © 2020 by Brenda Joy Davis

All rights reserved. No part of this book may be reproduced or transmitted in any form or by any means without written permission of the author.

ISBN 978-1-7361604-0-4

Front cover photo by Courtney Davis
Back cover photo by Shannon Montgomery

BY FAITH
these people overthrew kingdoms,
ruled with justice, and received
what God had promised them.
They shut the mouths of lions,
quenched the flames of fire,
and escaped death by the edge of the sword.
**THEIR WEAKNESS
WAS TURNED TO STRENGTH.**
They became strong in battle
and put whole armies to flight.

Hebrews 11:34-35, NLT
Emphasis Added

CONTENTS

Foreword 1
Prologue 3
1   The Backstory 9
2   Diagnosis: Impossible 19
3   A Rollercoaster 31
4   The Advocate 39
5   An Army 55
6   Ahhhh, Routine! 61
7   It's Not Brain Surgery! . . . Or Is It? 69
8   The Loneliest Christmas Together 85
9   Whatever You Do, Don't Fall 97
10 The Ed Hit Slinky Saga 111
11 Since You Insist 123
12 Round Two! 139
13 To The "Mustard" Station! 159
14 Melted Cheese On The Sidewalk Of Life 167
15 Welcome To Our Crazy Life – Episode #342 179

16 I Survived 197
17 Preparing For A Marriage, Not A Wedding 207
18 Therapy And Lots Of Babies 217
19 A Story Of Redemption: The Escalon Youth Center 229
20 When Normal Looks Extraordinary 241
21 Continued Progress 255
22 Kidney Stone Havoc And The Hectic Holidays............... 267

FOREWORD

Grab a box of tissues. You will need them! This powerful and heartfelt story will pull you in, hook, line, and sinker. This true and tragic story is told from real and raw emotions experienced throughout the journey of battling Glioblastoma (brain cancer).

This is a must-read for anyone who ministers to individuals or families going through major trauma. It's also a must-read for anyone walking through loss and grief, to help bring hope to your situation.

God spoke to Brenda Davis very early on and told her to share the good, the bad, and the ugly parts of this story in honesty. She has certainly been faithful to that challenge, leaving nothing on the cutting room floor. She exposes her and her husband's most challenging moments, with the focus on helping you understand when you are going through your own firestorm that it's alright to be real before God and man.

Brenda will lead you on a journey that is not just for those who have lost a spouse. There are powerful truths revealed on maintaining your faith in the most challenging of times - from parenting skills, spiritual leadership truths, and how a real church should handle a challenging event in the life of its pastor, to a beautifully rare love story. Finally, you will see how one pastor's faith in action affected his whole community, which will impact and challenge many of you as you read this powerful work.

This book covers a five-year journey of the most brutal attack on one's faith and trust, and even feelings of betrayal by God. Follow Brenda as she deals with every challenge, emotion, and fear that comes their way.

My wife and I are standing with Brenda as she is "Still Expecting a Miracle!"

—Pastor Mark McLeod

PROLOGUE

I SAT AT MY desk, with a feeling of dread, staring at the chalkboard with the day's writing assignment written on it. It read "A Foggy Day." I stared hard at those chalky, white letters, thinking to myself, "Are you kidding me? Who wants to write about a foggy day? I hate writing!!!"

I didn't like this class. I loathed the morning creative writing assignments that sometimes ended up being a homework assignment later on.

It was Mrs. Panero's English class in junior high. I'm guessing that it was 7th grade, but I could be off by a year. Mrs. Panero was a pleasant teacher. She wasn't the problem. The problem was being CREATIVE and finding beautiful, eloquent, descriptive words to paint my story on the canvas for readers to enjoy. I saw no need for such words. They seemed superfluous and annoyed me.

"Fog. What can one say about fog? . . . Wellllllll, it's white! Yes, it's white! Awesome!!! Write that one down, Brenda! . . . Hmmmmm . . . Thick! Yeah, that's another good descriptive word. Add that one to the word bank for my short story . . ." And that was about all I had. Sad, but true. I counted down the minutes that I HAD to write my creative writing story in class. I penned some awful, droopy, short story because I was forced to, but it really wasn't anything I was excited about or proud of.

Days later, Mrs. Panero was elated to read another student's creative writing assignment from that same day aloud to the class. It was a brilliant story of a foggy day in Escalon, complete with the eloquent, descriptive words that Mrs. P was teaching us how to use. It told of a drive down McHenry (a major road that connects our small town to Modesto, a larger city) in the fog, across the McHenry Bridge, and then bammmm! an accident on the bridge that transported them into an alternate dimension, an alternate universe. The story proceeded to engage the reader in a fabulous, fictional tale and grip their attention tightly. Eventually, it wrapped back around to another spontaneous event that transported the main character back to the original scene - the accident on the McHenry Bridge. It was brilliant in every way - the model story for our teacher to use as an example for us of what she was teaching us to write.

I don't remember who wrote it, but you can safely assume that I was sitting at my school desk, cheering on this person's mad skills in my head. I was very impressed.

At that point in time, I was also telling myself, "I am NOT a writer! I'm horrible at it. I don't enjoy it - not one bit. I'll do what's required for these assignments, but being a writer is NOT in my future."

Since that day, I've witnessed other amazing writers, four of them in my own family. My mom has always been one who could pick up a notebook and quickly pen a skit for special occasions at church. At times, she would sit and write children's books and other articles. I was always intrigued by her beautiful gift, but never had the inclination to try my hand at it. My oldest daughter, Cara, can sit down and brilliantly pen thoughts that are on her mind, giving different perspectives on certain topics and holding your attention. Even my second daughter, Courtney, has this beautiful gift. I'm amazed when I read things she has written. My cousin, Marla, can sit down and "paint" you a gorgeous setting with her eloquent, descriptive words. Although I'm not the reader who necessarily needs the Michelangelo-like details in a book, I'm stunned by her creative ability to put you in the moment and help you experience everything the character is experiencing in each moment of the story. These ladies have incredible gifts and, in my opinion, the ability to write whatever they put their minds to.

Many times since we started this journey of battling Jim's brain cancer (Glioblastoma Multiforme, grade 4 cancer – a terminal diagnosis), I felt God asking me to share all of it – the good, the bad, and the ugly. After struggling with the assignment presented to me, because it would involve baring my soul and brokenness (even the ugliest of days), I resigned myself to be obedient and give updates about daily stuff as we went along. It didn't seem quite as difficult as I thought it would be and people seemed to enjoy, even anxiously wait for, my updates on Jim. But now . . . well, now sitting down to write this whole journey in book form . . . uhhh yeah, that makes me super nervous, uncomfortable, and self-conscious about my skills. As much as you may want to argue this point with me, it doesn't change my feelings of being unfit for the task. And then I'm reminded of other times in my life when I have wrestled with God about stepping out into unknown territory.

Flashback to Spring 2009:
Jim started sensing God's call to step into ministry full-time. He said that all he could hear was God saying, "I didn't call you part-time. I called you full-time." He had been working part-time at his job as a regional manager of a tile store chain and part-time as the associate pastor at our church. As this shift to full-time ministry started looking like more of a reality, I clammed up. I started telling God, "I think you've got the WRONG person! Jim is the perfect pastor, but I'm not designed to be 'the pastor's wife.' I don't have the skills to fill those shoes. I don't teach Bible study. I don't lead worship. I don't play the piano well. I don't counsel people well. You've got the wrong person." Although I didn't share these insecurities with other people, I argued this point with God frequently.

I attended Ladies' Retreat with our church that year. I enjoyed it and received a lot from what our speaker taught our group, but during a prayer time at the end of one of our evening services, I was slapped in the face with my own words I had been telling God for months. Our speaker, Cindy, in the process of praying for specific ladies, walked directly over to me and said, "You've been telling God that He has the WRONG person. He is telling you He has the RIGHT person! He has not made a mistake."

I was floored.

I still had this overwhelming feeling that I was not capable of the duties that lay before me if my husband was to move into a senior pastor role, but how do you contradict what God has spoken to you from the mouth of a person you never shared these insecurities with?

Fast forward a few years:
The departure of our worship leader left a hole in our worship team – the lack of a leader, as well as a keyboard/piano player. I had just started taking piano lessons again to learn a different style of playing the piano I hadn't mastered yet – playing by chords and a simple melody line rather than notes on bass and treble clef (which had proven to be a struggle for me in the past). The opening caught me by surprise, but I felt God gently nudging me in that direction. I fought hard against it. I battled with huge insecurities and the fear of botching our worship services. Even stepping up to LEAD worship, not even playing the piano at the same time, was scary for me.

One day, I specifically remember saying to God, "I'll step up and do this, but I'm still afraid of what it will turn out like. It may not sound very pretty!" I'll never forget the response God gave me: "Brenda, you're NOT responsible for the end result. I AM! I'm just asking you to be obedient."

Once again, how do you argue with that?

Soooo, as I come back to the subject of this book and my insecurities as a writer, I'll be the first one to tell you that I'm NOT a writer. I don't see myself in that light. I have never set out to be a top-selling author of multiple, amazing books. Never once has that been my dream.

Sure, now that I've started penning the pages of this book and seeing that God MAY have a purpose for me writing it, it's exciting to think of the possibility of publishing it and ministering to someone who may be walking treacherous, painful paths similar to ours. I assure you, though, that my first and primary goal for writing our journey in book form is to help me process the unending trauma we experienced for over 3 years. Trauma that I did not have the "luxury" of processing during the moments we endured them. Trauma that is still unresolved. My second goal is to give my children and grandchildren a detailed account of the things that happened in these years – possibly of events that they never heard of, or if they did hear them at one point, their fragile minds did not allow them to fully process them because of the ongoing trauma they were enduring at the time. My third goal, should God find purpose in it, is allowing it to be an avenue to minister to others.

As I wrestle with the idea of this book and struggle with my insecurities - each time I think about it, each time I sit down to type out the incessant drone in my head - I feel God continuing to tell me what He asked me to do from the beginning, "Share your story. Share it ALL – the good, the bad, and the ugly. You are NOT responsible for the end product. I AM!"

And so, here I am . . . filleting myself open for "the world" to see. Trying to be OBEDIENT. If God says I'm a writer, I AM A WRITER. It doesn't matter what I think about it and how uncomfortable it makes me feel.

1

THE BACKSTORY

June 4, 2015 – approximately 2:00 PM

"MR. DAVIS, YOU have a mass in your brain."
The words could barely sink in. We felt numb. It seemed as if this moment all happened in slow motion. We looked at each other, astonished. Words failed us as tears filled our eyes. The doctor's words stung. They cut deep. There is no adequate way to explain a moment as raw as this. Every possible feeling hits your chest like a ton of bricks and leaves you struggling to catch your breath. Your stomach turns and your heart aches to return to the moment that you knew nothing of this horrible, crushing, impending nightmare.

But, there was no going back. Only moving forward. No matter how painful . . .

About 5 ½ months before this day our oldest daughter, Cara, had returned from college. She graduated one semester early and was excited to jump into ministry. God had opened the door for her first pastoral job as a youth pastor just one town away from us. She stayed with us through the holidays, then she and our second oldest daughter, Courtney, moved into a small place on my parents' property together, leaving only our son Christopher at home. He was 11 at the time.

For one month the extra bedroom stayed empty. Only a month! You see, by God's divine orchestration of every detail of our life, He knew what was needed. He knew it long before we ever knew we needed it.

At the end of January, the 25th to be exact, Jim received a panicked phone call just a little after 1:00 AM. We were sound asleep and actually missed the first phone call on Jim's phone. The second call came to my phone. At that moment I knew something was terribly wrong. Little did we know how much this one phone call would change our lives forever.

The call came from Hanna, one of the daughters of a single mom in our church. Through tears she bravely explained that they needed Jim to come to their house immediately, because the paramedics were working on her mom. Jim was not only the senior pastor at our church, but also the volunteer chaplain for the Escalon Fire Department. We both jumped up. I prepared everything Jim needed while he got dressed, frantically grabbing his shoes, warm clothes, and anything else that I could think of that he would need on a cold January night. When he arrived on scene, the crew was still working on the girls' mom. He carefully directed the girls to the other room to console them and their frightened hearts. Then news came that the emergency crew couldn't revive their mother. She was gone. Calls were made by the authorities to notify the girls' half-sisters (who were adults), and ask them to come and take the girls.

That was a Sunday morning . . . a very early start to a sad day. It took some time to calm down once Jim got home. We TRIED to sleep a bit more before we headed off to church. A few phone calls needed to be made to notify those in leadership of the tragic events early that morning. Hanna and Americis came to church that day, at their own insistence, brought by their older sisters and brother. It was a service filled with worship and sadness, comfort and tears.

Let me explain a little more of our backstory before continuing on with this part.

At this time, we had three children: Cara (almost 22), Courtney (19), and Christopher (11). Christopher was adopted from China at the age of 4 ½. Our adoption story for him is one of God's leading, starting first with me and the overwhelming urge to add to our family. Our family didn't seem complete. Jim fought the idea for months, and during that time God told me to stop initiating any conversation about adoption so He could work on Jim's heart. Around August of 2005, out of the blue He dropped a date in my heart . . . November 19th. I wasn't quite sure what this date meant, except to say that I felt that I would receive confirmation one way or another by then. I continued praying and asking God to either remove this urge to grow our family or to change Jim's heart regarding adoption. For months I did my best to stay quiet and not say anything to hinder what God might be doing. On November 18th we were traveling to Yosemite for a Board and Staff Retreat. I was excited that the next day was possibly a day God would bring the answer. But, wouldn't you know it, God opened the conversation between us ONE DAY EARLY, on our drive to Yosemite. I can still picture the exact part of the road we were on when Jim announced that he was open to getting information about adoption. I just about peed my pants with excitement! (LOL. Ok, ummmm, maybe a bit too much information there.)

A sudden, life-threatening illness in January 2006 made it impossible for Jim to be able to attend the informational meeting I had counted down to for weeks, and to say that I was disappointed by this interruption was a huge understatement. But, by spring we were on the hunt to gather bamillions of documents for our international adoption dossier . . . expecting to adopt a girl, as young as possible, and even stating we were open to twins. The room was painted pink. I had purchased a few items here and there, trying to soothe my aching heart during the long wait with a few fun purchases.

After requesting to be considered for multiple children on the special needs list from our agency and not being matched, the next year was disappointing to say the least. In November 2007, we reviewed the new list and, after much prayer and conversation, we submitted to be considered for two different boys and one girl (knowing that we would only be matched with one child if we were selected).

The file for one boy always tugged at me. His impish grin and sweet face called to me as if I somehow knew this child who lived on the other side of the world. His file was always the last one I would peruse on the many days of waiting for news. His was the file I always placed on top before I walked away, glancing back at his photo on top multiple times each day until we received the news. But, we were supposed to adopt a girl, right?!?!

We got the call at the end of November, the week after Thanksgiving. Jim just happened to be at the church office when he received the phone call. He stepped into the fellowship hall, then returned to my office and shouted at the top of his lungs, "IT'S A BOY!!!!!" ... Long story short, we repainted his bedroom (because Jim wasn't gonna have a son in a PINK room), completed a bamillion more forms, waited, waited some more, tried to focus on learning some phrases in Mandarin to pass the time, completed more forms, and then began packing and preparing for our trip. We traveled to China in April 2008, to add our handsome son, Christopher, to our family - a happy, smart, funny, generous boy who attached to us from the first moment and never looked back ... The rest is history.

After this adoption, Jim was determined that we were done growing our family. He was content to continue on as a family of five. I told him that I chose to be soft-hearted and let God decide if He was done using us in this area. He replied many times, "If God brings us another child and drops them right in our lap, then I'll know He wants us to grow our family again. If not, then I think I'm done." So what were the chances that God would just "drop another child in our lap?"

I prayed many times from 2008 to 2014, that God would have His way in our family and use us how he desired. Over time, my prayer actually morphed to "God, if you want to add to our family, I'm willing to do what you ask, buuuuut you will have to speak to Jim first this time. I will take direction from him as You leading us. If You desire to do this in our lives, You have to talk to him and have him take the lead in pursuing it."

And here's where we rejoin the story of Hanna and Americis ...

Monday morning, January 26th, Jim got out of bed extremely early. I knew the death of Teresa from the morning before was still weighing heavily on his heart. He was there in the raw moments. He saw the first responders working on her. He saw the fear and desperation in the eyes of her two youngest daughters in those first minutes. It was not an image he could easily forget. I assumed that he needed to get up to think for a while and clear his head.

I got up at the usual time and got Christopher ready for school. Jim and I were off work, because it was a Monday, so he drove Christopher to school to give me a little extra time to relax before I started on my to-do list. Soon after he returned, he came in to talk to me, expressing that God had laid a heavy burden on his heart for Hanna and Americis, and that he felt we needed to add them to our family if no one else was planning to raise them. He asked me to make some phone calls and get information, to which I responded, "I told God I would not pursue adding to our family without you initiating it." His response: "Well, I'm initiating." Then he agreed to make the calls himself to find out if there were any plans made for the girls yet. Their maternal grandparents were deceased. Their father had been in and out of their lives, but nothing ever consistent or healthy. Their half-siblings were young adults and could try to parent, but they were barely getting their own feet on the ground in life. Their paternal grandparents had them at the moment, but were unable to parent them. They loved them very much and desired to be an active part of their life, but circumstances made it difficult to make a commitment long-term. After long discussions with their paternal grandparents, they felt having the girls join our family would be the best fit for them. Days later, on January 31st, they stayed their first night with us and our home became their home.

I'd love to say the months following were filled with joy and laughter, but that would not be the truth. Because Hanna (age 13) and Americis (age 12) came to our home with very little, we spent hours and hours buying new clothes; sorting through bag after bag of clothes from our family and friends; purchasing items and setting up their bedroom; and figuring out what was still needed.

As if this task wasn't daunting enough, there were new, healthy boundaries that needed to be set (and enforced) in their relationship with each other, and new rules needed to be established for their everyday lives. I don't know how to say it kindly and not be offensive to anyone, but there was a lot of lack in their lives prior to joining our family: in discipline, in their home lives, in responsibility, and quite frankly in their daily needs. They not only had suffered through the loss of their mother and were grieving it, but they lacked a lot. Our whole schedule had to be restructured to encourage an environment of minimal dysfunctional knock-down-drag-outs in one day (between the two of them and between them and us). Specific schedules were set to avoid unnecessary confrontations during the time they got ready each morning, homework time after school, and every other time they would be in close contact with each other. February through April were some of the most stressful months I think I've endured. I had to ask God for strength and wisdom just about every minute of every day during that time. Many times I went to bed in tears.

Now, don't misinterpret what I'm saying. They are good girls. They just needed healthy boundaries and structure to help them navigate life in a more productive manner.

During these months, we researched guardianship information with the state and completed countless documents to become Hanna and Americis' legal guardians. A hearing was set for June 1, 2015 to decide if we had enough documentation and reason to become their legal guardians. We counted down the days. We worried about the sufficiency of our documentation. We fretted that things would be turned upside down for the girls.

At the beginning of May, Jim started having abnormal problems with repeatedly biting his tongue and the inside of his cheek while eating or talking. He complained of numbness around the right corner of his mouth and up into the area of his right jaw. At his first doctor visit, the doctor reviewed all of his symptoms and felt that it fit with the diagnosis of Bell's Palsy. It would last a while, but it should resolve itself in a couple of months. He warned that if symptoms persisted, worsened, or changed, Jim should contact him again to do further testing. Near the middle of May, he noticed worsening symptoms, along with a few new ones – an odd feeling in his right hand, less control with his right hand,

and a slight scuffing of his right foot on the ground when he walked. The doctor was very concerned and ordered a CT scan for him. And then we waited . . . and waited . . . and waited.

On Saturday, May 30th, we took pictures with Jim's whole family. A photo shoot had been arranged by our sisters-in-law. Surprisingly, all five of our children were all able to attend and take photos with us. An impromptu lunch followed at an Italian restaurant and everyone had a wonderful time. You often hear people refer to the "Last Great Day" they had before they received life-changing news . . . well, THIS WAS OURS. It was the last normal day of fun and enjoying the company of Jim's entire family. We left with bellies full of pasta and smiles on our faces.

Monday, June 1st, finally arrived! We headed to the courthouse with Hanna, Americis, their grandparents, and their cousin, prepared to let the judge talk with each of them privately, if necessary. Waiting for our case to be called made me sick to my stomach. Our nerves were on edge. And then we were called, approved, and were excused to go on our merry way. It was official!!! Well, at least guardianship was official. We still wanted to complete an adoption, but . . . well, you know . . . life has thrown other crazy obstacles our way that have made it impossible to focus on paper-chasing for an adoption.

In fact, just three days later our lives changed yet again . . . .

While waiting for the CT scan to be approved, we continued living life and taking care of our responsibilities. Thursday morning, June 4th, rolled around – THE DAY. We took the kids to school. It was the second to the last day of the school year. The kids were almost on summer vacation. I went to work at the church office. Jim dressed in his fire department chaplain uniform for the funeral of an honorary member of the fire department. He headed to the station, then out to the graveside. I met him there.

The next few hours are forever engraved in my memory: Watching the procession and funeral ceremony. Standing next to My Sweet Love throughout the service. Holding his hand and running my fingers across his right hand and fingers. Knowing that we needed to make a decision that day about how to go about getting the care he needed, since the CT scan had yet to be approved by insurance. The time seemed to go by so slowly, not because of the funeral service, but because of the uncertainty of the remainder of the day. As I stood caressing his hand, I remember wondering how life was going to change from that day on.

After attending the service, we stopped at the funeral reception for a time. At that point, I called the doctor's office one last time to find out if the insurance had approved the scan yet. No. No approval. (Sigh!) So we decided to head to ER.

Jim still had his fire chaplain uniform on from the funeral. The nurse at the front desk was very kind to him and assured him that they would take good care of him. In a matter of minutes, he was triaged. He sat in the waiting room for a few more minutes, then was called to the back and placed in a bed in a unit that was completely empty. A quick review of symptoms was done, along with medical history and allergies. Within 15 minutes he was taken to get his CT scan and brought back to the unit. Our oldest daughters, Cara and Courtney, arrived and had just entered the room before the doctor introduced himself. He politely asked them to step out so he could talk with us privately, so they stepped into the hallway to wait.

And then the news . . . "Mr. Davis, you have a mass in your brain."

1st Photo as a Family of Seven (Disneyland – February 2015)

The Last Great Day (May 2015)
Photo Credit: Samantha Thomas

2

DIAGNOSIS: IMPOSSIBLE

THE NEXT MINUTES, hours, and days are a blur in my mind, speckled with moments of clarity.

Jim and I tried our best to pull ourselves together so I could ask Cara and Courtney to rejoin us in his ER room. The attempt was futile. As I rounded the corner to get them I lost my composure all over again. We broke the news to them and all cried together.

Next, it was time to contact family and friends. My parents were already planning to pick up Hanna, Americis, and Christopher after school, but I had to tell them what the doctor had found. Jim's mom had been waiting all day to hear some news on Jim. She knew we were going to the hospital, but we hadn't updated her yet. I couldn't bring myself to call her and break the news to her in sobs, so I called Jim's brother, John, to ask him to do it in person on our behalf. Unfortunately, I forgot that his oldest daughter's 8th grade graduation ceremony was that evening. Had I remembered, we could have waited a few hours until after the ceremony was over. A few more family members and friends were contacted throughout the rest of the day/evening. Later that night I posted the dreaded Facebook post telling the rest of our friends and family of Jim's brain tumor diagnosis.

Jim was admitted to the hospital and moved to a room. Cara went home after a while. Courtney stayed with us and slept on the couch-bed in the room. I climbed into Jim's hospital bed with him and snuggled him as we both slept. There were raw moments of tears and fear throughout the night and next day.

Friday was the last day of the school year. Our three youngest kids came for a quick visit after school, accompanied by my amazing mom. My wonderful dad brought them again on Saturday morning, and Jim and I walked to a nearby waiting room so we could visit with all of them together. Other family members and friends visited on Friday and Saturday as well. Some were so thoughtful to bring snack baskets and food so we would continue eating well and not have to go out to pick stuff up. Others brought money to help with meals and gas.

After more testing to scan for any other cancer in Jim's body and see exactly what they were dealing with, it was decided that he needed brain surgery. A neurosurgeon at the hospital came in to discuss the surgery. Taking the advice of my wise cousin, Sheri, we opted to be sent to a specialty hospital to do the surgery there, rather than to stay at our local hospital for it. Arrangements were made for Jim's transfer. Stanford had a bed open and the neurosurgeon agreed to take his case. Family and friends gathered to catch him before he left, and Jim was transferred there on Saturday evening.

I remember it like it was yesterday: walking to my car with our best friends at the top of the hospital's parking garage. Fear was starting to sink in. As we said our goodbyes, Arney and Dana expressed once again how much they wished they weren't leaving for our church's Mexico Missions Trip the next day. Their hearts were heavy. My heart was heavy. The unknown was spread out thickly before all of us. They prayed with me one last time, then we parted ways.

I'll take this moment to explain that I grew up in Escalon, California. . . . And here's where most people say, "Esca-what?" It's a small town of about 7,500 people.... I'm a small-town girl. I have always hated Bay Area traffic. I have always hated driving in heavy traffic or in unfamiliar areas. Jim was my chauffeur for any trips to the Bay Area, Los Angeles, and the like. I didn't mind driving anyplace else, but to drive in these places, no thank you!

Jim was loaded in the transport ambulance, headed for Stanford. Courtney and I needed to drive there in our own cars. We were going separately because Court needed to be able to leave if we stayed too long. Cara couldn't join us until Sunday afternoon because of obligations at her church on Sunday morning. My parents had our three youngest kids. Our best friends were finishing preparations to leave for Mexico with a team the next day. It was late in the day, so asking anyone else to accompany us seemed unnecessary. They'd just have to drive right back.

Court led. I followed. We navigated our way to Stanford, but took a wrong turn at some point, avoiding crossing any bridge. Pretty much, that means we took the long way around to get there. We should have crossed a toll bridge somewhere. Hahaha! I tried hard not to panic as we got further into unfamiliar territory for my driving skills.

Finally, we arrived at the hospital. Where do we park? Where do we go? Where is Jim? We had been told that a team would be looking for us. . . . What team? Where would they be? How will they know we are the ones they are searching for? . . . We found the underground parking garage. I grabbed my bags (because we had been told we would be able to stay at the hospital with Jim) and searched for the elevator, the entrance to the hospital, the wing Jim was supposed to be in, and then found Jim's room.

No team. No one searching for us. No cheery greeting. But, whew, we had finally arrived!!!

Woohooo!!!

I'm pretty sure a gold star was put on my driving record that day. We had arrived and Jim was here, too. Relief. I could breathe a bit now, right? I could tell Jim of my courageous drive to Stanford and breathe. Or so I thought . . .

Court and I stepped into Jim's room. It was immediately evident that two other patients were in this small room. Hmmmm, ok. Well, I'm not sure where I'm gonna sleep, but I guess a chair will do. As long as I can stay with my guy, I guess I can sleep anywhere. I smiled and stepped over to the left side of Jim's bed. Court went to the right. My bags were heavy and hanging from my arms. Within minutes, a nurse entered the room and announced that we'd need to step out so they could do a quick scan. We obliged and I squeezed out the door, almost losing the bags off my shoulders. The scan was complete and we were given permission to re-enter the room. We stepped in and tried to talk with Jim again. I asked the nurse about where we'd be able to stay for the night (as was promised to us), only to be told there was no place for us to stay during the first 24 hours. Jim would need to be assessed and he had to be in this observation room during that time. Ummmmm, come again? We have no hotel reservations. We don't know the area. We are two ladies alone. It's dark now. Annnnd, you expect us to leave our loved one?

Then it got even better. A member of the neurosurgery team stepped in and asked us to step out again. He was brief, but as he started to leave the room he mentioned that a brain biopsy would be scheduled for Sunday (the next day) or Monday. Biopsy? Not brain surgery? He explained that the tumor in Jim's head was spiderous and couldn't be removed whole. The tentacles from the tumor would remain. They were planning a biopsy to confirm their suspicions of the type of brain cancer Jim had. Cancer? This was the first time this horrible word was used in our journey.

So, let's recap: The big C. No surgery. Biopsy instead. No place to stay for the night. Can't stay with Jim. No team to help walk us through these devastating moments. Our emotions were raw.

Here's where I'd really like to say that being the mature adult that I am, I gathered myself together and handled the situation maturely and confidently . . . Yeah. That sounds great, but that's not quite what happened that night . . .

Standing in the hallway, waiting for Jim's nurse to tend to some things, I fell apart. Like, I seriously became the sobbing lady that was falling apart in the hospital hallway. Courtney followed suit. Soon we were brought one chair. I sat in the chair and continued sobbing. Courtney sat on the floor in front of me. Another patient was taking his walk through the hallway. He had a feeding tube in his nose and was pushing his IV pole. He thoughtfully offered to get me some coffee, then water, then asked the nurses station for tissues for us. (As if he didn't have his own problems!) At some point a nurse told Courtney that she really didn't want to be sitting on the hospital floor because of the terrible germs and bacteria on it. She wasn't concerned. In normal circumstances we both would have been completely grossed out by it, but we were too devastated to care.

Jim appeared in the doorway. He asked if we could go to the waiting area and talk. The nurses approved it. They offered to take my heavy bags and keep them until we returned. We walked a way down the hallway and found a large sitting area. Court and I will forever call that waiting space "The Crying Corner." We were the only ones there. Perfect. I was still trying to glue myself back together. Jim tried to encourage us to go find a hotel room. I continued sobbing uncontrollably. Jim cried. Courtney cried. We all cried together.

Courtney broke away and called our friend, Dana. Dana told her to put me on the phone. I took the phone and sobbed uncontrollably as she tried to convince me to leave the hospital for the night. I cried as she told me they should've just made the trip with us. I refused to leave the hospital. Nothing could console me. Nothing could console any of us at the moment.

Jim asked Courtney to go back and check on something at the nurse's station. She agreed to go. Moments later she ran back down the long hallway and said, "They're gonna move us to another room!" Finally!!! Finally, some answers to our dilemma.

Once Jim was moved to a private room, we started to calm down a bit. A rollaway bed was provided. Only one, as we were told there weren't many available AND the room wouldn't hold more than one. (We found out later, that we had to keep tabs on that bed so no one would sneak off with it for another family.) Court curled up on the rollaway bed. I claimed a small slice of Jim's bed, squeezing in next to him for most of the night. When I felt like he needed more room, I sat up in the chair next to his bed and tried to find a comfortable, upright sleeping position for a while.

Sunday crept in quietly. Blurry eyed, we all got up and tried to prepare for the day. More tests for Jim were ordered first thing. They had to stick small circles to his head that looked like lifesavers. These helped them to get exact locations on the MRI for his brain biopsy.

The neuro team finally made their first appearance. They squeezed into the room with us, about five of them in all (if I remember correctly). The team was friendly and caring. They notified us that Jim's biopsy would be scheduled for Monday due to scheduling issues. At this point, we had the first discussion of what they thought Jim had: Glioblastoma Multiforme, grade 4 cancer – the most aggressive type of primary brain tumors. No cure, only treatment to prolong life. I remember them telling us it was the same brain cancer that Vice President Joe Biden's son, Beau, died of just a week before. Welllllll, that's just grrreaaaat!!!!

Courtney grabbed her phone to search for information on this aggressive cancer, breaking into tears within moments. I just stood there thinking, "If this man wasn't able to get the best-of-the-best care to save his son, what are our chances?"

Of course, our first question was "How long does he have left?" The answer: "18 months is the median survival rate. Some people live longer, some shorter." . . . 18 months. Hmmmm. 18 months takes us MAYBE two more Christmases. It's weird the way we try to gauge time sometimes. Would he make it to that second Christmas? Would we be preparing to say our final goodbyes around Christmastime? MEDIAN survival rate? Would we be saying goodbye BEFORE THEN? Our thoughts raced. Our emotions ran amuck. There was no way to grasp this news - news more horrible than that we had received days earlier. We tried to hold ourselves together as the team finished their assessment and attempted to bring comfort. Then they gave the details for upcoming events.

Once they exited, the three of us had to take some time to recover. . . Silence . . . Tears . . . Muttered comments through the tears . . . Repeat . . . Again, there's just no adequate way to express the raw, bitter pain that comes in these moments. I just can't.

At this point, we devised a plan to help us stop our incessant crying and have full conversations. In an effort to redirect our thoughts, we started listing kitchen household items out loud, "Pots and pans. Towels. Forks and Spoons. Plates . . ." After a while, we usually only had to look at each other and say, "Pots and pans . . ." and we'd chuckle together, realizing the other person was trying to help us push past the emotional moment. It still works for us today.

Transport assistants came to move Jim for his MRI. Court and I grabbed a few snacks from the cafeteria to pass the time, then rested in his room while we waited for his return.

Once he returned, Jim walked the halls in his unit, back and forth. Sitting and waiting around was not happening. He was on the move. Sometimes we walked with him. Sometimes he walked alone. He was not gonna sit in that room all day. In fact, the nurses came searching for him most of the day because they needed to get vitals for his chart. At one point, they told me he HAD to go back to his room so they could record needed vitals before their shift ended. Once this was done, Jim was up and out the door again. There were halls to walk and people to watch!

Our friends, Cliff and Jessica, visited late morning, bringing gifts of a new phone charger and SOFT Kleenex. I emphasize the word "soft" because we could not bear to use one more rough, sandpaper-like, hospital-issued tissue without our noses falling off. I asked Jessica for the softest she could find (lotion on it, if possible). Our emotions were on overload and our noses were paying the consequences. Cliff and Jessica visited for a while, then headed back home.

The afternoon brought more visitors with it: Jim's parents and his oldest sister. My parents arrived a bit later, then Cara, then my brothers and sisters-in-law. By this time, Jim and Courtney were relaxing at "The Crying Corner." Since Jim was a people-watcher, it helped him pass the time a little better.

We had waited all morning to talk to Cara about the news we'd received, knowing that her responsibilities that day would be hindered if we tried to give her news over the phone – not to mention that she still had to drive a few hours to get to us. We decided it was best to tell her face to face. Moments after she stepped over the threshold of the hospital, I greeted her and whisked her away to an area away from the group so I could break the news. Stunned, she took the news gracefully, not fully knowing how to respond to the greeting mixed with some of the most horrible news you could ever hear about your dad.

We took turns breaking the news with our parents and siblings, sharing that the doctors thought it was aggressive cancer - keeping information somewhat open, but somewhat vague. We, ourselves, could barely process the information. How could we expect them to process it so quickly?

As for social media posts, those were kept extremely vague. For some reason I just couldn't bring myself to share the name of this horrific cancer that the doctors said was growing in my husband's brain. I think in some ways calling it by name showed that I acknowledged the dreadful news of the truth. And so I avoided it the best I could. "Aggressive Cancer." "Spiderous." "Biopsy tomorrow." These were all acceptable words, but "Glioblastoma Multiforme, grade 4 brain cancer with no cure" was not acceptable. In fact, I held out hope that the biopsy would show different results.

My brothers, knowing Jim's love for root beer floats, ran to the nearest store and bought everything needed for the gathering at "The Crying Corner." We had grown into quite a large group, taking up most of the sitting area. We enjoyed root beer floats together. Jim had a big smile on his face and MRI lifesaver-looking stickers stuck to his head. Eventually, the last bit of ice cream in the container started to melt, signaling the end of our family visit. Hugs, tears, and words of affection were shared.

Before they left, my brothers worked diligently to make hotel arrangements for Cara and Courtney for the night, as the four of us would not fit in the hospital room together and get any real sleep. Little was available in the immediate area because of special events and graduation ceremonies, but they were able to secure a hotel room not too far from the hospital. They escorted Cara and Court to the hotel to get them checked in and secure for the night, then headed for home.

Monday morning didn't creep in as quietly as Sunday did. In fact, it hit like a ton of bricks. Early morning arrangements were made for Jim's brain biopsy. Visits from the neuro team. (Jim reminded the surgeon to leave a gnarly scar on his head, not just a cute incision. His reasoning: "Chicks dig scars." Hahaha.) Check lists were checked multiple times. Then Jim was moved to the surgery prep unit. Soon he was taken off to surgery and I was excused to wait in the open waiting room, overlooking other areas of the hospital. Cara and Courtney were en route, as they had slept in a little bit that morning, understandably. My friend, Jessica, drove a few hours through Bay Area traffic just to sit with us while we waited. The family photos we had taken together the previous week had been edited and were available that day. My sister-in-law was kind enough to send me multiple pics while we waited. That helped to pacify me and make the time pass a little quicker.

After a while, the neurosurgeon came looking for us. His kind demeanor was calming. His words were not. The biopsy was done and Jim did well, buuuut then he proceeded to inform us of the results. He said that the initial, frozen part of the biopsy they did pathology on in surgery confirmed Glioblastoma (GBM), but that he would send the tissue off for pathology just to be sure. We waited another hour, then Jim was moved back to his room.

I don't remember much about the rest of the day, except that: I showered in the girls' hotel room before rushing back to the hospital; Cara headed back home so she could go to work the next day; and Jim and I convinced Court to do a dinner run to Panda Express. Again, posts on Facebook were kept vague. I could barely cope with the news. Having others panic alongside me was not going to help me process any better or faster. I convinced myself that I could share THAT news once it was confirmed by the final pathology report we would receive later.

Tuesday, June 9th, arrived. Jim was being released that day, so I was up early, getting ready, packing up our bags, and transporting them to the car 3,000 miles away (or so it seemed) to the underground parking garage. Once Jim was released – which, by the way, felt like being released into nothingness – we followed Courtney through the maze of streets out of Palo Alto, across the bridge, and finally to an area that was more familiar to me.

The pain in our hearts felt like a huge fog had fallen on us that we couldn't navigate through. Jim shared deep, cutting thoughts concerning his situation as it pertained to our relationship and his impending parting from this earth. Tears flowed as we navigated through Dublin, then Livermore, over the Altamont, and into Tracy. Reality. Fears. The unknown. They hovered thick and clouded every thought. We were heading home. Home to our beloved town that was familiar and comforting. But nothing about the days ahead would be familiar or comforting. Everything from here on out would be scary and unknown...

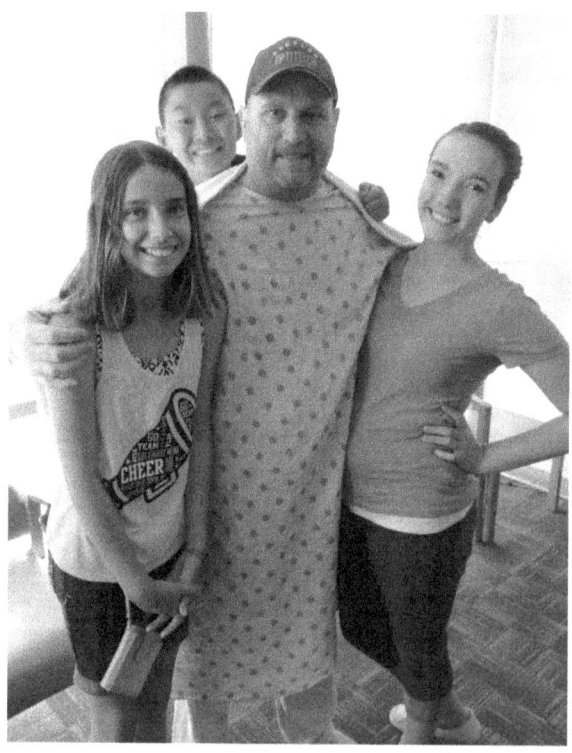

Jim at Memorial Hospital with Hanna, Americis, and Christopher – After Diagnosis (June 2015)

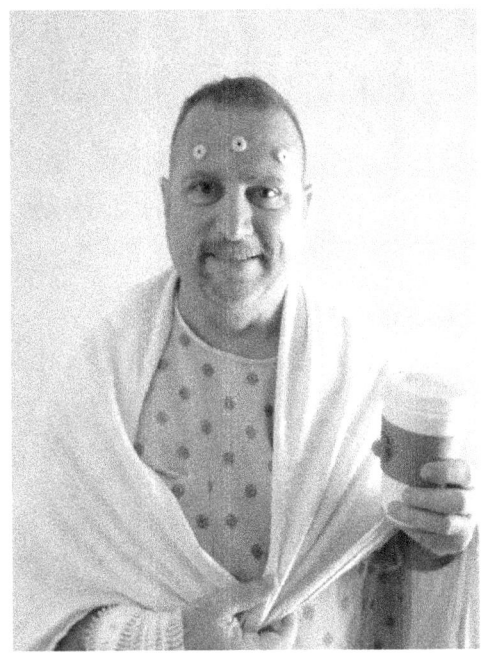

Jim - Ready for his MRI at Stanford (June 2015)

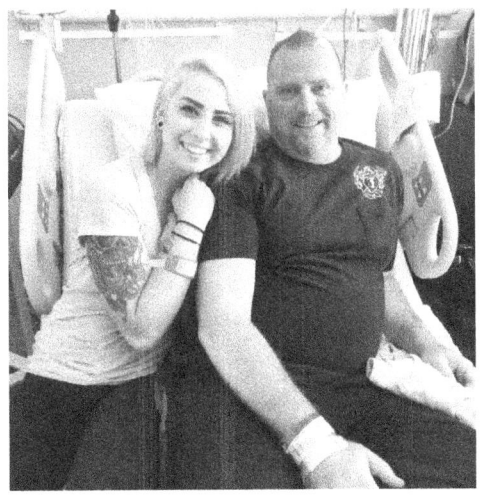

Jim & Courtney - Waiting to be Discharged from Stanford (June 2015)

3

A ROLLERCOASTER

HAVE YOU EVER been in line for a new, wild rollercoaster? Thoughts and fears grip you tight as you think of the dips, twists, turns, and upside down loops coming ahead. Screams from other riders ring in your ears. You don't quite know what to expect, but it's gonna be exhilarating and frightening all at the same time.

Maybe you're like me when I was in the fourth grade. My family made a trip to Southern California to see my aunt and uncle. While we were there, we all went to Disneyland. My parents, aunt, and uncle allowed my older brothers, my two cousins, and I to go ride Space Mountain together. It was my first time. "Space Mountain? Sure!!!" I was nine. Space? What could be wrong with a ride about space? It sounded fun . . . at least until we got closer and closer to the loading platform and I could hear the screams.

My heart started pounding. My hands were getting sweaty. I stopped talking as much because a lump of fear began to form in my throat. Then I started to object to this wild ride, saying that I didn't want to go. Nope, nope. Four, older teenage boys were not gonna let me out of this gig. They wanted to ride, so I was gonna have to ride with them.

Just before the loading platform I saw my chance. An exit sign. I thought through the route we had taken to the ride once we left my parents in front of the castle. I was only nine, but I was extremely observant and I definitely knew the way! Obviously, they were just ole', tired adults, so they would be waiting at the same place for us, right? I could go sit with them and nobody would miss out on the ride. So I bolted! I bolted out that exit door and ran as fast as I could through the long exit until I was almost out in the open again. My cousin ran after me, calmed me down, and cautioned me to stay with him because it was not safe.

Apparently, those adults had other plans for fun, without us. They would NOT be in front of the castle where we left them. Who knew???

Our journey with Jim's cancer diagnosis started something like my ride on Space Mountain (or lack thereof). I thought I could handle it. I thought we were strong enough to hop on the ride, expecting lots of dips, twists, turns, and upside down loops. We knew it definitely wasn't going to be a dull ride.

I had purposely chosen not to look up statistics on GBM at that point. I knew I couldn't handle "the screams of other riders" just yet, lest I bail prematurely. I had to stay strong and focused to help advocate for Jim. Statistics were not going to derail my efforts to tackle this "ride" with everything I had. Bolting out the nearest exit door was not an option. Our faith was in God, not statistics, so why set myself up for failure? But, I guess somewhere along the way I was counting on someone to be our fail-safe. Someone to be "over by the castle" if the ride got too scary, if I wasn't able to manage the details of Jim's care like I thought I could. In fact, we hopped on, trusting that even through the twists and turns, SOMEONE knew the way and would keep us on track.

I have always assumed that once a person is diagnosed with cancer, a nice group of helpful, informed people step in and help you with every detail, every decision, every twist and turn. A group of people who stick with you for the long haul. And I'm sure there are tons of groups out there that do their job well to help cancer patients and their families navigate the unknown road ahead. For us, we thought things were going to work that way. We depended on it! Then we hit an upside down loop right off the start.

A week later we found ourselves back at Stanford as planned, talking about pathology results (which confirmed GBM); discussing survival statistics; talking about where to go from here for treatment. It was a long day, full of a lot of information.

One of the medical assistants on Jim's team was put in charge of charting his basic information. You could tell from the moment he stepped in the room that he wasn't sure how to approach us. He appeared very serious, very professional, and was extremely careful with his word choice. Eventually Jim broke the ice with him as he asked about the statistics of GBM and started cracking jokes about how "lucky" he was to get such a rare disease – fewer than 200,000 US cases per year. Jim said he should go out and buy a lottery ticket, but quickly corrected himself and said that he wouldn't win the lotto. The medical assistant didn't miss a beat. He said he'd buy a ticket right after Jim and would probably win, to which Jim laughed and agreed.

Not knowing the boundaries of this new disease, Jim asked him about the possibilities of traveling. Of course, his first thought was of Disneyland. He asked about riding rollercoasters and suggested that he could get a helmet to protect his head. (Hahaha! That was Jim for ya.) But it didn't stop there. Jim added that he could have flames painted on the side of the helmet to make it look cool. By the time we left, the medical assistant was well aware that we intended to have the best attitudes we could – laughing when we could laugh, but crying when we couldn't contain it any longer.

We left Stanford with a series of new appointments that were scheduled for the end of that week – more tests, scans, and doctor appointments. When we returned later that week, plans were already in the works for a five-day intense radiation therapy, paired with oral chemotherapy. The radiation therapy would replace the usual six-week, five-days-a-week therapy, so we would only have to be at Stanford for one full week. It was a blessing! We still had three teenagers at home, two of whom had joined our family only months earlier and needed consistent rules and boundaries set for them. It would be a win, win situation – shorter therapy that still allowed us to be home most of the summer. Arrangements were made so we could stay in Stanford's patient housing for a week. Everything was good to go. Or so we thought . . .

Chemo and radiation were set to start the following Monday. Over the weekend, we received a call that put the brakes on everything. After careful review, they felt that the intense, five-day radiation therapy was not the best option for Jim. They reviewed his scans and felt that the size of the tumor was too big for the therapy they were offering. HOLD THE PRESSES! EVERYTHING YOU THOUGHT WAS GONNA HAPPEN HAS CHANGED. THE UPSIDE DOWN LOOP JUST MADE YOU LOSE YOUR LUNCH. It was a punch to the gut . . . But wait! . . . "Mr. Davis can still come for the next six weeks, five days a week to do the normal radiation therapy." After giving it a lot of thought and prayer, we decided THAT was not an option for us. Our whole family would suffer with that option (our parents, our kids, our extended family, our friends, and us), so it was time to find an option that would work for us – all of us.

And so we started back at square one.

Stanford was willing to work with their clinic in Turlock to continue plans for Jim's radiation and oral chemo, but that was easily 45 minutes to an hour away from our home . . . and we would have to travel it five days a week for six weeks. Other options? No. Any other option that was closer to us would take Jim out of Stanford's care. They would not work with local doctors to execute the treatment plan. So, on Monday morning – the day Jim was supposed to start his intense, five-day radiation in Palo Alto – I started making phone calls to search for another rollercoaster outside of Stanford's network . . . Hey! I'm just keeping with the theme here! LOL

I thought we were only looking for a radiologist. We were so new to this journey of cancer that I didn't realize Jim needed a care team that included both a radiologist AND an oncologist. I found a radiologist! A great one, by the way. But, once I contacted their office they kindly informed me that I'd need to select a local oncologist for Jim. Done! We were on our way. Both doctors were excellent and willing to jump on board right away.

And then we hit what seems best described as a dip, twist, turn, AND an upside down loop.

The radiologist's techs came up with the exact radiation plan that Jim needed. It hit the tumor at every angle they could think of. But, insurance didn't like the plan because of its title. Its title made it fall into the gray area of "experimental," even though plenty of effective radiation treatments were happening with this title. Multiple phone calls to the insurance company followed the news of this glitch. I got to the point where I just had to start saying, "If you can't help me, don't waste my time. Let me talk to your supervisor. I'm not taking no for an answer. I'm not hanging up until I get an answer. You need to authorize the needed treatment."

What did that get me? That got me a telephone babysitter – a sweet one, at that. Seriously, her job was to keep me on the line and pacified, while Jim's paperwork sat on someone's desk awaiting authorization/rejection. She talked about everything under the sun while we waited. She checked on the status multiple times. At the end of the work day we still didn't have any answers, so she gave me her direct line so I could call her the next day.

I called her back the next morning, right when she said she'd be at her desk again. She checked the status. My fingers were crossed. Uhhhhhh, nope! Not good news. Minutes after we hung up from our call the night before, her supervisors declined care based on the title of the radiologist's plan of care.

Ugh! How many twists and turns were we gonna encounter at the beginning of this rollercoaster. Don't they usually save the major spirals and loops for the middle of the ride?

Long story short, the radiologist tech painstakingly took the time to map out THE SAME EXACT TREATMENT on the traditional, insurance-approved plan with the correct title. Dumb, huh? Same plan, different name. Approved!!! I'm not sure how that even works, but it was my first eye-opener in the healthcare world concerning cancer treatment. Yaaay, 'merica!

Along with these twists and turns of getting treatment started, our emotions had jumped on their own emotional rollercoaster. Amid the overwhelming stress of the phone calls, I had major meltdowns, fearing I wasn't accomplishing anything to help My Love.

Then there were the nights we laid next to each other in bed, as we sobbed uncontrollably into our pillows, trying to stay quiet so the kids couldn't hear us. I wailed that I didn't want to be left alone and this wasn't the agreement we made all of these years. We seriously had always said that we were going to die together – whether that was realistic or not, that was OUR plan. Jim shared his deep grief over leaving me alone and the hurt it caused him to think that I'd possibly find someone to live out the rest of my life with. (Clarification: Not that he didn't want me happy, but that he wanted me to always be HIS. I hope that doesn't sound wrong. Please know that it isn't penned in that way. We understood each other. Don't search for something that isn't there.)

On one of those days in the first two or three weeks, we finally got to the point where we could start talking about Jim's wishes for his funeral. Talk about one of the hardest conversations you could ever have! This is close to the top of the list, I'm sure. We discussed details and I began writing them down at the back of the medical notebook I had started. We didn't get far. Our emotions were so raw. Our hearts were so incredibly crushed. We couldn't finish the conversation in one sitting, so we tabled it until we recovered. Upon revisiting the funeral details days later, we hit the high spots and Jim asked me to just fill in whatever was missing when the time came. It was much too painful to dwell on too long.

Early on, God started dealing with my heart about sharing our journey. Sure! I could do that. Then came the caveat: He was requiring me to share it ALL . . . the good, the bad, the ugly. . . Huh. An invitation not as inviting as I first thought. That would require me to be vulnerable. I would have to share my weakest moments. I would have to lay my weeping heart out for "the world" (actually just friends and family at the time) to let them feel my darkest feelings and see my weaknesses.

God continued to nudge me in this direction, cautioning me that if I didn't share it ALL He would not get the full glory He deserved for what He was doing as we walked this rocky path. If people only saw good reports, they wouldn't see the value of how He had worked to sustain us. I agreed and started doing regular posts to update friends and family on our status, eventually coming up with the signature line of "Expecting a miracle! ANY day will do!!!" Sound familiar?

Expecting a miracle? Yes. We had resolved ourselves that God was in control of Jim's life. Nothing would take him earlier than the days God had predestined for him to live. Our God is faithful and trustworthy. If we had preached His Word and proclaimed that from our very own lips for decades, why would we start questioning his character and trustworthiness now? How did that even make sense? Trust Him only when things are going well? Stop trusting Him when our world falls apart? NO! If there was ever a time to trust that our God was mighty, trustworthy, faithful, our provider, our healer, our hope . . . IT WAS NOW!!! If we didn't, everything we had ever based our lives on was a lie. We had counseled many other people in their times of crisis. We had urged them to press into God and trust Him. It was our turn to live it out. For lack of a better term, it was our turn to "put our money where our mouths were."

Radiation and oral chemo started the week after the Fourth of July, as it needed to be a full week of treatment before giving him a weekend break. Once Jim's face mask was molded, the techs were able to make the last adjustments to his radiation plan and get started. The mask was a full mold of the contour of his face. It fit tightly, pushing against his nose a bit. Radiation treatment would involve him lying on his back on the table and having his head fully strapped to the table. During treatment he wasn't able to move his head at all.

Monday through Friday you could find us at Dr. G-Y's office for radiation for an hour, sometimes two. Sometimes the kids were with us, working on craft projects or reading. Other days my mom took pity on them and let them come hang out with her for a couple of hours. (She really is the BEST!) After radiation, Jim usually took a nap while we diffused frankincense near him. As for oral chemo, that was an every-night thing for six weeks: 8:00 PM anti-nausea medicine, 9:00 PM oral chemo, with prayer beforehand.

We nestled in to our new routine pretty well. We even did our best to make it into the church office to complete work there throughout the week.

About three weeks into chemo and radiation, Jim started having more problems with motor skills in his right hand. It was heavy, hard to control, and hanging quite a bit. He even slammed it in between the car door and his seat a couple of times because it wouldn't cooperate with him. We acquired an arm sling for him to help him keep his balance while walking and to protect his arm from further incidents while getting in and out of the car.

Steroids were used to help with the inflammation in Jim's brain, both from the tumor AND effects of chemo and radiation. The doctors adjusted the dose up and down depending on the symptoms they saw. Slowly, over time, Jim's face began to puff up and eventually "moon face" was his normal appearance.

We counted down the days to the end of his first radiation/chemo cycle. On August 14, 2015, he rang the bell as he left Dr. G-Y's office, signifying the successful end of his treatment. Let me just say, the people in this office were TREASURES to us. They greeted us warmly each day and provided so much love and comfort that it truly helped to make our journey a better one. We felt lost as we exited the building, knowing that we would only be back for short, intermittent checkups after that day.

This rollercoaster had slowly come to a halt. Where we were going from here was a mystery. Only God knew the days coming ahead, the future rollercoasters that would test every bit of our faith, endurance, and trust in Him.

4

THE ADVOCATE

MY TITLES HAVE changed over the course of my life. Along with them, my responsibilities have changed. I've always tried to roll with each new season of life, doing my best to be flexible and learn as I went. Daughter. Student. Secretary. Wife. Mother. Pastor's Wife. Worship Leader. Each title has brought its own joy and struggles. I've learned to change each hat as needed, not necessarily searching for the one with the most authority, but looking for the one that was the priority for that moment.

My new hat: advocate.

Advocating for Jim's medical care was not something I had ever had to do. It was definitely a new hat. It was definitely out of my comfort zone. It was the most important hat I had ever worn, as my husband's life depended on my abilities to advocate for him the best I could. I did not possess a medical degree. I had no formal training, or rookie training for that matter!

I was the wife who couldn't handle medical emergencies. When our oldest daughter, Cara, split her forehead to the bone at eighteen months old, Jim was the one who had to hold it all together: calling 911, putting pressure on Cara's head to stop the bleeding, and keeping me from freaking out. I've never done well with blood. I'm the person who had to have him take the bandage off my arm after a blood test so I wouldn't get woozy. I had a looooooong way to go with this new, fancy advocate hat I was given. I had so much to learn!!! I would need to stretch more than I had ever stretched before.

Two weeks. Barely two weeks after Jim's first cycle of chemo and radiation ended, we faced a new dilemma. Jim didn't feel well. In fact, he felt just awful. We tried to get in to see his oncologist, but had to wait.

In the early hours of Sunday morning, August 25th, while I was taking our puppy out to the backyard to go to the bathroom, Jim decided to take his own trip to the bathroom. As I stepped back in through the sliding glass door in our bedroom, I heard a loud thud. I scrambled to put the puppy back in her kennel. Running to check on Jim, I found him on the bathroom floor, lying on his back. I told him I was calling 911, but he convinced me that it wasn't needed, he just got dizzy from getting out of bed too fast . . . or at least that was the story. He further convinced me to get back in bed, relax, and go back to sleep. Everything was "just fine" and "no reason to panic."

We went to church that morning, took our special guest, Dr. Jay, to lunch (he is the Secretary-Treasurer of the NCN Assemblies of God District – a sweet, trustworthy man who loves people and serves the Lord with all he has), then went home so Jim could rest. For the remainder of the day Jim continued to feel "off" – sleepy, dizzy, thirsty, and just plain awful.

Monday morning, we headed off to see his oncologist. Jim barely made it into the examination room. The doctor was running a little behind. Jim crawled up on the examination table and just laid there, hardly moving. The oncologist examined him, sent him for additional bloodwork, then for a stat brain MRI. They couldn't fit Jim in for an MRI for an hour, so we hopped in our car, drove to grab a bite of lunch to hold us over, and Jim slept in the car. Minutes before we re-entered the building, Dr. S (Jim's oncologist) called me urging me to take Jim to Urgent Care (same building) immediately after his MRI appointment. The reason: His blood glucose was 543.

And this is the point where this advocate learned that long-term steroids can increase blood glucose in the body. Who knew? Add that one to the list.

Jim's MRI appointment was quick and painless. The techs were kind enough to transport him via wheelchair in the back halls to Urgent Care. Upon our arrival, I notified the registration nurse that Jim's blood glucose was 543 and that Dr. S had urged us to bring him over immediately. They registered him, did some basic tests, then notified me that indeed his blood glucose was extremely high and they could not treat anyone over 300 in their facility. He would need to be transported down the street to the hospital. . . . Ummmm, excuse me? Really??? Was I not clear when I said his results an hour before were five hundred and forty-three? Read my lips!

I asked to transport him to ER myself, not seeing the need for the ambulance to transport him one mile down the street and send us a bill. Nope. Not gonna happen. It's a liability thing. He has to go in the ambulance. Jim, feeling lousy, told me just to let it be. He would be more comfortable being wheeled out, than trying to load himself in our vehicle one more time.

My brain was on overload as I texted multiple friends and family to notify them of our newest emergency. I hopped in our car and drove the full mile down the street to the emergency room. We waited together in the ER unit, while additional tests were done and the results from his MRI were processed. The MRI showed a slight brain bleed at the tumor site. The blood tests continued to show elevated glucose levels. A sinus infection was detected (or so they thought – put a pin in that one until later. I'll explain more as our story unfolds), and they started antibiotics. And, surprisingly, they also showed that he needed a few units of blood. We would be staying in a unit one step down from ICU, called CMU.

We shared the room with another patient. I stayed, sleeping on a chair-bed next to Jim's bed. I learned from that point on to notify the nurses in ER that I would NOT be leaving – "If Jim stays, I stay."

He slept a lot and was so weak he could barely get out of bed. After his transfusions, he started to feel a little better, but still remained extremely weak and was very quiet. They started treating his steroid-induced diabetes with insulin and a controlled diet. A dietician was called in to consult with us on meal planning. Another person was scheduled to come show me how to test Jim's glucose and administer insulin shots, since he could not do it with only one hand. A new record notebook was started so I could record Jim's glucose readings and insulin doses. I was overwhelmed by the new responsibilities. Completely overwhelmed. I wanted to cry. I probably did cry at one point. It was more than I could handle. Let's just add a nurse hat to my collection of hats. Why not? I've got nothing better to do, right?

They attempted to discharge Jim the next day. It was waaaay too soon. He could barely muster enough strength to get out of bed and walk a couple of steps. His day nurse kindly pulled me aside and tried to warn me that he might not want to go home because of his diagnosis, notifying me that some patients have a hard time with that so they drag their feet when being discharged. Nope. I was certain that was not the reason. I knew Jim too well. I could read him like a book. He just felt awful still. There was no feet dragging happening here. And, I was right.

The next day, when prompted to do so, Jim got out of bed and showed that he was able to walk to the door and back. It took a lot of effort, but he was motivated to get out of there and go home. He was on the mend.

The weeks and months following that hospitalization were full of many changes: glucose monitoring four times a day; a special diet to keep his blood sugar in check; reading every label on every item I bought; still keeping our household going; sleeping on our couch (Jim in his recliner); and getting to work as frequently as I could. It was draining. Absolutely draining. Without the help of friends and family, we wouldn't have survived such a horrific time in our lives.

At that moment, I thought this drastic change would be one of the most stretching moments in our journey. It was absolutely overwhelming. What else could happen that would stretch me so much?

I dared to ask it, and I soon had my answer. It was not an answer I wanted to hear. And, honestly, if I had known all the things coming for the next few years I would have given up hope at that very moment.

Where's that rollercoaster exit door? The battles were just beginning. The challenges we had seen so far were nothing compared to the ones that were coming our way. Not even close.

We had planned for many weeks to attend the NCN Ministers' Retreat in Seaside, California on September 9-11, 2015. I NEEDED the break. Jim NEEDED a change of scenery. It was going to be a stretch to make it happen, but we decided to run with it. The Secretary-Treasurer that had been a guest at our church weeks before generously made arrangements for us to have his room so we could be in the same hotel as the conference, making it as easy as possible for us. The hotel was sold out, so without his and his wife's generosity, we would've had to use the hotel on an adjoining property. This would've posed an additional challenge because of Jim's need for a wheelchair for long distances. Hotel room secured, we headed off to the retreat with our best friends, Arney and Dana. They taxied us around and helped with Jim the best they could. (We sure have amazing friends!)

Jim reported that he felt weak, extremely short of breath, and just plain ole' crummy. He missed a good portion of the services. He stayed in the services as long as he could, but then asked me to take him to the room to rest on the couch.

He kept complaining of something draining into his mouth. It was a vile smell. One of the most disgusting smells I can recount. Oh, how I loathed that smell. On the final morning of our stay, we all decided that we should head home a few hours early. Arney drove. Dana and I sat in the back of their suburban. Jim barely talked the whole way home. I knew he didn't feel well.

We arrived home early afternoon, just in time for me to pick up the kids from school. It was Americis' 13th birthday, so we had planned to celebrate the next few days as a family, including a sleepover at our house with 3 of her friends on Saturday night. Jim did his best to stay alert and join in the celebrations, but he struggled.

By Sunday, he was feeling worse. We decided to go to church and then we'd head to ER to see if they could check Jim. We thought his "sinus infection" had not cleared and that was the only thing causing him to feel horrible. The craziness from that point is almost indescribable. I'll do my best to do this briefly, and not belabor the point.

We packed up (making sure to have Jim's insulin and glucose monitor and a change of clothes for me). We drove to church. When I hopped out to get Jim's wheelchair, our vehicle slipped out of park and almost rolled over me. Jim, not feeling well but still quick on his feet, stopped the car before it rolled back too far. I loaded him in the wheelchair and took him up the handicapped access ramp to our church. Once I got him settled in the church and service had started, Jim notified me that he had left his phone at home and needed it. I drove back home to get his phone, then back to church. I settled in for a few minutes and tried to catch my breath, but I had missed most of the service by this point.

After service, we searched out my parents to ask them to keep the kids a few hours. We told the kids goodbye. I told them, "Don't worry! It shouldn't take us long. I think they just need to give dad some more antibiotics for his sinus infection." Unbeknownst to me, that was wishful thinking... very wishful thinking.

We arrived at the hospital half an hour later. Jim was triaged and taken in quickly because of the immune system risks from his recent chemotherapy treatment. I retreated to the restroom to change. At church, I was given two new shirts designed especially for me. The front said, "Expecting a miracle. Any day will do!" The back had the verse Joshua 1:9 written on it. I slipped on a pair of jeans and one of my new shirts for the first time.

Once inside ER, it was determined that Jim's blood count was VERY low again. He needed more transfusions. He needed more antibiotics for his "sinus infection." He needed to be hospitalized. Ughhhh. Again? Yup, again. They started his transfusions while they arranged for his room, as he couldn't be placed in a room with other patients due to his compromised immune system. They found a room. It was in the pediatric ward. We laughed about that because Jim was a big kid at heart. It was a very large room with two hospital beds and a large window that gave us great views of the sunset each night. Since Jim couldn't have a roommate, the other bed would be vacant the whole time. We asked about a tentative discharge date. The response: "Oh, maybe about three days."

Jim was settled in, but I was not. Truth is, Americis and Christopher were supposed to leave with their school class the next morning for Science Camp. They would be gone for a week, and with all of the hustle and bustle of the weekend, nothing had been prepared yet. I ran home; washed clothes; searched for "old clothes and shoes" that still fit the kids (which proved to be a serious challenge since Americis had only been with us for a little over 6 months); packed their bags furiously; packed bags from myself; and asked my mom to bring the kids home to stay with Cara for the night. Jim's mom was super helpful and purchased travel-size deodorant, shampoo, conditioner, and soap for the kids, then dropped them off to me. Everything was set to go, so I returned to the hospital to sleep in an awkward reclining chair for the night . . . but only after hiking halfway around the outside of the hospital to the ER entrance because I had arrived so late that the other door was locked. Another lesson learned. Check.

The next morning, I left the hospital bright and early to go home. I picked up the kids; took them all to school; walked Americis and Christopher through the luggage drop-off area; comforted them with words along the lines of "Dad should be home before you get home"; hugged them; and sent them on their way to Science Camp.

We spent the next few days in the pediatric ward of the hospital. I eventually gave in to the extra bed in his room that was calling my name. No one could be placed in his room with him because of his compromised immune system, but I was told the extra bed wasn't for me to use. After a night or two of trying to navigate the weird reclining chair that kept folding up on me, I succumbed to the sweet call that said, "Come sleep here! You'll get good rest!" Now, I know that's against hospital rules, but I'm just gonna say that having a family member stay with a patient; helping care for them all day/night long; and not getting adequate rest themselves is not an ideal situation. That is especially true if said family member is the main caregiver once the patient is discharged to go home. I'll get off my soapbox now.

Jim was given another transfusion and they were monitoring his blood count. He remained short of breath and very tired. I didn't give it much thought because I figured everyone had it under control. I didn't have a medical degree and this advocating thing was still very new for me.

Only, they didn't completely have it under control.

By Wednesday afternoon/evening we felt we were getting closer to Jim being released from the hospital. In fact, I think there was talk that he could go home the next day. They were monitoring his blood count and had asked for a chest CT earlier in the day, but as far as we knew Jim was slated to leave the next day. The CT was to check on something they saw on his scans the day they admitted him. Up until that point, no one sounded concerned. Thankfully, someone decided to double check!

My mom and Hanna came to visit for a little while after school. Courtney came by later and brought us Panda Express for dinner. She ate with us and visited.

As we finished our dinner, packing up our cartons to throw them away, the nurse popped in to talk. She mentioned something about Jim being moved to another room. This was the first we had heard of it. Our first thought was that they needed the room for a pediatric patient, but that was not the case. We found it odd that they would move him one night before discharging him.

The nurse excused herself and said she'd return in a minute. She came back in holding her phone and telling Jim that the doctor needed to talk to him. This was not a sign of good news. I stood holding my breath, straining to hear any bit of info the doctor was giving Jim. Nope. Nothing. All Courtney and I could hear was Jim's side of the conversation. Upon hanging up, he shared that the doctor said they found blood clots in his lungs and they needed to move him to a different unit to monitor him closely. Tears followed. Fear gripped us once again and my dinner decided to take a speedy exit from my body.

I don't remember when Courtney left. All I remember was gathering everything we had in Jim's room, being transported to another room on another floor . . . a much, much smaller room, and the nurses setting up a full cardiac monitor on Jim to keep close watch on him. The Telemetry

Unit was no joke. They had techs watching the stats from Jim's monitor every minute.

Now, when I say the room was much, much smaller, it really is an understatement. There was barely room for Jim's hospital bed, a night stand, his rolling hospital tray, and a chair. To make it even better, they moved a chair-bed into the room for me, making it almost impossible to move about the room without feeling like I was on some extreme obstacle course. Once it was expanded into a bed, it blocked the door to the bathroom. Super!!! This was gonna be interesting. I'm sure my face showed the look of "Are you kidding me?" I was trying hard to hide it and just be thankful that they had a chair-bed for me to sleep on - more comfortable than the reclining chair that attempted to fold me up in it. I wasn't leaving Jim alone, so I needed some place to sleep that would be semi-comfortable.

After Jim was all set up and settled in, I made my way to his restroom so I could change into my sweats for the night. That is, of course, after I folded up my chair-bed so I could get through the door. I stepped inside and seriously could barely turn around. Inside: a toilet; a trash can; a large, covered soiled linens container; and me. I struggled to change without touching everything in sight (as I'm very aware of hospital germs).

As I looked down, I noticed the irony of the moment: I had my Superman t-shirt on that day. Coincidence? I think not!!! Trying to keep my humor in a moment of duress, I found myself chuckling as I continued to struggle to change. When I emerged from the restroom I told Jim, "If Superman can change in a phone booth, I guess I can change in THAT tiny bathroom! I just can't figure out how he changed into his stretchy pants so quickly, in such a confined space, without pulling a muscle!!!"

The humorous moment didn't last long. We both settled down and had a moment to process what was actually going on. Jim had blood clots in his lungs! And, according to the nurses, he would not be able to get out of bed for any reason until the doctor gave the clear. How 'bout sitting in a chair next to his bed? Nope. Not gonna happen. He wasn't even allowed to put his legs over the side of the bed for fear that his blood clots would move. This was serious. Super serious. We wouldn't even understand HOW serious until the days to come.

As this new reality began to sink in, our spirits began to sink as well. We needed God. Jim and I had a time of prayer and sang some worship songs.

We were finally able to say goodbye to Wednesday and get a little sleep. On Thursday, the doctor ordered scans of Jim's legs and they found blood clots there, too. Diagnosis: Pulmonary Embolism and Deep Vein Thrombosis. Blood thinners were started. Jim was still not allowed to get out of bed or sit on the side of his bed. Minimal movement was best. Another transfusion was needed as well. His blood count was still too low.

So, here's a good time to get up and take a break from reading this. Stretch. Play a little music. Put the laundry in the dryer. Make dinner. You choose. Just take a deep breath. I know I need one. As I recount this journey play by play I just feel the need to stop and BREATHE. The tedious details boggle my mind. The incessant drone of my own words recounting these moments starts to wear me down. Here's where I wonder, "Who would ever want to hear these stories? Why would they want to take their precious time to pour over the words on these pages?" And yet, I feel compelled to write them.

So, have you taken that deep breath so we can continue on? You'll need it for this chapter, I assure you. I haven't even been able to sit down and pen the words without taking multiple breaks. I'm ready to skip to the next chapter, but there's much more to the story of this hospitalization that has to be shared.

Deep breath. Annnnd go!

Enter Dr. O . . . Dr. O was my next lesson in learning to pay attention to all of Jim's care and to advocate for him to the best of my ability. Although I thought I had the list of my responsibilities down pat, in fact I did not.

Dr. O was the hospitalist assigned to Jim's care while he was in the hospital. She was a short lady who signaled that she was near by the sound of scuffing shoes coming down the hallway. She was pleasant as she introduced herself to us and started to review Jim's chart. The nurse would usually enter the room when Dr. O visited so she would have the information she needed for Jim's care, but she was detained in another room on this day. After the doctor had reviewed everything with Jim, we had a chance to ask questions. Knowing that Jim was frustrated about being confined to his bed, I asked, "How long will it be before he can get out of bed?" I was surprised by her response, "Oh! He can get up today if he'd like to." Huh? We understood that he would be confined to bed much longer, so I asked, "He can sit in a chair to eat?" She replied, "Oh, yes. That's fine." Then she exited the room.

Minutes later, as we were deciding how/when Jim would get out of bed and where he would sit, his nurse rushed into the room with a panicked look on her face and frantically announced, "I know she said you can get out of bed, but you can't!!!" Apparently, the doctor mistook Jim for another patient in the same wing with similar symptoms/diagnoses. Allowing Jim to get up would possibly send blood clots to his heart, so that was definitely not an option at the moment. He had barely started blood thinners, so there hadn't been enough time for the clots to start dissolving yet.

And so we waited.

The next day, Dr. O made her rounds again. This time the nurse (the same nurse) made sure she was in the room with us. Still wanting to know how long it would be before Jim could get up - annnnd I have to admit that I was checking to see how much I could trust his doctor – I asked, "When can he get up out of bed?" Again, she replied, "Oh, he can get up today!" "He can?" I asked. Then the nurse immediately spoke up and mentioned that he had only been on blood thinner for a couple of days. The doctor quickly corrected herself and made sure we understood that he could NOT get out of bed yet, then exited the room again.

And that, my friends, is when I had my internal panic attack.

I spoke to the nurse after the doctor left. She understood my urgent concerns and took note that NOTHING would be done with Jim unless it was verified by Dr. S (Jim's local oncologist). We needed a fail-safe. We needed someone to advocate for us and double check everything. I could no longer trust that this doctor remembered which patient she was dealing with at the moment.

Christopher and Americis returned from Science Camp on Friday, with many stories to tell of their amazing experience. Their luggage arrived before the student buses, so I searched for their suitcases and sleeping bags in the school cafeteria with the help of some other kind parents and loaded them before the kids arrived. They desperately needed showers and non-camping clothes, so we headed home. I had the chance to update them on Jim's status while they got ready, then we grabbed a snack at Burger King and I took the kids to the hospital for a visit. They told Jim a few of their fun stories from camp; we played cards; and then Jim needed to rest again. Jim's brother and sister-in-law came to pick up the kids to watch the school football game and spend the night.

Over the weekend, a few other visitors funneled through Jim's quaint room. I walked a few of them to the elevator to say goodbye one night. As I was rounding the corner, heading back to Jim's room, the nurse caught me in the hall and notified me that orders were in Jim's chart to bring in a physical therapist to get Jim up and walking again. She saw the orders late in the day and sent a message to Dr. S for verification. By the time she heard word back it was too late to call PT to come in, so she warned me that they'd be in the next day and she wouldn't be working that day. She further warned me that if the physical therapist didn't see the results they were looking for, they might recommend for Jim to go to a rehab center until he was stronger.

As I prepared for bed that night, changing in my "Superman Booth Bathroom" and moving things around the room so I could extend my chair-bed, I just cried. I talked with Jim about my extreme concerns that I had to advocate for him. I did not have a medical degree. I did not know the details of our rights to ask for second opinions or if I should be questioning the doctor's orders. I was not fit for the task. How was I expected to assume this much responsibility for Jim and not know anything? How was this possible? We were ALONE in this and no one had prepared us!

Jim allowed me to continue expressing my shortcomings and fears out loud, then we prayed. We prayed that God would go before us and send us someone to help us navigate the ins and outs of these medical details I had no clue how to navigate. We asked that He would give us wisdom and peace. We asked specifically for an advocate.

Soon Jim was ready to go to sleep. I stayed up a while, posting our prayer request for friends to see on social media. Throughout the night, I woke up multiple times (partly because that's what happens in the hospital, and partly because I had the weight of the world on my shoulders). I prayed each time, cried, and tried desperately to go back to sleep.

I was weary. By this time, we had been at the hospital for over a week. My chair-bed, although much better than a hard plastic chair or a reclining chair that tried to make me into an accordion, was starting to take its toll on me.

We awoke the next morning to the sound of a cheery voice coming from behind the curtain around Jim's bed. "Gooood morrrr-ning!!! I'm your Nurse Advocate for today. Let me know if there is anything I can help you with!" My eyes were still closed as I processed this information. An advocate? Yes!!! That's what we asked the Lord for all night. He had sent us an advocate! My heart raced as I struggled to open my eyes and sit up. But even better than just an advocate, I KNEW THE CHEERY VOICE BEHIND THE CURTAIN! I could trust that person!!! God had sent us an advocate we could trust: It was a sweet friend, Patti, who had attended the same church with us years ago.

I opened my eyes and desperately announced, "WE NEED YOU!!!" In her sweet, calm, sing-song voice she replied, "I heard that you might." The nurse who had helped us the days before put in a word that someone needed to help us navigate the challenges we were facing. Patti wasn't usually assigned the position of Nurse Advocate, but when she was asked to fill the role for that day she had accepted it. She was exactly what we needed. God knew it. He had gone before us and prepared a way.

After Patti had checked on a few things and we had a chance to get ready for the day, she returned to Jim's room. She reviewed everything that had happened with Jim so far (his diagnosis and medical care), then she confirmed that PT was indeed coming in for an assessment that morning. She asked about our concerns and expectations. I was uncertain of what to do regarding the doctor. I didn't want her on Jim's case any longer, but I didn't want to be THAT wife – you know, the one who tells everyone off and fires everyone on her husband's case. It worried me. Patti consoled me and reminded me of Jim's patient rights. We set reasonable expectations for the physical therapists: They would get Jim up once in the morning and once in the afternoon, to give time to accurately assess him before assuming that he needed to go to a rehab facility. As for the doctor, she could be fired from his case . . . Well, that was the plan.

Dr. O came to visit again. I squirmed in my seat as I had to confront her about the reasons we were uncomfortable with the care she had provided. I conveyed my concern of not having a medical degree, but feeling the need to protect Jim because of the mistakes she had made. It was hard to look her in the eye. I don't like confrontation like that if I can avoid it. She took it very professionally and apologized for her actions. Patti had previously explained to me that it might actually work out easier for Jim's hospital discharge to have her remain on for a few more hours, instead of bringing another doctor up to speed before discharging him, so we agreed to keep her so we could expedite the process.

Shortly afterwards, the physical therapists entered Jim's room. Jim's first round of getting up and attempting to walk after about five days of being in bed did not go well. In fact, the charge nurse came to visit me during their first assessment, asking me to contact our insurance company regarding percentages and copays for rehab facilities. She further informed me that the type of facility Jim might need would not be local. My heart sank. I got on the phone and struggled to retrieve the needed info. I didn't know all of the correct terms, so it was frustrating. I jotted down all of the details I could get and walked down to the nurse's station to give them to her.

To my dismay, when I returned to Jim's room, his therapists were already discussing the need to go to rehab. They assured me that they'd try to get him up again in a few hours, but warned that I needed to start preparing for the fact that he wasn't going home directly from the hospital. I was falling apart at a rapid rate. My friend, Dana, called and I unloaded my heavy heart, sobbing inconsolably while I recounted the details of the morning and the fact that they might be moving Jim to a rehab facility out of the area. She hopped in her car and headed to the hospital right away to help me.

After lunch, the physical therapists came to do their second assessment. They helped him up out of bed and stood by to support him if he needed it. Surprisingly, he made it out his hospital room door and a little way down the hall. Dana arrived and passed him in the hall on her way to come talk to me. She was surprised at the quick change in our situation from the time she called to when she arrived. Things were starting to look up!

Some time passed before we were discharged later that day. The charge nurse carefully oversaw every detail. Patti stood by to make sure we were alright with the decisions being made. As Jim was wheeled out to our car, the nurse escorting us assured us that the situation with the doctor would be dealt with, not overlooked.

And, once again, we were bound for home with a wonderful packet full of new information.

As I look back at these moments of despair, a new truth of these experiences emerges. I thought I was Jim's advocate. I falsely believed I was it! I knew I needed to chart his every move, have notes for the doctors when they asked for them, and step in to speak up for Jim when he needed it . . . but I lacked. I lacked the medical education needed for these circumstances. I didn't KNOW what was right in some situations. I didn't know what to ask for.

For a time, I believed that God sent us Patti as our advocate. She was just what we needed. She was a person we could trust. We knew her heart and her dedication to others. We could trust her medical expertise and advice. She stepped in and accomplished everything we needed. What a blessing God had given us!

But then, as I have given it more intense thought, I have come to realize that neither one of us was the TRUE ADVOCATE. You see, I had prayed to the True Advocate the night before. The True Advocate had provided the exact people we needed to coordinate Jim's care. The True Advocate never leaves us and we can trust Him. He is faithful. His ability and character do not change based on our circumstances. Our God had supplied for us in our moment of dire need. I was not capable, but He was. Sweet Patti was the tool He used to meet our need. He knew we needed a familiar face in front of us to calm my panicky heart. She was the face and hands of Jesus in that moment – something I could see/hear/feel tangibly in my distress.

Maybe you need God big time for something you're facing today. I don't know. I just know that my revelation in these moments was not something for me to keep silent. I believe that it was meant to encourage others on their challenging life journeys.

I pray that this speaks to your heart today and meets a need that only you know of – the need you can barely speak of because it hurts too much to say it out loud. He's trustworthy. Ask Him to be your Advocate and to put people in place to meet your dire needs . . . And then wait. Wait expectantly for Him to show up and provide for your needs.

God was . . . and continues to be . . . our Advocate.

5

AN ARMY

I HAVE ALWAYS LOVED the Bible stories found in 2 Kings 6 and Exodus 17. They were among some of my favorites as a child, but in the past few years God has revealed new meaning - new depth - to me in them.

> *The king of Aram became very upset over this. He called his officers together and demanded, "Which of you is the traitor? Who has been informing the king of Israel of my plans?" "It's not us, my lord the king," one of the officers replied. "Elisha, the prophet in Israel, tells the king of Israel even the words you speak in the privacy of your bedroom!" "Go and find out where he is," the king commanded, "so I can send troops to seize him." And the report came back: "Elisha is at Dothan." So one night the king of Aram sent a great army with many chariots and horses to surround the city. When the servant of the man of God got up early the next morning and went outside, there were troops, horses, and chariots everywhere. "Oh, sir, what will we do now?" the young man cried to Elisha. "Don't be afraid!" Elisha told him. "For there are more on our side than on theirs!" Then*

Elisha prayed, "O LORD, open his eyes and let him see!" The LORD opened the young man's eyes, and when he looked up, he saw that the hillside around Elisha was filled with horses and chariots of fire.
   2 Kings 6:11-17

Moses commanded Joshua, "Choose some men to go out and fight the army of Amalek for us. Tomorrow, I will stand at the top of the hill, holding the staff of God in my hand."

So Joshua did what Moses had commanded and fought the army of Amalek. Meanwhile, Moses, Aaron, and Hur climbed to the top of a nearby hill. As long as Moses held up the staff in his hand, the Israelites had the advantage. But whenever he dropped his hand, the Amalekites gained the advantage. Moses' arms soon became so tired he could no longer hold them up. So Aaron and Hur found a stone for him to sit on. Then they stood on each side of Moses, holding up his hands. So his hands held steady until sunset. As a result, Joshua overwhelmed the army of Amalek in battle.
   Exodus 17:9-13

I have purposely saved this chapter as the very <u>last</u> to write. Although it falls in the lineup of the first handful of chapters in this book, it is one that I have wrestled with so much that I chose to set it aside over and over again. I hoped by doing so that I would find an adequate way to express the numerous thoughts and feelings reeling in my head and heart regarding this topic.

It is the only chapter left, and yet I still feel unprepared and immensely inadequate to tackle it. The eloquence that is needed for such a chapter of honor eludes me.

As I look at the scriptures above, huge tears form in my eyes and leave me struggling to catch my breath. The picture of how they apply to MY life hits me square in the face and is extremely humbling.

The excerpt from 2 Kings reminds me that although I have felt extremely alone many times in our journey with Glioblastoma, I was not. As I read and reread the words in this passage, it squeezes my heart with a vicious clenched fist. I feel God telling me that if I could have seen the view that He saw from day one, I would have seen a vast, fierce, well-equipped army of faithful warriors that He had already laid out on the hillside before us – an army prepared to battle and stand with us every step of the way. Each person on the hillside served a purpose. Each person on the hillside was not only personally invested in our journey, but they were each <u>divinely placed</u> in our story by God.

Maybe you are one of those people.

The second set of scriptures stabs as fiercely at my heart as the first. Tears flow freely each time I read the portion that says "Moses' arms soon became so tired he could no longer hold them up. So Aaron and Hur found a stone for him to sit on. Then they stood on each side of Moses, holding up his hands. So his hands held steady until sunset." I clearly see a picture of those closest to us standing by our side and holding our arms up when we were so weary and in so much pain we could no longer hold them up ourselves. It sounds so cliché, but I assure you that it is the most accurate description I have found to depict what some of our family members and close friends did for us in the years we battled the wretched demon of Glioblastoma Multiforme - grade 4 brain cancer. Just as I assume it was exhausting and painful for Aaron and Hur to hold up Moses' hands <u>until sunset</u>, I am certain that the people God placed in this position in our lives were exhausted and in pain. And yet, they remained faithful to us and served us with their whole hearts.

I am humbled by the two vivid pictures God has revealed to me about our lives in these events chronicled in the Bible. So humbled, that it physically hurts me in the very core of my being and honestly brings me to tears every time I have tried to visit this topic in the years I've spent writing this book. And, once again, that is why I've set this chapter aside for so long.

Every single person that did something for our family on this journey has touched my heart in ways they cannot fathom. When I start to recall

all of the things that people have done for us along the way and try to form a chapter that honors each person, I freeze dead in my tracks. You see, I strongly fear that in mentioning only certain people, the people I fail to recognize will have the misconception that we forgot what they did for us and that we didn't appreciate it. It couldn't be further from the truth, friends. It hurts me to even go there; to even think of that atrocity. I want each person to know how much they matter to ME, how much I love them for who they are, and how grateful I am for their many acts of kindness and generosity.

The precious army of people God has placed in our lives is better than anything I could have imagined, anything that I could have thought to ask for in preparation for this enormous battle. Some people purchased groceries for us and delivered them to our house during the months and months of chaos. Others took our kids at a moment's notice and never made us feel guilty about it once. Some friends and family members spent hours putting fundraisers together to help alleviate the pressure of accumulating medical bills that threatened to suffocate us.

The offers and kind gestures of family, church family, close friends, acquaintances, and those in our amazing little community were endless. I had offers to clean our house and wash our laundry (although I was seldom able to take advantage of these offers because I'm way too stubborn). We had delicious meals delivered to our home many evenings, thanks to an ongoing meal train that was arranged for us. Two ladies even helped me with Easter baskets for my kids on different years, because the ongoing, traumatic events made it impossible for me to get to the store to collect the items I needed for the project (and, quite frankly, was too exhausted to complete). Yard work was tackled by a few. Thoughtful gifts and cards were received frequently, of which some included extremely generous monetary gifts to help us.

And then, there was the group of people who stood by and followed our journey through my posts. These sweet souls may never know their special place in our journey. They may never fully understand the value of their extended hands to us via a simple social media platform. They prayed for us, left encouraging comments on my posts, and anxiously awaited my next update - at times biting their nails because of the brutal descriptions of our latest and greatest challenges.

I had people stop me in the grocery store, at the bank, or around town, begging for the latest update on Jim with such love and concern in their eyes that it poured out into my soul. It left me in shock at the number of people who cared about what was happening in our lives. We really aren't that special! We're just normal, ordinary people. I am awestruck at the compassion and encouragement people stopped to show these "normal, ordinary people." It was like having wet cement poured into our lonely, empty souls to infuse us with the strength we needed to endure the days ahead.

Then I think about our church family and church board and I'm left speechless. You have no idea of the selfless decisions they made to stand by us UNTIL THE VERY END, waiting and praying for a miracle, standing beside us and expecting the miracle along with us. They would not relent. They would not accept Jim's attempts to resign. They were steadfast and immovable. They exemplified the true Body of Christ to us in every way. Again, to say that I'm "humbled" seems so weak and frail. They have my heart.

The first responders from Escalon's fire, police, and ambulance department were no exception in this matter. As you will see throughout the pages of this book, they went above and beyond their duties to serve the Davis family. Their kindness and compassion to us in the unexpected emergency moments we experienced is to be greatly commended. They will forever have a special place in my heart, as well as my utmost respect. I lack the capacity to express it adequately.

Friends, in my feeble attempts to give you examples of those who have blessed us in our hours of dire need, you may find that I failed to touch the category you fit in on our journey. That has been one of my greatest fears. I assure you that if you did ANYTHING to help us on this brutal journey, it was appreciated. Pleeeeeease do not discount the value of your place in this army. It would crush me into a thousand pieces. If God placed you on our path, it was for a reason.

The vast, fierce, well-equipped army of faithful warriors God provided for us is unlike any other force I have ever witnessed. It is second to none!

God knew the part that each warrior would fill. He strategically placed each soldier on our hillside, knowing the strengths they had that would fortify us and hold us up on our weakest day. I'm grateful for every single one of them. I'm grateful for YOU!

6

AHHHH, ROUTINE!

AS WE FINISHED September, trudged on to October, and slid into November, we began to find a new normal. There was time to breathe in between doctor appointments. There was time to settle into our everyday routine again.

Ahhhhhhh! Routine!!! Although the to-do list was never ending, we could somewhat count on what to expect day to day. There was comfort in that, no matter how mundane it seemed.

Since I'm naturally a creature of habit, the mundane, routine things bring me much peace. If I know what to expect, I'm not grasping for how to plan things out in the spur of the moment. I can put my ducks in a row and take care of each one of them – even stepping outside of the box and tackling my "ducks" out of order. . . . Shock! . . . THAT is spontaneity in my life! (Go ahead and laugh. I know it's funny. I can laugh at the absurdity of it, but I still choose to love order and structure.)

My days were filled to the brim with: monitoring Jim's blood glucose levels multiple times a day; administering meds; finding the right kind of food for each meal by checking and re-checking nutritional content on containers; getting the kids to and from school (and any other place they needed to go); maintaining my responsibilities at work; and balancing any responsibilities for Jim's job that he was not able to keep up with at the church.

Since the beginning of June I had been learning how to juggle the various tasks of the day and multitask my little heart out. I was getting pretty good at this juggling act. In some ways it felt like an intricate dance, remembering each step and movement and executing every detail of it with precision - because our lives depended on my ability to execute it well. Sometimes my brain felt so full I thought it was going to explode. I always worried that I would forget something important and our family would suffer the consequences of it. This "dance" stretched every part of me to maximum capacity: physically, emotionally, mentally, and of course, spiritually.

Much of our lives changed drastically after Jim's two hospitalizations in August and September. Jim required more assistance with moving about the house; showering; dressing; cutting his food; opening containers; getting in and out of the car; and the list goes on and on. He absolutely hated relying on me to help him with these things. If you knew My Love, you know he strived to make my life as easy as possible, not to mention that there is a certain dignity that is lost when you suddenly need assistance with such a wide variety of tasks. The look in his eye when he needed help but wanted to do it himself was torture enough for both of us.

Showers. Oh, showers . . . they became my workout! . . . I helped Jim undress while balancing him against the bathroom counter behind him, so he wouldn't fall. At this point, he had lost a tremendous amount of weight and looked like a Holocaust survivor – pale, thin, bones showing that never showed before. His strength was gone, so I monitored every part of his showers. He would carefully step over the small threshold into the shower. A friend loaned us a shower chair for him to use, and I have to say that that thing was a lifesaver for us! I stood outside of the shower stall and he sat on the chair. He washed up, or if he wasn't able to do it I would lean into the shower and wash him. Once he was done, he'd stand so I could rinse him off with the handheld shower head.

But, then came the challenging part: I had to help him dry off because his right hand couldn't hold the towel. (Have you ever tried drying yourself with one hand? Try it next time when you shower. It's almost impossible.) Even if his hand were functioning, bending over to dry the lower half of his body would've thrown him off balance. Maybe it doesn't sound very challenging to help him dry off, but I assure you it was. Imagine drying off your slippery 5-year-old child, except now imagine that they are taller and heavier than you. . . . Oh! And they aren't stable on their feet . . . . It wasn't easy.

After he was dry and I helped him step over the shower threshold again, we started the task of getting him dressed. I wised up and brought in a folding chair for him to sit in while we struggled to get his deodorant and clothes on, piece by piece. Sitting down helped him to reserve some energy for the rest of the day. Oh, I thought it was difficult to put my daughters' socks on their tiny feet when they were little girls, but once I attempted this with my full-grown husband's feet, I soon realized that it WAS possible for it to be a more difficult task than I had experienced with my girls! I recall sitting on the floor, wrestling his feet to get those darn socks on. Eventually I would win the wrestling match only to start the same struggle with his shoes. So, to say that I was exhausted by the time Jim was fresh, clean, and ready to leave the house, is a serious understatement, but this became as normal for us as anything else in life. It was necessary. It had to be done.

Did I mind doing these things? I absolutely did not!!! I was honored to help my sweet husband. It was my joy to cover anything I could for him. I never wanted him to feel like he wasn't worth it. I never wanted him to feel that I wasn't committed. I meant every part of our marriage vows "In sickness and in health." I know he did, too. And, I knew if the roles were reversed, he would've stepped up to the task and would've done all of that AND MORE for me. He probably would have doted on me excessively, because that's just the amazing guy he was and how much I know he loved me. He wouldn't have given it a second thought.

Jim completed two more rounds of oral chemo in October and November. Because Temodar tanked his blood count so drastically, Dr.

S (Jim's local oncologist) had to delay the start of Jim's next treatment by a week or so both times. And, although our normal daily routine was established, Jim's body was not experiencing "routine." He suffered from fatigue. He napped often and struggled to move about the house.

We tried some in-home physical therapy to aid in his mobility, but Jim never seemed to click with the therapists coming in. Looking back, I believe much of it was because he just didn't feel well and wanted to be left alone. He only obliged because he knew it was necessary to keep him going, and Jim was all about fighting to keep going. He didn't fight for himself. He fought for me. He fought for his family. He fought for more time with us.

During this time, like I mentioned with his showers, we also started noticing the diminished capacity of his right hand and arm. It hung next to his body as he stood. When he walked, it swung freely as if it were an empty coat sleeve that was not being used. It looked as if it were no longer even part of his body. This skinny appendage lacked any muscle tone and hung in an ominous way, needing support any time he moved about. As he entered/exited his recliner, he would have to pull his right arm in close to him so it wouldn't throw him off balance as he sat down or stood up.

We continued sleeping in our family room for almost a year. Jim had difficulty getting in and out of bed, so he opted to sleep in the recliner. I slept on the couch a few feet away from him. Unfortunately, the wooden handle to recline the chair was located on the right side. This required Jim to flop his right arm over the side in an awkward fashion, lean as far over as he could to grip the handle with his left hand, and release the handle to put his feet down. Then he would have to gather his arm next to his body again and prepare to stand up. I frequently offered to help him, but he wanted to be independent and chose to do it for himself most of the time.

Early one morning, Jim needed to get up to use the restroom. He didn't secure his right arm well enough before he attempted to stand up. Instead of coming to a full standing position, he rolled himself forward onto the ground. Surprise!!! This is a scary and frustrating situation to wake up to in the wee hours of the morning when my brain wasn't functioning properly. Thankfully, since he was so low to the ground already, he didn't injure himself. I had a front row seat to the show, watching from the couch as I was standing to go help him. From then on, I helped him out of his recliner night and day, supporting his limp arm for him as he scooted to the edge of the recliner and positioned his feet under him for good support before standing.

Although the daily challenges in our routine continued, we tried our best to navigate them gracefully. Our new motto should have been "Adapt and Overcome" because we soon found that it was required with every turn we took.

Leaving the house with Jim became its own ordeal. It became necessary for me to help him down the two steps into our garage; escort him to the car; help him safely aim to sit down in the seat; carefully tuck his right arm onto his lap; buckle him in; annnd I discovered that I needed to double-check the position of his right arm before I closed his door to ensure that I didn't hit his right elbow with the car door armrest. That happened a time or two, to my dismay. Once he was in the car and buckled in, I loaded whatever assistive device he needed for the day (hemi-walker, cane, or wheelchair). Check. Double check. If we had everything we needed for the outing/appointment, then we were off and running.

As the days moved on, work became another new challenge. Many days it was difficult to leave Jim home alone because his mobility was hindered so much. I soon found that I had to find ways to work from home; track my weekly to do lists for the office; then break away when it was convenient to go to work to print, fold, and set up the items I had been working on all week or gather more work. My love for compartmentalizing specific areas of my life, and organizing them in their own space soon became a thing of the past. Over time, as I learned to tackle these tasks - out of order, out of my normal work space, out of anything that symbolized a typical working environment - I began to expand myself and became more confident in juggling whatever was on my list wherever I was planted for the moment. Later on, throughout 2016 and 2017, I became known as the wife who accompanied her husband to EVERY speech/physical/occupational therapy session and brought her work with her. The therapists became accustomed to it and started asking, "So, what are you working on today?"

Getting out to get groceries (besides the occasional gallon of milk or fresh produce from our local grocery store) became another challenging aspect of life. I'm happy to report that none of us starved because of this new obstacle. Like I've mentioned in a previous chapter, we had the support of an army. We had multiple people asking if we needed groceries when they went grocery shopping, so they would drop off items to us on their way home. My mom and Jim's mom were constantly checking in for a list of anything we were lacking, so I didn't have to be out of the house for a long grocery shopping trip one town away.

As crazy as it all sounds – and I'm sure it sounds pretty crazy - we eventually learned to master all of the new ins and outs of our new routine gracefully. Crazy became normal. You read that correctly: crazy became normal. Sad, but true.

On a side note, Cara and Marcus got engaged in October 2015. Marcus had elaborately planned an extremely romantic proposal; drove six hours from Southern California to ask us in person for Cara's hand in marriage; then executed his plan to the tee. It was the sweetest! Sunset. Handmade paper lanterns with luminary candles. A fun treasure hunt for Cara that a friend helped make possible. Flowers. A beautiful ring. And a romantic proposal. Our son-in-law is pretty amazing, and his deep love for Cara was very evident in the well-planned day. It was a bright spot in time, considering everything else that was going on!

Jim had a new MRI in November of 2015. He was still with his local oncologist and radiologist, so that MRI was done one week and we didn't receive the results until the next week.

One week? One hour? It never mattered. The waiting was always grueling. Many people battling cancer call this "Scanxiety" and I think that title fits just fine! We always struggled emotionally the days/weeks before Jim's upcoming scans.

A month before the MRI, Jim and I decided to ask Dr. S how he felt about referring Jim to UCSF to see if additional treatments were available.

He approached the idea thoughtfully, but said he'd prefer to wait for the MRI results before making that decision. We had prayed about it before asking him, so we felt a peace about his answer.

The MRI results were in on November 20th. Dr. G-Y said Jim's tumor looked a little different, but it was hard to determine exactly what was going on still. There was a possibility that what remained was necrotic (dead) tissue, instead of live cancer cells, but we'd have to wait three more months to see a comparison of two MRIs to get a better assessment.

A few days later, Jim saw his primary care physician again because he was still battling an ongoing "sinus infection." The foul-smelling drainage was back again. The doctor prescribed a new antibiotic to help him fight it.

Dr. S met with Jim on December 7th to assess how he was doing and discuss continuing treatment. We weren't expecting to bring up the question about UCSF again. We were surprised when he said that he was on board with referring Jim to UCSF. And, even better, Jim could be seen by UCSF, but Dr. S could remain on as Jim's local oncologist to help bridge the gap that can occur when you have specialists so far away from your home base. Win! Win!

The referral was submitted to UCSF and we were told we would hear from them soon. We were not expecting HOW SOON. Within five days we found ourselves reeling with excitement, nervousness, and facing a lot of hard decisions.

7

IT'S NOT BRAIN SURGERY! . . . OR IS IT?

"IT'S NOT BRAIN surgery, ya know!"

I'm sure we've all heard the phrase used numerous times in our lifetime. A phrase here which means it's not that complicated or difficult; it's easy.

But what if it IS brain surgery, like for reals brain surgery, not the one we joke about all the time. What then? How do you process something like this when you or your loved one is going under the knife, and the neurosurgeon will actually be delicately removing a large mass from the brain? Of course, in that situation, you would think the opposite terms: complicated, difficult, far from smooth or easy. And you would be right.

Five days after we left Dr. S's office with knowledge that he was sending a referral to UCSF, we found ourselves sitting in the waiting room in the UCSF neuro-oncology wing for an 8:30 AM appointment.

Only. Five. Days. Later.

Jim was the first patient for their first Saturday clinic day. This required me to brave the Bay Area traffic once again. We were up early to be sure we arrived on time. Thankfully, since it was Saturday, the traffic was lighter and easier for me to navigate. I was nervous, but willing to stretch myself to get Jim to his appointment.

Dr. B, Jim's new neuro-oncologist at UCSF, was a thin, young-looking doctor. His bedside manner was comforting. His demeanor was calm. He seemed extremely knowledgeable and ready to help Jim.

"Mr. Davis, I think your brain tumor is operable."

Up until this point Jim had been told that the brain tumor wasn't able to be resected safely. He was told that operating in that area of his brain could further impair his speech and the motor functions for his right side. He was told that the spiderous tumor would be an impossible task to remove.

Dr. B went on to explain all of Jim's options for treatment: listing continued chemo, pairing chemo with another medicine, clinical trials, and the like. Then he summed it up with the short list of the most effective treatments he would advise. As we continued discussing the option of brain surgery, he stated that he would like the neurosurgeon to look at Jim's most recent MRI to get his opinion before proceeding further. He explained that the neurosurgeon wouldn't be available until late afternoon on Monday and promised to call us by Tuesday morning.

That made for an impossibly long weekend!

This news was a wonderful surprise that brought many complicated emotions along with it. At first it was, "Surgery is a possibility!" (excitement). Then it was, "Surgery is a possibility!" (extreme fear). Although you cannot hear the inflection in my voice when I say this same sentence in two different tones, I'm sure you can guess what each would sound like, as well as the look on my face when I express the excitement or extreme fear in each.

Once again, every possible emotion flooded us at the same time. It took the full weekend and Monday for us to talk through the option of surgery and prepare for the best/worst news we could receive from the neurosurgeon's assessment.

Tuesday morning arrived – December 15th to be exact – and Dr. B called as promised. The answer? Yes, the neurosurgeon felt brain surgery was a valid option for Jim. He explained that if we were on board, the neurosurgeon's office would call to set up a surgery consultation for Jim.

Oh, they called alright! They called on the same day.

"When can we be seen for Jim's surgery consult? Oh, Thursday? THIS Thursday? Like, two days from now?" Yes. Yes. This Thursday, December 17th. We were in shock. Everything was speeding down the track like a runaway freight train. It was too much to process so quickly, but we were giving it our best.

Furthermore, as we discussed possible dates for surgery, Jim and I decided that it might be best to complete it before the end of the year, as our medical insurance deductible had already been met for the calendar year, and we wouldn't have additional medical bills tacked onto the growing stack we were accruing at a fast rate. We presented the idea to Dr. A's team and they approved it.

The surgery date was tentatively set . . . Tuesday, December 22nd. Again, let me confirm that you read that date correctly: Tuesday, December 22nd - ONE week away! (Insert my panicked face here.)

I immediately jumped into planning mode. Everything needed to be organized by the weekend. Christmas was gonna have to happen early this year. It was a good thing that I was almost finished with purchasing gifts for our children. I had started early, not knowing what the days ahead would hold, not knowing if we would have week-long emergency trips to the hospital like we had experienced in September.

Thursday, December 17th arrived, and we made our way back to San Francisco for another 8:30 AM appointment, leaving extremely early to avoid the morning commute traffic. We met with Dr. A and his staff for the first time. After they reviewed Jim's history and assessed him physically, Dr. A confirmed that he still felt surgery would greatly benefit Jim.

Then came the surgery details.

An awake craniotomy - Jim would have to be awake to answer questions; verbally identify photos; recite the days of the week, months of the year, count, say his ABCs; and move certain parts of his body on command, while they stimulated certain areas of the brain and mapped it. This would help the surgeon effectively remove the tumor without damaging vital parts of his brain that controlled his speech and motor skills. Surgery would take about 4-6 hours. Jim would be in ICU for a minimum of one night, then moved to a hospital room on the neuro floor. Overall, he would be hospitalized 3-4 days... Yes, we would most likely be spending Christmas at UCSF.

We left with very full brains that day. While I navigated Bay Area traffic, we discussed the plan for the coming days and tried to brace ourselves for the unknown - the unknown weighing heavily on us. We expressed a variety of concerns to each other, but I'm sure we still internalized our deepest, darkest concerns, knowing that the risks of surgery were very clear: brain damage, or even death, were both possible with such an intricate surgery.

As if the day wasn't full enough, Christopher had a guitar concert at school that evening. Our three youngest kids were at my mom and dad's house. Once we got back into town, I barely had time to get Jim settled in, eat dinner, and rush off to meet my parents and kids at the concert. Jim was worn out from the day and couldn't muster enough energy to attend. We recorded the highlights so he didn't miss out.

Home again. Showers for the kids. Bedtime.

One would think that I would have been so exhausted from the day that I crashed out immediately and slept through the night and a good portion of the next day, but my body was in fight mode. My adrenaline kicked in fiercely and my brain needed to organize everything that was needed for Jim and our family in the coming days/weeks ahead. We needed a dog sitter! That was DEFINITELY something that had to be coordinated at 1:30 AM. (Yes, you are sensing a bit of sarcasm there, but my brain was on overload and I needed order. Oh, and I'm totally admitting to the fact that I was panicking over the need for a dog sitter at 1:30 AM in the morning.)

I finally had to come to terms with the fact that I wouldn't survive the next week without sleep, so I prayed that God would help me manage everything that was on my list well. And I specifically prayed that He would help me find someone to watch our dogs. I needed that item checked off my mental list that night before I slipped off to sleep... for a couple of hours.

I recall waking numerous times a night over the next few nights, sobbing uncontrollably in sheer terror, thinking about what the days ahead potentially held. I stifled my cries the best I could, trying not to wake Jim. He had enough to worry about. He was the one undergoing brain surgery!

Friday was the last day of school for our kids before Christmas break. I made the best of my time while they were at school by running laundry; writing thousands of lists; contacting everyone I needed to contact; cleaning our house; packing; making plans for the kids while we were gone; wrapping gifts; finalizing Christmas shopping for the last items on my lists; covering important details for the church; and resigning myself to the fact that I may not be able to cover EVERYTHING before we left on Sunday afternoon.

That last one is always a difficult one for me, but I did have a few things that were left undone. I specifically recall that there were a few unwrapped gifts and that stocking stuffers were sparse that year. As I type this and truly realize the absurd, monumental task I was faced with, I am trying to give myself adequate credit for surviving it and doing the rock star job that I did. (I'm not so good at recognizing that, but I'm working on it.)

Sunday arrived and surprisingly we were all still in one piece. Our bags were packed. The kids bags were packed. It was Christmas Sunday, and we were up, dressed, and ready to head off to church (just like every Sunday).

After church, we headed home. We had time for a quick lunch and planned to have "Christmas" together before Jim, Court, and I drove to San Francisco to check into our hotel room.

Before we got the chance to get to our family Christmas presents, the Escalon 4-H group leaders stopped by to bless us with gifts they had been collecting for us. It was such a sweet surprise! They enjoyed watching us open them before they left. There were gas gift cards, food gift cards, clothes for the kids, coats for the kids, a FasTrak device to pay for bridge tolls going to/from San Francisco, money, and so much more! They really blessed us and we were so grateful! In January, we were able to purchase a power recliner for Jim with the money they gave us. The big thing about that was that it had the buttons on the left side of the chair, which made it easily accessible for him with his functioning hand/arm.

Our 4-H friends were on their way out the door when Cara and Courtney arrived to open gifts with the family. I quickly grabbed all of the unwrapped items I didn't have time to get to from our bedroom. We read the Christmas story from the Bible; had a few moments together; then proceeded to open gifts. Soon it was time to start picking up the empty boxes and bits of wrapping paper that littered the family room. Hanna, Americis, and Christopher rushed to tuck the items they received into the bags they had already packed.

And, one would naturally think that we were off to San Francisco after that. But, no, we weren't done yet. We were supposed to meet Cara's in-laws-to-be for the first time! We had yet to meet Marcus' parents! They are missionaries to South America and live there most of the time. Due to that and Jim's diagnosis/battle, there hadn't been adequate time to get together yet. They were available for Christmas week, so we originally planned that they would come and spend time with us so we could get to know each other. With Jim's brain surgery, the week-long visit was no longer on the table because we'd be in San Francisco. We decided to improvise and met them briefly at our home before we traveled. We enjoyed our visit and deeply regretted having to cut it so short.

Eventually we were on the road, bound for San Francisco with high winds, rain, and all the fun stuff that adds to driving in areas where I'm uncomfortable. A quick stop at Panda Express for dinner helped to pacify our growling tummies and bring a little comfort for the rest of the trip. As we crossed the Bay Bridge, the wind and rain came down in full force. The rain beat down persistently on our windshield, while the wind took turns tossing us back and forth.

When we got to the area near our hotel, we searched around aimlessly for a bit, routing down one-way streets in circles until we located the entrance to the hotel unloading area.

A friend of the family generously arranged for the week-long hotel stay for Cara, Courtney, and me (and whoever else we needed to cram into the room, if needed). I was elated to have them coordinate the arrangements, as I didn't know exactly where to stay and was panicked about selecting a hotel in the wrong location of the city. Jim, Courtney, and I would need to stay at the hotel the first two nights, but the third night Jim would be in ICU and I would not be allowed to stay with him.

We unloaded Jim on a flat area near the hotel entrance; scrambled to grab all of our luggage; checked into the hotel room; and navigated up to our room for the evening. We were all exhausted, and the next day was going to be pre-op day.

Monday, December 21st started bright and early with an MRI at 6:30 AM. That was on the 3rd floor of the hospital building. It was followed with bloodwork on the 1st floor, which proved to be easier said than done, so they shipped us across the street to another building to complete it. Jim's veins were hard to find after chemo, and it took many attempts for them to find one that would give enough blood for the required tests. Then back to the Echo Lab at 11:00 AM on the 3rd floor of the hospital building. We had a brief break for lunch across the street before we had to be back for an ultrasound of Jim's legs to check for blood clots (3rd floor of the hospital building) at 1:00 PM. No blood clots could be seen. Yaaay!

Back and forth. Back and forth. By this time, Jim, Courtney, and I were already exhausted. Jim was in and out of the wheelchair all day long. I was pushing the wheelchair. Court was helping me hold extra paperwork, backpacks, and food, as well as assisting with the wheelchair when my hands were full.

We thought we only had one more appointment for the day - a language mapping appointment. Before we finished the ultrasound of Jim's legs, I received a phone call telling me that Jim needed an additional test in the university side of the hospital. Once again, we scrambled to load Jim in the wheelchair, gather our belongings, and search for the location we were told to go to for his next test. Although, for time's sake, I won't go into all the details of this test, I will say that it was tucked into a rather odd room. Court and I waited while Jim complied with a grueling test that required him to answer a lot of questions. I drifted off to sleep sitting up. I think she did, too.

Back on course with the original appointments of the day, we were slated to be at the medical building across the street for Jim's language mapping – this would assist him during his awake craniotomy. We had time to cram granola bars down our throats and guzzle a bit of water, then we reluctantly headed across the street ONE MORE TIME to make the 4:00 PM appointment.

Jim, very tired by that point, struggled to get through language mapping. He had exhausted all of his strength for the day, and now they needed him to identify pictures; say his ABCs; recite the months of the year; count to a specific number; and so on. They had to get a baseline on his speech so they would know what was out of the ordinary during brain surgery.

About 6:30 PM we dragged our tired bodies to the car and loaded everything in it. We didn't have the energy to locate a restaurant for dinner, so we resigned ourselves to eating at the hotel's restaurant, hoping to find something that we liked.

Dinner finished, we trudged up to our room. To my dismay, we still were not done for the day. I had evening meds to administer and needed to help Jim shower thoroughly with Dial soap before hopping in bed.

Physically, mentally, and emotionally exhausted, one would think that we crashed out for the whole night immediately upon finishing Jim's shower. Instead, Jim and I sat at the edge of our bed, my head leaning against his as he held and caressed my hand. Tears filled his eyes as he shared his fears with me about the next day's surgery - knowing that there was a chance surgery could change his speech and mobility for the worse, or more importantly, that it would possibly change his personality and the way he related to me and our family. There is a deep heaviness that hangs in the air in moments like these. The pit of one's stomach is tied up in knots and the brain cannot properly process the anxiety and fear of the unknown events to come. The gravity of the situation was not lost on either of us. We knew the risks all too well. In this moment, he did not hold back in reminding me of how much he loved me (something he loved to say frequently). For a while we just sat in silence and held each other.

We finally resigned ourselves to TRY to go to sleep. There was much tossing and turning throughout the night for all three of us. Against our valiant efforts to get a good night's sleep before the next day, we were not as successful as we had hoped to be. Many times throughout the night I felt Jim's hand searching for mine or his foot extended out to nestle next to mine - as was his normal custom on many a night - but that night was different. The comfort of lying next to each other, hand in hand, was everything we needed as we anxiously approached dawn.

Morning came much too soon.

I awoke early because I knew I had a full list of things that needed to be done for Jim after I finished showering and getting myself ready. The hospital staff had given me a full list of meds that Jim should take on the morning of surgery, as well as meds that he should skip. Then there was glucose monitoring. On this particular morning I had to watch his blood glucose to be sure it didn't get too low, because he wasn't allowed to eat anything before surgery. I was given complete instructions on what he could have if it dipped below such and such number. I went through my list I had jotted down days before while talking to the pre-op nurse. I checked and double-checked everything on the list that Jim needed to do before we left, then I gathered my backpack and the things that I needed for the day. It was going to be a long, grueling, emotional day.

The Corbins had arrived at our hotel on the night before. Our amazing friends were always beside us on the most difficult days. Their oldest son, Denton, agreed to drive Jim, Courtney, and me to the hospital on the morning of Jim's surgeries. I was elated that I wouldn't have to navigate the dark streets of San Francisco this time. It was nice to have a break from that chore on such a stressful morning. Even if Denton did accidently run a red light in the middle of San Francisco, I'll never tell. (Sorry, Denton!)

Before long, we were pulling into the driveway at UCSF. My heart raced. I immediately clicked into high gear to brace for the events of the day that were rushing at us at the speed of light. Jim did the same.

As we walked through the front doors of the hospital we could see that Jim's parents and brother, John, were already in the waiting room to the left. Jim walked over to greet them, and I bolted in the other direction to get him checked in for his first surgery. Once the nurse gave me the necessary documents for Jim, I joined them and was able to greet Jim Sr., Becky, and John briefly before we headed upstairs.

We delivered the documents to the third floor, and Jim was given a green-striped hospital gown and pants to change into. He and I escaped into the changing room so I could assist him. We emerged soon after – me carrying his clothes and shoes that were carefully tucked into a plastic bag, and him wearing his new, fashionable hospital garb, including fancy, non-skid hospital socks.

His name was called within a few minutes. They started his IV, then he was whisked off for his first procedure - the installation of a fabulous IVC filter to protect him from the risks of blood clots for the period of time that he wasn't able to take his blood thinners.

The surgery went smoothly and didn't take long. Before we knew it, he was excused from the procedure room and we were heading back down to the first floor again to finish registering for his craniotomy surgery.

The next half an hour or so is a blur to me. Greeting more friends and family in the main waiting room. Completing forms for the surgery. Being called to another floor for Jim to be prepped for his brain surgery. Although I can tell you bits and pieces of these moments, they seriously are blurred together in my mind, as my emotions were once again put on hold to brace for the next few hours that Jim, our families, our friends, and I were about to embark on.

Once in the pre-op room, multiple people came to check off items on their individual check lists for Jim. We met a few members of the neurosurgery team again and they proceeded to recap the basics of Jim's craniotomy, checking to be sure that they had everything correct in their notes. The nurses checked his vitals, adjusted his fluids and meds for his blood glucose, and charted everything that was needed. Jim's mom was allowed to join us in pre-op after the initial items were checked off.

And then, it was time to address the wedding ring on Jim's left hand. Months before, his meds started making his hands swell. We had tried on numerous occasions to remove the ring, but had been unsuccessful. His nurse tried multiple times, but failed. She said she could ask one other nurse who was well-known for her success in removing rings that others couldn't. I pleaded with her to do so because I couldn't bear the thought of them cutting Jim's wedding ring off of his finger. I realize that in the whole scheme of things it really was not the most important item of the day, buuuuut TO US it was precious. For me it was gonna be the straw that broke the camel's back. I was holding it together fine at this point, but I had no assurance that I was going to be able to hold my composure if they had to cut that ring off. Thankfully, the last nurse was able to remove it with a fancy trick – using string to wrap around his finger to compress it enough to slide the ring off.

But, the victorious moment was fleeting. As the ring was placed in the palm of my hand, we were told it was time to wheel Jim off to surgery. My mother-in-law and I were able to walk alongside his bed out into the hallway, then were given instructions of how to get to the elevator to return to the main waiting room. The goodbyes were brief. Jim and I snuck in one last kiss before he and his bed were escorted through the doors to the surgical arena. Becky and I followed the directions and headed back to the waiting room where . . . wellllll . . . WE WAITED . . . and waited, and waited some more, in the company of many family and friends.

By this point, our family and friends had pretty much occupied most of the space in the main waiting room. I'm guessing there were roughly 25 of us in all. Of course, Jim's parents and brother were there (like I already stated). Courtney had been with us the whole previous day and remained by my side on surgery day for anything I needed. Cara and her fiancee' Marcus joined us. My parents had arrived, and they brought our three teenagers with them: Hanna, Americis, and Christopher. Arney, Dana, and Connor Corbin had now joined Denton at the hospital and were assisting us with crowd control and the needs of my teenagers. My brother and sister-in-law made the trip to UCSF to wait with us. Then there were a couple of friends from our church as well.

The group that shocked me the most when they arrived was a group of friends from the Escalon Fire Department. About 5-6 of them had carpooled together to come and sit with our family on this important day. It was very touching for me. Jim and I didn't expect that they would come and wait for such a lengthy surgery with me and our family. They waited patiently with the rest of us. As the time passed, we tried to encourage them to get back on the road before traffic was too difficult to navigate, but they sweetly insisted on waiting with us until the surgery was complete.

Minutes ticked away into hours. We all found our own way to pass the time and keep our minds occupied. Some played games on their phones and listened to music. Some of us chatted to pass the time. Others walked around and checked in periodically at the waiting room.

Eventually, my kids went across the street to grab lunch and insisted on bringing me something to eat as well. It's funny that I can remember exactly what I ate for lunch that day: A Panda Express orange chicken bowl with chow mein, complete with a soda to wash it down. I reluctantly forced it down my throat, knowing I needed to eat something and wouldn't hear the end of it from our family and friends if I didn't eat. But, I wasn't able to finish all of it. The remainder was sitting on a shelf in the corner of the waiting room when I received the first phone call from the operating room.

I stepped around the corner to hear the news, but was still within view of our friends and family through a clear glass divider between the two spaces. The nurse on the phone was kind and calm. She stated that surgery had started and that they had already opened Jim's skull to begin the tumor resection. I expected that type of update, as the neurosurgeon had mentioned such updates when we talked in his office the week before.

Then came the message from Jim. The nurse said she asked him what he wanted her to tell his wife, and he replied, "Tell her I love her very much." Upon receiving this portion of the update I will definitely say that I cried. I quickly followed up that crying moment with a big smile, as everyone in the waiting room was trying to get a read from the look on my face, and crying at a moment like that is not a good thing for friends and family to see at such a tense moment.

The nurse wrapped up the phone update. I rounded the corner back to the waiting room and quickly reassured Jim's parents, then the rest of the group, that Jim was indeed doing well in surgery and it was just a scheduled phone update for us.

More hours passed.

Once again, I received a phone call from the operating room to give me an update on Jim's status. By this point they were wrapping up his tumor resection and would start closing soon. The nurse assured me that things were still going well and that they would call me as soon as Jim was moved to the neurosurgery intensive care unit.

Tick tock. Tick tock.

After about a total of 6 hours of surgery, a member of Dr. A's team called and asked me to meet him upstairs, near the neurosurgery ICU, to get a full update on Jim's surgery. I could bring one person with me, which I immediately knew should be his mother. Becky and I headed upstairs and quickly found Dr. A waiting in the hallway. He explained that the surgery went well and they were able to resect 90-95% of the tumor in Jim's brain. He was pleased with the results and said that they would keep Jim in ICU overnight, as planned, and would evaluate him the next day to see if he could be transferred to a regular room.

Of course, my question was, "Can I see him now?"

I walked into Jim's room for the first time after surgery. The top of his head was completely bandaged with gauze, resembling a turban. His eyes brightened as he recognized me and he motioned for me with his left hand to come close so he could tell me something important. What was this important thing he needed to almost whisper to me? Oh yes, his important message for me was, "I'm NOT doing THAT ever again!!!"

I chuckled and told him that he didn't need to worry about that for the moment. I told him that Dr. A said he did such a good job and he was very happy about the amount they were able to resect, to which Jim replied, "I had to tell him I couldn't take it anymore. I just couldn't go on any longer!"

In later days, Jim recounted the horrific experience of hearing/feeling/smelling them cut into his skull to open a portion for the tumor resection, then being grilled over and over again with requests to count, say his ABCs, identify pictures, and much more as they worked to identify areas of the brain they could cut safely, with minimal damage. He said he had a small tube-like hole that he could see out of to communicate with the surgical team member asking him the questions. Jim had nightmares for many months after surgery and developed post-traumatic stress disorder because of the events that he experienced during surgery – even getting severe anxiety about upcoming MRIs which required him to be in a confined space (something that wasn't much of an issue before his surgery).

Dr. A told me that if I took in people from the waiting room by twos to greet Jim and see him briefly, that they would allow everyone in our group to see him. I was elated to break the news to our family and friends. All of them had been so concerned about Jim. You could tell that their minds were immediately put at ease as they rotated in to greet him personally. He conversed briefly with each of them, but was still experiencing a lot of speech challenges. Within a few minutes, everyone had had a chance to say hello to Jim. With thankful hearts, they all hopped in their cars and headed back home. A handful of us remained.

My parents had previous plans to meet my Aunt Donna at Disneyland for her birthday (which is on Christmas Day). They considered canceling their plans once they learned of Jim's scheduled surgery, but I urged them to go and spend the time with my aunt, knowing that we would be at the hospital until the end of the week. So, once my parents knew Jim's surgery went well, they started their long trip to Southern California to meet up with my aunt and her family.

Arney and Dana graciously agreed to keep Hanna, Americis, and Christopher for the following days – even hosting them for Christmas! – and until after Jim was released from the hospital.

Cara, Courtney, Marcus, Denton, and I had a few moments with Jim before we had to leave ICU for the night to give Jim a chance to rest. We talked, laughed a bit, and snapped a few pictures together with Jim before we left.

It was absolutely agonizing for me to walk away from the hospital that night, but I had no other choice. Staying with him overnight in ICU was not an option.

We stopped for Subway sandwiches on our way to the parking garage, then parted ways. Cara and Marcus headed back to Escalon. Courtney and I went back to the hotel room for the night.

Surgery was over. Jim was doing well. We were all extremely tired from a long day of waiting anxiously. We needed sleep.

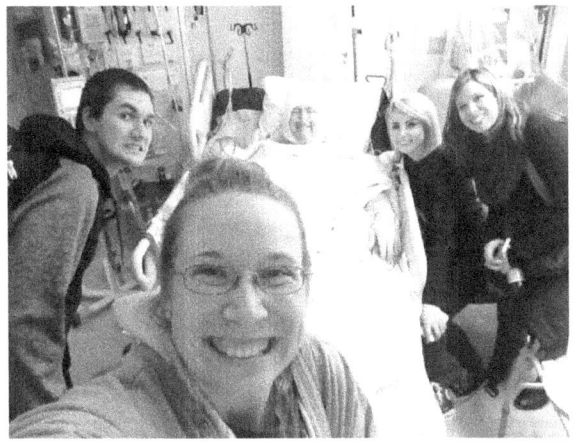

After Jim's Brain Surgery at UCSF (December 2015

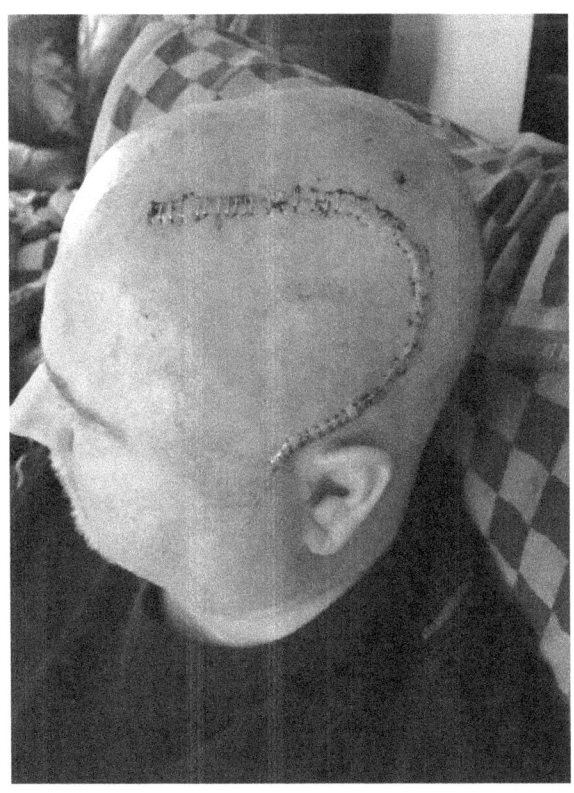

Jim's Incision Post-Surgery (December 2015)

8

THE LONELIEST CHRISTMAS TOGETHER

OVER THE YEARS Jim and I had our share of slightly disappointing Christmases. In almost 30 years of being together, from time to time one of us was sick on Christmas Day or one of our kids ended up being sick. Overall though, we had a good track record for successful holidays together, and even on "disappointing years" we made the best of our circumstances. We knew that Christmas wasn't based on how many gifts we received/gave, who was able to attend our family gatherings, or how tasty the special holiday meal was. Those were bonuses for a season that we set aside to celebrate the birth of Christ. And, although we knew the correct center of Christmas was the tiny baby who became the Savior of the world, we still took time to decorate a tree, put up Christmas lights, exchange gifts with those we loved, and enjoy Christmas songs throughout the month.

If anyone ever loved Christmas, it was Jim. He was like a little kid at this time of year. He thoroughly enjoyed it once I had our decorations in place in our home. He loved the smell of our Christmas tree, and usually insisted on a freshly cut tree to be displayed in our home, lest he miss out on the amazing smell. He lit up when Christmas songs were played, and he made sure he played them often (starting them on the night before Thanksgiving and always keeping that tradition alive for us). He loved getting together with our family and friends to celebrate, too. But one of the things I can say he loved most of all each year was driving around our town to look at all of the beautiful Christmas lights neatly strung on the houses in every neighborhood. You could always count on him to spontaneously issue the decree to our family that we were all hopping in the car to drive around town to see the various light displays. I truly loved the intense excitement that he brought to this beautiful holiday. He brought fun to the holidays for me.

But, Christmas 2015 was anything but a fun or exciting Christmas.

On Wednesday, December 23rd, I awoke to the feeling that I had been hit by a Mack truck. The stress and anxiety of the days leading up to Jim's surgery were finally catching up to me.

I drug myself out of bed and somehow made it to the shower. The hot water spraying on my disheveled hair and running down my back should've been quite enough to help me wake up, but I fought the idea of being completely awake, knowing that I would be forced into the day's reality much quicker than I was ready to face it. After drying off, dressing, drying and styling my hair, and applying makeup to a face that clearly needed many more days of sleep, I packed my suitcase and headed out the door to collect my vehicle from the valet attendant.

Courtney assured me that she would be joining me at the hospital later in the day. She was feeling the effects of the previous day's events and needed to rest longer. I envied the fact that she was still nestled snug in her bed, but the fact that Jim was waiting in ICU across the city was enough to tear me away from the hotel room.

I bravely navigated through the streets of San Francisco. I was alone this time, but I was determined to get to the hospital so I could see Jim and check on his status. I will honestly admit that I had a short, private celebration in my Expedition as I parked in the UCSF parking lot and turned off the engine. I thanked God for helping me navigate there quickly and successfully, without any wrong turns, then I gathered a few basic items and walked to the nearest elevator.

By this time, I was getting more familiar with the layout at UCSF's Parnassus Campus. Once the elevator doors opened, I knew I was on the street level, so I took a left to make my way to Starbucks. (I had called the hospital a few times in the middle of the night to check on Jim. He asked for me to bring him an iced coffee from Starbucks when I came to see him that morning, so I had that on my list of things to do before I went to see him.) I had his iced coffee and my hot chocolate in my hands, so I trudged across the street to the hospital. Jim was still in ICU on the neuro floor, so I located the correct hospital elevator and proceeded up to his floor, entered the unit, and slipped into his ICU room.

Jim was happy to see me and with broken speech proceeded to update me on the events I had already missed for the first few hours of the morning. He said he felt good. He ate dinner the night before and had already had breakfast that morning. Talking was still difficult, especially putting full sentences together. Naming items and remembering things didn't seem to be a problem, so that was good news. He finished a speech therapy assessment and then started physical therapy to see if he could get up and walk. He did pretty well with that.

He complained that his head, jaw, and back were all hurting, but he tolerated it well with the pain meds they offered him.

After his morning appointments and visiting with me for a bit, he was tired again and needed to rest. I was happy to sink into the chair in his room, slip my feet up on the end of his bed, close my eyes, and enjoy the quiet for a while. We were both running on fumes.

Later in the morning, they took Jim in for a new MRI to check for brain bleeds and accurately assess how much tumor was able to be resected the previous day. After the tight squeeze for his MRI he stated that his head and jaw were hurting him much more for the rest of the day.

Lunch was served and I fed him, as his IV was placed in his good arm and made it difficult to use his utensils.

A bit later, Jim looked down the hall and could see Courtney approaching his room.

This would be a good time to interject the fact that Courtney had adamantly warned Jim before his surgery that pretending not to recognize us after his surgery was definitely NOT going to be a funny joke. But, in true Jim fashion, he couldn't resist the opportunity to tease Courtney with his cruel joke. As he saw her approaching his room, he turned to me quickly and whispered to go along with whatever he said. I didn't have the heart to disappoint him.

Courtney entered the room with a tired smile and greeted Jim. He looked at her, got a puzzled look on his face, then turned to me and said, "Who's that?" Since he was in such a good mood and was really enjoying his untimely joke, I replied, "You don't know who that is?" He looked at her again and plastered another puzzled look on his face. I could tell she was getting very distraught, so I tried to encourage him to stop teasing her. He laughed a lot and was very pleased with his own funniness. Courtney was not amused. In her tired state, it was all she could take. She joined us for a while, but decided to leave later and take a break from the hospital setting. We still had a couple more days of our luxurious stay there, so I'm sure it was better for her to regain her bearings.

Jim was transferred to a regular room on the neuro floor in the evening. There was some concern that he wouldn't get a private room and I couldn't stay with him that night, but at the last minute they worked it all out. I think his nurse in ICU pulled some strings for us. That was a relief, because I was prepared to sit in a chair all night if I had to. His new nurse said Jim was her best patient all day . . . He arrived 15 minutes before the shift change.

I retreated to the car to gather my duffel bag. Now that he was in a regular room I would be able to stay with him all day and all night. I was relieved! I didn't like being separated from him and not being able to advocate for him. Since Jim's speech was such a challenge, many people liked to "help" him by filling in the words before he could say them. This only frustrated him and caused him to repeat whatever the other person said, no matter if that was really what he wanted to say or not. His brain couldn't filter it out and allow him to express his own thoughts once someone else tried to fill in the blanks for him. Because this was such an issue, I was hyper vigilant to advocate for him and/or encourage others to take the time to listen to what he was attempting to tell them. Being in the room with him night and day was a huge help in this matter.

I don't remember much about the 23rd after we settled into his new room. At some point in the evening, we prepared for bed; Jim was given his evening meds; and we drifted off to sleep – occasionally being wakened by the night nurse for additional pain meds and necessary monitoring. Before long, we slipped into the morning of Christmas Eve.

I got up when the day shift nurse came into Jim's room and introduced themselves. I showered, dressed, put my makeup on, did my hair, and tidied up his room for the day.

The surgeon's resident came in halfway through the morning. He removed Jim's head bandage and said the surgical site looked good. Jim got the huge scar he wanted, that's for sure! It looked like a huge question mark. It started from the top left of the left side of his head, extending to the top right, curling down and back over the top of his ear, and finally coming to an end in a straight vertical line in front of his left ear. Although I didn't know it at the time, he had 53 staples in his head! 53!!! The sight of it made me nauseous, so I avoided looking directly at it as much as I could. After the resident checked everything, he said that the initial results from the MRI the day before confirmed that they had been successful in removing 90-95% of the tumor. We were elated! Then he reported that they needed to keep the drain in place at the surgery site for a little while longer, as there was still a lot of drainage.

Jim's speech was very difficult. He struggled to find words when he told me or the nurses what he needed. They said the brain swelling from the surgery would cause this. His right arm was still weak, but since it hadn't been used for a while we could safely assume that it would take some time to rebuild strength in it. He said he had more feeling in the area on the right side of his lip. Numbness in that area was one of the first things to appear when he started having symptoms in May. It even appeared that he could open his mouth much wider to eat and brush his teeth.

We endured the usual rounds of the nurses, doctors, and a member of the neurosurgery team for the rest of the day. At one point Jim asked the nurse if he could go on a walk when they were available to accompany him. The continued pain in his head and jaw was intense, but he endured it all with much grace.

At some point, I wandered around the campus and decided on something for lunch. I spent most of the day parked in my chair-bed next to Jim's bed, waiting for whatever he needed and keeping him company, resting when I was able.

Courtney returned in the afternoon, bearing gifts of REAL Pepsi (not diet – Hallelujah!) for me and other treats. I vaguely remember that she and I shared a box of See's candy I had found in the gift shop earlier, although we didn't put much of a dent in it. She worked on Sudoku puzzles and chatted with us.

As afternoon turned to evening, we knew that Jim's family would be gathering for their traditional Christmas Eve get-together. We had advised them, my family, and the Corbins not to come back to UCSF that day because we thought Jim would be discharged from the hospital early the next morning. Jim turned on the TV in his room and searched for a Christmas movie to watch, settling on one of our family's favorites – A Christmas Story (with Ralphie and the Red Rider BB gun).

Soon we received a FaceTime call from Jim's entire family. Oh, how we longed to be with them that night. Our aching hearts were searching for something normal, something familiar on that evening, but there was nothing to soothe the ache. It was almost torturous to see everyone together and know that we were missing out on the evening. The FaceTime call was one of the two highlights of our evening, and it didn't last long enough for our lonely little hospital room.

Court left soon after that call.

Realizing that nothing else was going to happen that night, I changed into my sweats, washed my face, and snuggled up in my Monopoly quilt to continue watching TV with Jim.

In the next moments we experienced the second highlight of the evening ... carolers in the hospital hallways. I heard the voices begin faintly down the hallway. As they neared Jim's room they got louder. Although I have always loved to hear Christmas carolers, I cannot tell you of another time when carolers were such an enormous blessing to me. On this lonely night, those people sounded like angels approaching Jim's room. They stopped and greeted us when they noticed how much we were enjoying their singing. One of the ladies offered me a pan cookie from the Pyrex dish she was holding. Now, I don't usually take baked goods from strangers, but on this lonely night it was the only gift I was being offered. Jim couldn't have one because of his glucose levels. I eagerly scooped up the cookie and placed it in the napkin my new angel-friend handed me, overjoyed at this tiny gift I was holding . . . only to find out later that the cookie contained coconut, and I hate coconut. That night, I ate as much of the cookie as I could, trying to pretend that the coconut was not in it to spoil the texture and taste. Try as I might, I wasn't able to finish it.

I wish I could go back in time and tell those carolers how much they meant to both of us on that lonely night, when we were separated from our family and friends. Their simple gesture made such a difference for us. Jim and I reminisced and spoke fondly of them the next two Christmases.

Jim and I wished each other a Merry Christmas, then drifted off to sleep for another night in his hospital room. Once again, we were awakened periodically for charting vitals and administering meds. Jim's pain was very high that night, so he was awake every hour or two.

To my surprise, I awoke at 6:00 AM on Christmas morning to a slight dilemma. Jim, not quite awake yet, had stretched his arm and accidentally caught the surgical drain that was connected to his scalp, ripping it out of his head. Of course, doing so amazingly well with anything relating to blood, I remained completely calm and helped him contact his nurse. . . . Ok. Ok. That's not how it really happened . . . . Instead, I gave him a panicked look; tried to figure out where the tube had slithered off to; stopped for a minute to bend over, place my hands on my knees, and express that my stomach was feeling rather queasy and I needed to regroup; THEN I calmed myself and rang for the nurse to have them send someone to help us. . . . There. That's the REAL story.

The nurse entered the room within a few minutes and assessed the situation. Jim's drainage tube was reinserted quickly, only to be taken out a couple of hours later when they decided he could be discharged.

We got a good laugh out of that, realizing that there really wasn't much reason to panic about it being ripped out in the first place.

Here it was, Christmas Day. And here we sat, waiting in the hospital room. Courtney had rejoined us and was keeping us company. We were all tired and ready to be back in our normal surroundings. We missed our family and dogs. It didn't feel like Christmas Day. Annnnd, my hair felt disgusting – I'm totally sure that was the least of my worries, but it really did feel gross. I had tried my best to get ready that morning and look decent for the day, but I really needed a full shower; some clean, hospital-free clothes; and my own home.

Throughout the morning the nurses and residents worked to assess if Jim could be discharged that day, or if he needed to wait until the next day before going home. Eventually the news came that he was getting his "Get Out of Jail Free" Card (a joke we used frequently). Because it was Christmas Day, there were a lot of challenges to route around because certain departments in the hospital were closed for the holidays.

One issue was the fact that they felt Jim needed a specific arm sling to protect his weak, dangling arm. They wanted to ask a member from that specialty department to come and fit Jim with a sling that would assist the poor, overstretched muscles in his shoulder and give them a chance to heal. Unfortunately, that specialty department was closed for the day and the remainder of the weekend, so we agreed to skip that requirement on his discharge paperwork.

The next issue was regarding his prescription medicine. Jim's nurse wanted to ensure we were able to get all of the meds he needed before going home. Again, due to the fact that it was Christmas Day, the pharmacy they usually send patients to before going home was closed. On top of that, we found that not many pharmacies between UCSF and home would be open that day either. The nursing staff worked tirelessly to locate a few pharmacies I would be comfortable with trying to navigate to in the Bay Area on our trip home. They provided me with a printed list of pharmacies and addresses.

Eventually all of the boxes were checked for Jim's discharge. I signed the discharge papers and was handed a copy to add to my growing stack of medical paperwork. I helped Jim get dressed, then the nurse removed his IV. I had already made a trip to our car in the parking garage to load my duffel bag and other belongings, so once Jim was snug in his wheelchair Courtney and I escorted him out of the hospital, into the cold December air, across the street to the parking garage, and out to our car.

WE WERE FREE!!!

As I climbed into the driver's side of our Expedition, I immediately resolved myself to keep from looking directly at Jim too much on the way home. His surgery site on the left side of his head was no longer covered, and lucky me, that just happened to be the area that faced me as I hopped in our car! Grrrrrrreat! I knew that if I focused on it too much I would be feeling quite squeamish for the rest of the ride home.

Courtney still had her belongings at the hotel. I followed her back so we could collect her stuff and complete our checkout. Checkout complete, we hopped on the road, bound for home.

We drove across the Bay Bridge and eventually arrived in Dublin. Courtney called me and we decided to stop in an area near the movie theater to locate a little something for a late lunch. That area has numerous restaurants, so we were sure to find one open on Christmas Day. Round and round we drove, slowly searching for signs that any restaurant was open. At last, we found ONE small pizza place that was open. (I laughed as it reminded me of the scene from "A Christmas Story" when they had to eat dinner in the Chinese restaurant because their turkey dinner was snatched up by the neighbor's dogs.)

Courtney and I found a place to park. I jumped out and retrieved Jim's wheelchair from the back of the vehicle, then helped him move carefully from the car to the wheelchair. We walked into the small pizza place, ordered our meal, and discovered that the only seating for the place was located outside of the building. It was a good thing that Jim already had his sweatshirt on. The dining area was small. Most of the tables were already taken, but we found one open table available. We settled in and devoured our lunch, filling our hungry bellies.

I remember one customer at this restaurant that day – a lady who noticed the enormous wound and staples on the side of Jim's head. I was worried that it would repulse people as they were getting ready to eat their meal. Instead, as this sweet lady passed Jim, she kindly patted him on the shoulder and gave him a smile. I have no idea what she thought had happened to Jim. We chuckled together as we thought of all the horrible things she could have surmised he had been through, and finally concluded that she must have thought he was in a terrible car accident or something.

With full bellies we were back on the road. Now that we were in Dublin, the trip home was relatively easy for me, so Courtney notified us that she wouldn't be making the next stop with us. She would continue back to her house so she could get some rest.

Jim and I still had to stop at the pharmacy for his prescription meds. We had located one just a little way off the freeway that was easy to find. I ran in to deliver his prescriptions, then found myself waiting for about 30-45 minutes for them to be filled. During that time, I made multiple trips out to the car to check on Jim. He was comfy in his seat, and dozed off and on while we waited. Soon I had prescriptions in my hot little hand. I gave him the ones that were due immediately once I reached the car.

Next stop – HOME!

We made our way back to the freeway, then up and over the Altamont and into Tracy. From Tracy to home I struggled to keep my eyes open and stay on the road. I desperately needed a nap, but we were so close to home it made no sense to stop. I would need HOURS of sleep before I could get back on the road, and having Jim stay in the car for that long was not an option. So I focused on the road the best I could, played games in my mind to count down the minutes to our destination, and worked desperately to keep my peepers open until we arrived home.

We pulled into our driveway around 4:30 that afternoon. We were so exhausted that it took every ounce of energy to get both of us into the house, use the restroom, and plop ourselves down onto our comfy furniture. Jim sat in his recliner, as usual. I scrambled to get on the couch and cover myself with a blanket. A couple of hours later we awoke to a pleasant feeling of hospital hangover.

I struggled to search for something we could call dinner, got Jim his next round of meds, unloaded the car, then made a phone call to check on our youngest kids.

As you may remember, the Corbins took Hanna, Americis, and Christopher home with them the night of Jim's surgery. They loved on our kids; supported them on these difficult, emotional days; and graciously provided a wonderful Christmas Eve and Christmas Day with their extended family – even taking the time the week before Jim's surgery to quickly gather gifts for our kids so they wouldn't feel left out when they exchanged gifts with their family.

I wanted my kids home. I wanted to see our family. I wanted to see our friends. We had entirely missed Christmas. But, unfortunately, we didn't have an ounce of strength to change any of those situations that night. We didn't have the strength to carry on a semi-coherent conversation with each other, much less anyone else. The previous two weeks had definitely caught up to me and I couldn't even muster enough energy to drag myself in to take a much-needed shower. I felt disgusting, but I lacked the capacity to do anything about it.

The good news was we were finally home!

The bad news was we were finally home . . . and now all of Jim's care was up to me. Me, the person with NO medical degree. I was terrified when I realized how much was riding on my shoulders. Once again, the success/failure of Jim's recovery was my responsibility.

9

WHATEVER YOU DO, DON'T FALL

SINCE JIM'S DIAGNOSIS of GBM, I have always felt that whatever the doctors and nurses said shouldn't happen or wasn't likely, was always the thing that actually DID happen. Over the years that he battled bravely, it just seemed that those "least likely situations" were always the situations banging on our door, begging to be let in every time we thought we had a moment to breathe.

We BARELY had a chance to catch our breath between battles. Seriously, I can't even express this strongly enough to allow you a glimpse into the constant state of chaos and trauma we were thrown into time and time again. As I proceed to write out the next few chapters and describe the first seven months of 2016, you'll get a better idea of why I say this. As I pen these events, I can't even believe that we survived the brutal attacks that seemed to be never-ending. I can only tell you that we were not capable of surviving them alone, in our own strength. We were only able to continue pushing through these dark, treacherous waters because of the prayers of those who surrounded us, because God was faithful to see us through those difficult days and provide supernatural strength and perseverance.

When we left UCSF on Christmas Day, part of the orders Jim was given verbally before his discharge were, "Whatever you do, don't fall."

The instructions seemed easy enough. Jim wasn't PLANNING to throw himself on the ground anytime soon. He was already avoiding that at any cost throughout his daily routine. Whenever we went out, I acted as his Border Collie, circling him continuously, watching for anything (or anyone) that might possibly pose a threat and throw him off balance, and barking information to him that would help him navigate his path safely.

After I tie up some loose ends, I'll come back to that....

Hanna, Americis, and Christopher returned home the day after Christmas, and we were all ready to spend some time together; get good rest; and to try to get back into a little bit of a routine.

I called our primary care physician to make an appointment to have Jim's staples removed the following week (January 4th). I explained to the receptionist that there were A LOT of staples and they would need to reserve enough time for the doctor for this appointment. She asked me, "More than 15, you think?" Up until this point I hadn't really taken the time to count them because the incision looked so gross, but I indulged her and started counting as quickly as I could (not looking for accuracy at that point, but just a general idea). By the time I got to 50, she just said she'd put in the notes "over 50." Of course, once I realized the enormous amount of staples in my sweet guy's noggin, I just couldn't stop with "over 50." I needed an ACCURATE COUNT because I had gone to so much trouble. I started counting over again and found that the official count was 53! I was shocked by that.

Jim was able to get his scalp wet during his shower on December 28th. That helped me to clean up some of the mess that was still evident from his surgery. I struggled with the blood, but pushed past it once again. I was never meant to be a nurse.

Over the next week we had to adjust pain meds, steroids, and insulin to keep up with the changes in Jim's body. He started asking for only half of his pain meds because they were so strong they made him sleepy. At bedtime he was fine with a full dose. The neurosurgeon had increased his steroids after surgery to help with swelling and inflammation. Due to the increase in steroids, his blood glucose levels were elevated once again and I had to start administering insulin at every meal.

Within a few days I was helping Hanna pack for our church's Youth Winter Camp and attempting to find warm clothing and snow boots for her. Cara and a few students from her youth group were going, too. That was a problem for this lady here because Cara had been the one who was helping me keep Jim's incision clean and applying Neosporin to it daily. I still felt like I had worms in my stomach every time I tried to look at it and use the Q-tip to wipe the dried blood off of his surgery site. The plan was that Cara would do that chore for me and I would do all the rest. BUUUUUT, that wasn't going to work if she was supposed to be out of town for 3 days! Courtney was no help with that kind of task because she was even squeamish-er than her mother. (That is a real word. You just don't know it yet.)

I resigned myself to the fact that I would indeed need to put my big girl panties on and take on the task of keeping Jim's wound clean. I had to do it in segments, but I eventually was able to complete the job each day. I always finished it off with a little shiver dance to shake off the yucky feeling in the pit of my stomach and throat. Jim would laugh and applaud my efforts to stretch out of my comfort zone to take good care of him. Not to toot my own horn here, but I'm pretty sure I met the requirements for the Not-A-Nurse-But-Acting-Like-A-Nurse Award. And, yes, this is where I pat myself on the back and say, "Well done, Self. Well done!"

Soon the kids were back to school from the holiday break, and I was tending to Jim, taking down Christmas decorations, working on my office work from home, making phone calls to set up necessary doctor appointments and therapy, and, on occasion, we got out of the house to ease our cabin fever.

On January 4th, I took Jim to have the 53 staples removed from his noggin. His primary care physician teased Jim and asked him why the surgeon cut his head in the shape of a question mark. We joked that we would start calling Jim "The Riddler." Our doctor knew the severity of

Jim's condition and loved that we still enjoyed laughing about the little things in life.

Later that week I made phone calls to Dr. B to get instructions for starting chemo the following week. Appointments had been made to see Dr. B in his office, but I guess his new scheduling coordinator double-booked him. We were flexible and decided to have a phone consultation to get the necessary information.

That week I also started the referral process to get Jim into speech therapy with a therapist near us. In the middle of coordinating all of that, I had to make a doctor appointment for Hanna because she had a severe sinus infection AND Christopher had to stay home from school for a couple of days because he wasn't feeling well. At the same time, I was trying to do a marathon preview of Bible study materials for our Ladies' Bible Study, in an attempt to prep for the new series we were starting. And, wouldn't you know, it was also the week that construction was starting at the Escalon Youth Center. Jim was super excited and wanted to go watch the team work for a while. (I'll say more about the youth center in another chapter.) I felt like I was running in circles!

To make matters worse, the appointment with Jim's local oncologist, Dr. S, was also cancelled. It was due to a family emergency for Dr. S. He was supposed to authorize Jim's next chemo session after thoroughly checking his labs and seeing him in his office. Thankfully, that cancellation turned out to be a huge blessing! Read on and it will make more sense.

And, now that I've tied up all of those loose ends from the three weeks between Jim's surgery and January 14, 2016, we can return to our regularly scheduled program. Annnnd, go . . . .

When January 14th rolled around, we were doing well to operate in our new daily routine. In fact, I was just getting to the point that I felt it was manageable again and I wasn't panicking as much about caring for his wound. It was healing quite nicely.

I drove the kids to school that morning. Later in the day, I took Jim out to Sutter Gould to get his blood drawn. This was necessary to check his blood counts before he started chemo. After I taxied him in and out of the building and loaded him and his wheelchair in the car, I stopped at Target to pick up some much-needed groceries for our house. Many people had offered to help with grocery shopping and meals, but at this point I just wanted to make my very own shopping trip to stock up on stuff for our house. I can't remember if Jim waited in the car for me that day, or if he used the electric wheelchair at Target. I just know that in a matter of about 15 minutes I was done and loading the car with the precious purchases that I had made all on my very own. (I guess it doesn't take much to make me happy. Hahaha!)

I started the car and headed back to Escalon to pick up our kids from school. Once home, I parked in the garage and asked the kids to each grab a bag or two of groceries on their way into the house. I needed to help Jim out of the car and hold his cane for him while he stepped up the two steps into our laundry room.

The kids exited the car and grabbed the groceries as requested. Jim got out of the car and I walked with him to the steps of the house inside our garage. I walked up the steps into the laundry room and reached to take his cane from him so he could grab the door frame with a firm grip before he navigated up the two steps. He successfully climbed up both steps and was standing firmly inside the laundry room. I shifted the items around in my hands so I could hand his cane back to him, but as I did I saw the oddest thing I've ever seen. Standing firmly on both feet, Jim suddenly leaned backwards, starting from the chest and shoulders, as if someone had placed a hand on his chest and pushed him back in slow motion. I scrambled to release the items in my hand and catch him, but it happened so fast I couldn't react quickly enough. To my horror, he fell completely backwards past the two steps without being able to brace himself. He landed on his rear and lower back, forcefully rolling all the way up his back to his shoulders before he struck the cement with his head. His legs flew up briefly before he came to a full stop. His floppy hand/arm got caught in the mix and hit the cement hard.

What did I do while this was all happening? I screamed bloody murder. Yes, I screamed high-pitched, bloody murder screams multiple times from the moment I saw him falling back until a few moments after his body came to a sudden halt on the cold, cement floor in the garage. He laid there stunned from the fall, as I continued my high-pitched intervals of screams. (Yes. I told you how amazing I am in crisis situations. You still don't believe me, huh?)

Jim quickly came to his senses and told me that I needed to stop screaming. I was traumatized. While the screams were exiting my mouth, my mind was running 3000 miles an hour. I knew he was on blood thinners. I knew he hit the ground very hard and I had no way of knowing if he broke a hip, or his hand, or if it affected his brain when his head hit the ground. He had just had brain surgery. I thought to myself, "Oh goodness, they said, 'Whatever you do, don't fall!' He fell. Now what? What do I do now?!?!?!"

Hanna, Americis, and Christopher obviously knew something had happened when they heard the blood-curdling screams coming from the laundry room. It was hard to miss the fact that their mother was yelling like a crazy woman. They had made it to the kitchen with their bags of groceries and barely had a chance to set them down on the counter before the commotion started. They came running to help.

Jim was attempting to sit up, but I cautioned him to stay put and not move. I grabbed my phone and dialed 911 to ask for medical help. While I waited for them to answer I simultaneously checked Jim for severe injuries and instructed the kids to start putting the cold items in the refrigerator for me, knowing we were on our way to the hospital in a few minutes. They finished unloading the last couple of bags from the car and followed my directions to the tee.

Meanwhile, I gave the information to the dispatcher, including the information that he had just had brain surgery three weeks before this. Since we live in a small town, we quickly heard the sirens heading our way. Help was coming! Once the dispatcher had all of the information they needed, I was able to hang up to start greeting our town's amazing first responders. Many of them already recognized our address when they were dispatched and they were thoroughly prepared to help us.

I started making phone calls to those I needed to notify immediately, knowing I would need someone to come get the kids if I was making the trip to the hospital with Jim. After giving the first responders a quick synopsis of the situation, I knew I needed to give them our insurance card and the papers I always had handy with Jim's medical history and list of meds. I left Jim in their care and went into our office to grab said items, using the time to multi-task and finish the short list of calls.

The Corbins arrived first and were able to take the kids for us. Jim was assessed by the ambulance crew, helped off the cement floor, and loaded onto a gurney to be transported into the back of the ambulance.

I gathered the things I needed for the hospital, knowing the list all too well by this point, then Courtney and I drove to the hospital.

We had also learned the routine at our local hospital, knowing that even if we arrived at the same time that the ambulance did we would have to wait in the waiting room until they moved Jim to a bed in ER and started evaluating him. For most people this wouldn't be a problem, but because Jim's speech was so challenging (and that challenge increased with stressful moments) I was always chomping at the bit to get into that room to help him communicate effectively with the nursing staff. I knew that most of them would get impatient while going through his basic health history and waiting for his replies. I feared that they would try to fill in his words before he could answer their questions completely. That would be very dangerous if they assumed specific information, tried to help him fill in the blanks verbally, but only caused him to switch into repeating what they were saying instead of answering accurately.

Let me explain to help you better understand the risks involved with Jim's speech challenges: If I were to ask Jim, "Do you want a hot dog or a hamburger?" the fact that I said "hamburger" <u>last</u> would cause Jim to answer, "Hamburger!" whether or not that was what he truly wanted. Or if Jim got stuck on a certain word in the middle of a sentence and I tried to finish the sentence for him, he would immediately repeat the portion of the sentence I filled in, whether that was what he intended to say or not. Once I interrupted him by saying out loud what I assumed he wanted to say, it derailed his train of thought and it took him some time before he could think through it again to be able to express it. It was extremely frustrating for him. I had learned to allow more time for him to express what he wanted to say before I offered to help fill in his words. Every time we arrived at the hospital for a new emergency, I was panicking, fearful that speech situations like this would cause them to fill in his chart incorrectly.... Now that I've explained that challenge a little more in depth, you can definitely get a better picture of the danger in leaving Jim alone in an ER room for too long while a nurse proceeded to run through their check list of questions. Now, you can see that I wasn't just the typical, freaked-out family member who was pushing to get in and see their loved one in ER.

Courtney and I checked in at the security desk, asking about Jim's location. As usual, we were told that we would have to wait. I explained the situation of Jim's speech challenges to the security guard, but after he briefly checked for Jim's ER room number he proceeded to tell me that I still needed to wait a few minutes. I learned at these times to continue standing nearby to remind them that it was urgent for me to get in as quickly as possible. In a few minutes, the guard let me in to see Jim and start reviewing his medical history and the details of his fall with his nurse, then with the doctor.

The hospital staff checked Jim over thoroughly and ordered a brain MRI and x-rays of his floppy arm. They called UCSF, at my request, and consulted with them to see if they wanted additional scans or tests. By the time they finished up with Jim, they found that he had sprained his right wrist, had a tooth infection, and had a "sinus infection" (the recurring situation he had been facing since September – that we were about to get real answers for in the days to come).

Unfortunately, they missed the fact that he had broken his right pinky finger. Jim didn't notice that was the case until many months later, after he had been doing hand therapy for a while and was getting some mobility of his hand and fingers back.

But, I'll leave the description of our hospital visit to my trusty social media posts. I don't think I can improve on them or give you any more of an accurate description than they give, so here goes:

January 14, 2016 – Evening

Home now. Jim was finally released from the crazy house (also known as ER). He is hungry, sore, has a sinus infection, has a tooth infection (caused probably from chemo and radiation), a sprained right wrist that was put in a splint (his bad hand/arm even before the fall), and we. are. exhausted.

I've decided a few things today:

- I'm done with hospitals. We've seen too many of them (and doctors' offices) over the last 7+ months.
- I could probably be hired as a screamer in a horror film. I did pretty good at that today . . . until Jim, lying on the garage floor, had to tell me to stop screaming.
- I truly need a few weeks to ONLY SLEEP and to look at pretty scenery. And then I need lots of fun. I'm missing fun in my life. Hmmmm, what IS fun? It has become a foreign word to me. Help!

If I feel up to it tomorrow, I'll indulge you in a few great one-liners we heard from the crazies in ER tonight. I seriously thought we were getting sucked into the vortex of craziness.

Thanks for your prayers today!!!

Expecting a miracle! Pleeeeease be soon!!!
♥ **Jim and Brenda**

January 15, 2016 – Morning

Here is an assortment of the crazy events and comments we witnessed in ER last night . . . You're welcome!

Guy 1 (who was very loud and obnoxious the entire time we were in ER): "WHY AM I FLATLINING OVER HERE?!?!?!" (His monitor didn't sound any different than anyone else's.)

Lady 1: "Do you understand me? Do you understand me? Do you understand me?" over and over and over for at least 5 minutes. Then they had to clean her and change her and she said a new phrase continually for 5-10 minutes. It was in Portuguese, but I assume she was telling them she was cold. She seriously didn't stop in between the phrase, over and over and over again.

Guy 1 (who had been yelling and moaning loudly for hours himself): "I just can't take this anymore. It's so loud in here. I just need 30 minutes of peace. Can you give me that?"

The doctor went in to talk to guy 1, but got called out because the patient on the other side of us stopped breathing. But instead of being patient and waiting till they finished with her, he continued to yell that he needed this or that. So the nurse explained they had an urgent situation. To which he responded, "I've got an urgent situation too!!!!" The nurse said firmly, "One second!" To which he replied maturely, "ONE SECOND BACK!!!"

Security was called in multiple times for guy 1. At one point he said he was just going to leave. But when the nurse came in to remove his IV to leave he said, "I can't believe you're not going to treat me!!!" After much more crazy conversation he decided to stay, but his best comment ever was to the doctor: "I think because my mind is racing, that's why my back hurts and I have abdominal pain."

In between all of these other chaotic moments an elderly lady was brought in from a nursing home. She had just been transferred there that day and was not happy. Some crazy ordeal transpired and she had a knock-down-drag-out with the nursing care staff and the paramedics. She came in strapped down. Her husband arrived quite some time later and she tried to convince him that he could just wheel her out of the hospital and escape. Then she started accusing him of damaging something that was hers, to which he replied, "We brought those in so we could prove that you still had them and they hadn't been stolen like you said! YOU were the one who broke them when you hit so-and-so and started everything!" Conversation calmed for a while, but when he navigated out of her curtained area and left ER, he threw his hands up in the air and said, "Lord, deliver me!!!!"

Annnnd then, of course, as we were leaving ER, we were waiting for Court to bring the car around to load Jim, and a nice-looking, elderly gentleman made eye contact with us from sitting in his wheelchair by the door. He smiled normal-like, but then started signing to us. We tried to be polite and give gestures to him that we didn't understand what he was saying, then he laughed and started talking. He told us he was trained in martial arts and could make a weapon out of almost anything. ". . . Even CDs and DVDs! Ya wanna know how to do that? You break them in half and you can cut someone really good!" . . . To which I responded by telling Jim that we needed to wheel him outside and wait in the cold for Courtney to bring the car around.

And that, my friends, was our interesting entertainment during the night at the looney bin!

See, I told you I couldn't convey that hilarious chaos any better than I already had!

The next few days were extremely stressful as we managed Jim's pain from the jolt of his fall and kept an eye on him for additional signs of trauma to his brain and body. His eye almost swelled shut. It started at the top of his eye, near his eyebrow, then over the next 24 hours it pooled into and under his eye. The hospital staff didn't give me clear directions on exactly what to expect to happen, or parameters for when to call. I was ready to take him back to ER, because I feared damage to his brain or a possible brain bleed, but after speaking to a doctor at UCSF they put my mind at ease. Sure enough, the next day the swelling started to decrease.

Five days after Jim's fall, he was scheduled to see his local oncologist, Dr. S. It was the appointment that had been rescheduled from earlier in the month. It also gave us a chance to bring Dr. S up to speed on Jim's brain surgery, discuss this possible tooth infection and how it would affect his pending round of chemo, talk about decreasing his steroid dosages, and update him on Jim's recent fall. Dr. S said that Jim would have to be seen by a dentist and get the tooth infection under control before he could proceed with chemo. He asked him to continue on his current dose of steroids, and set an appointment for him to come back in two weeks.

Two days later – January 21st – we were at our local dentist office for a consultation on Jim's tooth/teeth. The dentist confirmed an abscess between tooth #14 and #15, adding that both teeth would require extraction from an oral surgeon. He provided a referral for Jim, and he was scheduled to see the oral surgeon in Modesto the next day.

On January 22nd, we met with the oral surgeon. Jim had a horrible headache and struggled to get through the appointment. We would have cancelled it, but knew that it was important to get the teeth pulled immediately to resolve the issue so he could resume his chemo regimen. The oral surgeon reviewed the x-rays from our dentist office and agreed that oral surgery was needed. He discussed the procedure and reviewed Jim's prescriptions, noting that he would not need to stop his blood thinner for the procedure. By the time we left, oral surgery was scheduled.

Four days later – January 26th – Jim had two teeth extracted. He did relatively well with the procedure and the oral surgeon was diligent about taking good care of him because he knew our situation.

The surprise came after the procedure, when the oral surgeon told us that the abscess between the two teeth was extremely large. ***AND

HERE IS WHERE WE FINALLY GOT THE ANSWER TO THE ISSUE WE WERE DEALING WITH SINCE SEPTEMBER 2015!*** He said that the abscess was a long tunnel that went all the way from his gum, between the two teeth that were extracted, and extended up into his sinus cavity!!!

You can imagine our extreme shock at that crazy information. For FIVE MONTHS we had been treating Jim's "sinus infection" off and on. He had had multiple MRIs: a routine check after radiation, in preparation for his brain surgery, after his brain surgery, and finally at the hospital after he fell – but somehow no one ever caught that he had a long tunnel that extended from his mouth into his sinus cavity. His "sinus infection" was actually a huge abscess! No wonder the foul drainage he kept experiencing was so disgusting! No wonder we weren't able to get that infection under control!

I actually forgot to add back in October, that Jim had even seen an ENT (ears, nose, and throat specialist) to see if anything else was going on regarding his "sinus infections" and the horrible drainage. He didn't see anything on the scans we brought him and suggested that Jim start using a nasal saline spray, Claritin, and to put a humidifier in the room close to Jim to keep his nasal passages clean and moisturized. As I look back at the information in his medical notebook I kept for him and discovered that little tidbit of information I had forgotten, I'm more than disappointed that a specialist like himself couldn't have looked into Jim's case a little deeper to help him out at that point in time.

I am cautious as I express the following statement, not knowing if it is reality or not: I often wonder if Jim's fall was meant to reveal the huge abscess that no one had discovered yet. I know that sounds weird to express, but as I think back about the moments of his fall . . . recalling that both of his feet were firmly planted in the laundry room once he climbed up the stairs . . . there is no doubt in my mind that at that moment he was stable and was only waiting for me to hand him his cane before he proceeded into the entryway from our laundry room. I shudder as I recall that it looked to me like someone had shoved him from the top of his chest/shoulder area, and that he fell backwards from the top down, realizing that his feet never stumbled. It leaves me baffled and wondering if the discovery of that awful abscess between his mouth and his sinus cavity was actually the result of an angel intervening on his behalf. I'll never have the answer to that question this side of heaven, and by the time I get there I will have forgotten that I even had the question.

I consulted with Dr. B (at USCF) by phone regarding Jim's recent tooth abstraction and findings after the procedure. Jim's body needed time to heal. The tunnel in his mouth needed time to close completely and seal off the area to his sinus cavity. It couldn't do that while he was on chemo, so his next chemo cycle was delayed again.

Jim had two follow-up appointments with the oral surgeon over the next week and a half. He also visited Dr. S again to get him up to speed on the recent findings and discuss the issues that had been tabled from his last appointment. Dr. S confirmed what Dr. B had already decreed, Jim's chemo would need to wait. We were on board with that, knowing that God was in control and was directing our path. We had been jostled around, to and fro, for so many months now that we had <u>almost</u> learned that fighting what was happening in our lives was in vain. Almost.

On February 1st, Jim had his first speech therapy appointment with Jim S. Jim S was a brilliant man. He was kind and easy to talk to. It was evident in our first session with him that he was interested in Jim's ENTIRE well-being, not just the speech end of things.

You may find that I use the words "we" and "our" a lot when it comes to descriptions of Jim's therapy sessions from here on out, because I attended every one of them and was an active part in them: speech, physical therapy, occupational therapy. I was present for almost every single one of them. It was extremely rare for me to ask someone else to take Jim to therapy because I used the information from his sessions to help him throughout the week. I took my job as his caregiver very seriously.

Jim S reviewed Jim's health history and recent surgeries, asking a lot of questions to get a good baseline on him. As he worked with Jim in his sessions, he was extremely patient and encouraging. He found ways to hit topics that Jim would feel comfortable talking about, even asking him to attempt reciting Scripture verses, singing a song (which helps with tempo in speech), or talking about things he did as a pastor. As long as Jim was engaged in conversation, the topic at hand did not matter to his therapist, and he found great pleasure in getting to know Jim. Jim and I enjoyed him, too. We settled in to the routine of speech therapy once a week with Jim S, and Jim and I worked on speech homework at home in between his scheduled sessions.

Once again, we thought we were back on track to a somewhat normal life. We had a brief chance to breathe . . . or, in reality, at least to take half a breath before the next emergency. We falsely believed that things were finally settling down and we could attempt a normal routine.

And here, I almost feel like Lemony Snicket in <u>A Series of Unfortunate Events</u> cautioning his readers to stop reading if they were looking for a happy, uplifting story with a beautifully resolved storyline. I feel compelled to share the first paragraph of his book "The Bad Beginning" because it is so appropriate for the long saga of unfortunate events I'm recording:

> "If you are interested in stories with happy endings, you would be better off reading some other book. In this book, not only is there no happy ending, there is no happy beginning, and very few happy things in the middle. This is because not many happy things happened in the lives of the three Baudelaire youngsters. Violet, Klaus, and Sunny Baudelaire were intelligent children, and they were charming, and resourceful, and had pleasant facial features, but they were extremely unlucky, and most everything that happened to them was rife with misfortune, misery, and despair. I'm sorry to tell you this, but that is how the story goes."

We, like the Baudelaire children, had many more battles coming our way.

We just didn't know it yet.

10

THE ED HIT SLINKY SAGA

Sunday, February 7, 2016:
We need prayer RIGHT NOW.

Jim is on his way by ambulance to the hospital. He had a seizure just a bit ago. Ed hit slinky need prayer for him, but for our family. All three youngest kids witnessed this and are having a really difficult time. Cara and Court are going with me to the hospital. We're just a bit behind the ambulance.

YES. YOU READ every word of that post correctly. I'm sure it left you wondering who Ed and Slinky are, and why in the world Ed would hit Slinky. Furthermore, did he punch him with his fist? Did he hit him with a bat? Did he hit him with his car? Did Slinky deserve such treatment? What in the world did Ed do to Slinky ... and WHY? INQUIRING MINDS WANT TO KNOW!

This is the post that went out to all of our friends and family begging for prayer on the night of February 7, 2016. It left many of our friends baffled. I didn't realize my error until many hours later. And, THIS is the post that was shared by multiple friends and family so people would pray for us because of the new emergency we were facing. I was embarrassed when I realized what I had accidentally typed... or, rather, what my phone had autocorrected for me in my frantic state, on the way to the hospital.

One person surmised that Ed was the ambulance driver and Slinky was our cat, hence deducting that Ed hit Slinky with the ambulance and our kids witnessed it and were having a difficult time. That was very creative reasoning! I laughed at that when I read their reply later, but that was not the story. I found it even funnier that they thought we were on a first name basis with the ambulance crew at that point because we had made so many trips to the hospital. Unfortunately, Ed was NOT Jim's driver that night, so that was not accurate either.

And so started the "Ed Hit Slinky" Saga.

Before I get too far along in this story, I'll clear up the mistake. The strange "Ed hit Slinky" sentence should have read more along the lines of "He had a seizure just a bit ago. **We not only need prayer for Jim**, but for our family."

Sunday morning, February 7th, I woke up and started my usual morning routine. I headed for our restroom and started the shower, only to find that we had no hot water. None at all. Only clear, cold water streamed from the showerhead that cold winter morning, and I was having none of that! Try as I might, I couldn't force myself to take a freezing cold shower, so I resigned myself to wash up the best I could and get dressed for church.

I woke the kids and they started getting ready. Courtney arrived before we left the house. She was always a big help to me, and she stayed with Jim every Sunday morning while I went to worship practice. After practice, I usually darted home to help Jim get dressed and ready for the day, then loaded him in the car to take him to church with me. And, that was what happened on this cold February morning.

After church, we headed home to plan for a fun day with our kids. It was Super Bowl Sunday. We had a big dinner planned together, with lots of fun finger food laid out for the whole day. Not that I care, but in case you were wondering, the Panthers were playing the Broncos. If the google results I have are accurate, the Broncos won 24 – 10. (You're welcome.)

Jim was raised in San Leandro/Oakland area and was a die-hard Raiders fan, but he could never pass up the opportunity to watch the Super Bowl, no matter who was playing.

We all settled in together, nestled in blankets on the couches and floor of our living room.

My dad came by that afternoon and found the explanation of our hot water problem from earlier that morning: For some odd reason, the pilot light on the water heater was out. Simple fix. He lit the pilot light and was on his way home. (What a great dad!)

I don't know how to describe the rest of our day together, except to say that it was one of the best days we had had as a family of seven. We laughed. We laughed A LOT. We joked with each other. No one got their feelings hurt. Everyone was in a great mood and enjoyed the day. Nobody felt like they were in competition for Jim's or my attention. We all just enjoyed the day together and felt at peace.

Peace. That feeling that we didn't get to experience very often with the ongoing traumatic events that kept interrupting our lives, but here it was! On February 7, 2016 the Davis family experienced a peaceful afternoon and evening, filled with lots of fun and laughter. Mark that one on the calendar!!! We cherished it. We even talked about what an amazing day it was as we were wrapping up the evening.

Hanna, Americis, and Christopher started rotating through shower shifts. I pulled a card table over to my recliner so I could continue working on a Disney puzzle I had started a few days earlier. Jim was relaxing in his recliner. Cara and Courtney decided they would head for home and said their goodbyes.

Peaceful day complete.

I wish that was the end of the story, but it was not. Apparently, the evening was NOT finished for us. More trauma was lurking around the corner, waiting to catch us off guard at the end of a beautiful day.

About ten to fifteen minutes after Cara and Courtney left, as I was working on my puzzle, I started hearing strange sounds coming from

Jim's direction. I turned to my left and was briefly paralyzed with fear as I identified that Jim was having a grand mal seizure. His body was convulsing uncontrollably. His arm was stiff and flopping toward me, back and forth. He kept making short, guttural sounds.

I started talking to him immediately, calling out to him and assuring him that I was there and everything was alright. I held his hand, then placed my hand on his chest, continuing to call his name and assure him I hadn't left. I retrieved my cell phone from the cup holder between our two recliners and immediately dialed 911.

Although I cannot tell you who was in the room when Jim's seizure started, eventually Hanna, Americis, and Christopher had all joined me. Suddenly, I heard wails from my children. One of them begged me through sobs, "Make it stop. Make it stop. What's happening to him?!?!" As I tried to navigate the details of the 911 call, I instructed my kids to step into the family room, just around the wall, if they needed to be slightly removed from the situation. It was a traumatizing sight! I was barely coping and keeping it together at that point.

I continued hovering over Jim and placing my hand on his chest, hoping to bring some sort of comfort to him. Once I finished on the line with the emergency dispatcher, I started through the mandatory list of family I needed to notify immediately – starting with a phone call to Cara and Courtney to ask them to come back to our house. By this point the seizure had stopped and Jim had fallen into a deep sleep, snoring rather loudly.

My adrenaline was pumping again. I had switched into emergency mode and needed to coordinate everything that needed to happen in the next minutes. I called to the kids to help me kennel our dogs and unlock the front door for the first responders. I grabbed the puzzle table and moved it out of the way. Then I started gathering the items Jim and I would need for the hospital. I repeatedly stopped to check on the kids, as they were still crying and traumatized by the horrific scene they had just encountered. My mom was on her way and said she'd stay at our house with the kids for the night.

It had only been 3 ½ weeks since the ambulance had last been dispatched to our house! This was getting to be INSANE! How much more could Jim handle? How much more could our kids handle? How much more could I handle? We were ALL on overload.

Familiar faces lined the entryway and living room of our home again. That is one thing that I can say always brought us much peace in the emergency situations we faced. Our town's ambulance, police, and fire crews were familiar with us and took such amazing care of our whole family, offering their comfort and excellent services to each of us in those crisis situations. You don't get that personal touch just anywhere, and I never took it for granted. Many times in these situations (including the ones I haven't written about yet), the fire or police crew would stay at the house with me until I had finished grabbing everything we needed. They made sure I had locked the doors to our house, and double-checked to be sure I (or whoever was driving) was in a state to drive safely. Upon departure, they would always offer their support if there was anything else they could do to help us.

Jim was quite confused when he was awakened from his deep sleep and had multiple strangers standing around. His speech was more difficult than usual. He recognized me, but was reluctant to follow my instructions as they attempted to get him up and onto the gurney. He always searched frantically, looking for me. He needed me to provide guidance in those stressful moments, knowing he could trust whatever I was telling him. The scared, confused look in his eyes was enough to sear a huge hole in my heart. Eventually, I was able to convince him that it was alright to do what the paramedics were asking him to do. I assured him that I would grab everything he needed and would meet him at the hospital. Once on the gurney, they wheeled him outside and loaded him into the back of the ambulance. Cara and Courtney helped to supervise as I scrambled to continue comforting the kids and gathering items from the house.

My mom arrived at our house and stayed with Hanna, Americis, and Christopher. Courtney was going to follow the ambulance in her car. Cara, knowing I was extremely shaky from the whole traumatic experience, offered to drive me to the hospital in my Expedition, so I would have a vehicle to drive home when Jim was released from the hospital (or when I needed to come home to shower – depending on how long Jim was in the hospital).

Sitting in the passenger seat of my car, still shaking from the adrenaline rush I had experienced, I began typing out the urgent plea for friends and family to start praying. I had no idea what this seizure meant for us in the days to come. I had no idea what it meant for Jim's physical capabilities. Would it affect his speech more? Was there something going on in his brain that was creating this havoc – a brain bleed or some other complication from his surgery a month and a half before? Would he be able to walk still? My mind was spinning, and somehow in the process of posting the urgent plea to join us in prayer, my phone decided to turn my post into "Ed hit Slinky."

Sunday Update #1:
We're at the hospital. He is alert and answering questions correctly. He was EXTREMELY confused when he was leaving the house, but doing much better now. We are waiting for them to run tests. They've started an IV. I assume that they'll keep him through the night for observation, but I don't really know at this point. THANK YOU FOR CONTINUING TO PRAY!

Sunday Update #2:
The doctor has received the CT results and consulted with UCSF. They are keeping Jim here overnight. I don't know if we will be able to be transferred to a regular room or not. It all depends on space.

If possible, they'd like to do an MRI before he leaves. If they can't fit him in while he's here, we'll need to schedule one soon.

The doctor and staff have been FABULOUS this time around. We're doing ok. Just really tired.

My mom is with our 3 youngest at our house - my sweet momma. Cara and Court are heading home for the night now. Jim's parents and sister are leaving in just a bit too.

Thanks for caring for us and lifting us in prayer!!! We KNOW God is faithful!

Monday, February 8, 2016 - Morning Update:
We were in ER all night. He just now got moved to a regular room. His tongue hurts really bad and he's starting to complain of a headache.

We didn't sleep well. I barely slept at all. I think I finally really went to sleep around 6:30 this morning and missed the whole shift change. When I woke up, no one looked familiar except Jim.

It sounds like he's staying throughout the day. I don't know anything about the length of time beyond that. I'm just going by what I've heard so far.

Oh! And for those who might be confused about what happened, Jim had a seizure last night while sitting in his recliner. The kids were still awake and were terrified. It was very scary. He came to the hospital via ambulance. I don't know why my post decided to autocorrect last night and tell a strange story about Ed and Slinky. (Still giggling about that.)

That's all I've got for now.

Monday, February 8, 2016 - Afternoon Update #1:
So, it looks like Jim will be spending another night at the hospital. They still have an EEG ordered and haven't been able to get it completed yet today. Plus, they'd like to keep him at least 24 hours for observation and that's not until late tonight.

They moved him from a double room to a private room this morning, shortly after he was moved up from ER. His room is very comfy and has lots of space. It's muuuuuch different than the one he had back in September that barely had enough space to change your mind.

The hospitalist came by and discussed the plan of care and the MRI results a little while ago. The MRI looks fine, only some inflammation that remains from his brain surgery. Nothing else is noted that would be cause for concern. So that's great news!

Right now the nurses are in the process of getting someone to put in another IV, because the one they put in his thumb in ER last night came out a bit ago when they were trying to stabilize it. It was bent and the nurse almost had it fixed, but sadly it didn't work. It's so hard to get IVs in him. Poor guy! We tried to tell the nurse to use the vein in his forehead.

The nurses just came in to try to readjust Jim's bed back to the normal height. It was a pretty hilarious moment with his bed going up and down, over and over. Cara told him he was on Tower of Terror, except it was Hospital Bed of Terror and they were going to drop it any minute. We all laughed pretty hard. You have to have some fun, right?!?!

I went home around noon to shower and grab clothes for tonight/tomorrow. Jim napped most of the time I was gone. Cara stayed in his room and answered questions for nurses and caseworkers. I also had to cancel 2 appointments for Jim for today and 1 appointment for Hanna tomorrow.

Monday, February 8, 2016 - Afternoon Update #2:
To add insult to injury, when I got back from showering, getting stuff at home, and picking up a late lunch for me and Cara, she informed me I have a rip in my jeans. Really?!?!?!?!?! And not just a rip, but it's right on my bootie. Nice!!! That's just about all I can say. Nice!!! Good thing I packed an extra pair of pants. The problem is that I picked up lunch in my ripped pants and walked into the hospital (with people behind me)! How do these things happen to me??? Maaaaybe Ed and Slinky messed them up during their fight last night. Hahaha!!!

Tuesday, February 9, 2016 – Morning Update:
Jim's EEG was completed first thing this morning. We're waiting for the results now. We still have to consult with the neurologist as well.

Jim has been sleeping most of the morning again. He complained that his head hurt a little earlier. He didn't eat much breakfast.

After the shift change this morning, the nurse wrote tomorrow's date on the board for the expected discharge date. I'm hoping she's wrong. We'll see!

Tuesday, February 9, 2016 - Evening Update:
We just talked to the hospitalist again. He's very nice. It looks like they're waiting for the EEG results from this morning. It hasn't posted in the system yet. The neurologist who is coming to consult with us and give the information from the EEG doesn't usually round until after 7:00 PM. Because of this, they are relatively certain he won't be discharged until tomorrow.

Jim was finally awake and ate lunch a little after 1:00. He slept ALL morning. The hospitalist said the anti-seizure meds can make you sleepy until your body adjusts to them, so it might just be from that. I'm sure the seizure itself took a lot out of him, too.

We've been in great hands all day (yesterday too). When I was heading downstairs to grab lunch, I found out that a family friend is our charge nurse for the day.

My big disappointment today is that sad fact that I paid for a bowl of chocolate pudding with my lunch, but left it on the weighing scale when I left the cashier. Some things are just unbearable! (Maybe Ed and Slinky grabbed it and ate it for me so it didn't get wasted.) Hahahaha.

Still expecting a miracle! Today would be great!!!
♥ *Jim and Brenda*

The neurologist did arrive to see Jim later that evening. He ran a few more tests and did a neuro assessment on Jim in his hospital room. He was rather bossy and cold. As he reviewed Jim's pain meds for his back (one that he had taken for years for degenerating discs, and hadn't experienced any seizure activity), he abruptly came to the decision that Jim needed to cease using that prescription immediately. Jim, with broken speech, tried to object to the doctor's conclusion, but the doctor talked over him and didn't want to wait for Jim to finish his sentences.

Moments like those were when you could be sure I had something to say. As Jim's caregiver I was not about to let someone disrespect him like that. I took a deep breath and resigned myself to speak as slowly and calmly as possible to speak up for Jim. I tried to hide the fire in my eyes that was eager to jump out and consume this neurologist. If he only knew! How dare he disrespect my husband and not pause to listen to his objection!

I explained that the prescription medicine he was advising Jim to stop taking for his back pain was the only one that he had found that didn't make him sleepy all day. It helped to decrease his pain, but also kept him alert enough to function well throughout the day. The doctor, continuing in the same manner as he had since he entered the room, gave up his argument against the pain medicine, but very quickly, but firmly, stated that we'd have to triple Jim's Keppra dose (anti-seizure meds) if he wanted to continue with the same pain meds. Then he packed up his small examination case and excused himself from the room as quickly as he had entered. And that was that!

We sat there in utter disbelief.

To say that I was seething at this point would be an accurate description. Having someone talk to you like you're nothing and bark orders at you is very degrading and frustrating. It took a few minutes for Jim and I to calm down.

I still had questions for the doctor, but he didn't stay around long enough to field those questions. He had decided that Jim's Keppra dose should be tripled, and that was what was going to be added to his discharge paperwork the next morning. Only, they hadn't even tried this new dose for Jim yet and were discharging him the next morning. The current dose he was on made him feel sleepy already. What was a tripling the dose going to do to him? No one knew. No one cared. He would be released to go home and it would be my responsibility to figure it out.

I resigned myself that I would call Dr. B at UCSF as soon as we got home the next day. Dr. B would have the answers we needed.

Wednesday, February 10, 2016 - Morning Update:
It looks like Jim is being discharged from the hospital today. We're waiting for the nurse to complete the discharge papers and such. We should be home soon.

Once home, I called Dr. B's office. He returned my call later in the day. The phone call to Dr. B proved to be exactly what I expected. Dr. B was kind and caring – quite the opposite of the neurologist we had just encountered the night before. He fielded a few of my questions and gave us permission to continue Jim at the original dose of Keppra the hospital had started him on when we arrived in ER a few nights before, stating that if we noticed any seizure activity, it would confirm the dose needed to be increased. He realized I was panicked and searching for the answer to numerous medical questions for Jim, so he agreed to meet with us the following week. He encouraged me to write down all the questions we needed answers to and bring the list with us. He would help us get the information we needed.

And that, my friends, is an AMAZING DOCTOR. I cannot even express the deep respect I have for that man and the compassion he always showed us. At the appointment the following week, my respect grew one hundred times over.

Our 25th wedding anniversary was on February 16th. We resigned ourselves to the fact that we would have to make due with our limited options for celebrating. Jim's appointment at UCSF was set for the 17th. Our three teenagers were on a week-long break from school, so we decided to take them with us and head to Monterey for a brief overnight trip. There wasn't much of a fanfare to celebrate such a momentous milestone in our marriage. We visited Cannery Row and then ate at Bubba Gump's that evening. When we got back to our hotel room in Seaside, I went to the indoor pool with the kids until bedtime.

The next morning, we had a delicious breakfast at the hotel, then hopped on the road, northbound to UCSF.

The kids brought tablets and books to keep them busy in the waiting room while Jim and I visited with Dr. B. They did a great job of staying quiet and waiting patiently for us.

The appointment with Dr. B was over-the-top. He greeted us warmly upon entering the room, then acknowledged that the last month had been an enormous challenge for Jim medically. He sat back, pushed himself away from his desk and computer, facing us and giving us his full attention. He indicated that he was ready for the list of questions, so I proceeded to ask them one by one. He calmly answered each question, waited for me to jot down the answers or get more clarification, then patiently paused. I would ask if he was ready for the next question, to which he would respond that he was, so I continued. On and on, down the list of eleven items we had come up with prior to the meeting, Dr. B answered every one of them and offered words of kindness, encouragement, and compassion as he fielded each one. He only excused himself briefly for one question, rolling his chair over to the computer to enter a note about scheduling to have Jim's IVC filter removed – one of the questions that had never been answered up until that point – then pushed himself away from his desk once more to face us.

By the time we left his office, we had answers to the questions we were struggling with regarding Jim's Keppra and steroid doses, his current MRI, having his IVC filter removed, details about chemo in regard to his open sinus cavity, the tingling sensation in Jim's head at his surgery site, problems with dry skin (caused by the steroids), and much more.

We happily collected our kiddos from the waiting room, then piled into our car for the long drive home. We were stuck in rush hour traffic, so it would take over 3 hours to get home, not including a stop for dinner on the way.

Dr. B's office called the following week to give us an update on having Jim's IVC filter removed. He was scheduled for the procedure on March 2nd at the Mt. Zion UCSF Campus, on the second floor. In an effort to save space for more important events that I'm attempting to journal in this book, I'll condense that experience here. Once Jim was done and in the recovery room, the staff reported that it took a little longer for the procedure than planned because it was difficult for them to retrieve the device. Jim reported that it was another traumatic experience and that he hoped he'd never have to go through that again.

Jim had a routine appointment with Dr. S (Jim's local oncologist) on March 4th. My notes from this visit indicate that Jim was fatigued, had a loss of appetite, and was feeling very nauseous. Dr. S chalked it up to the fact that Jim was having steroid withdrawals – he had finished tapering off of them and hadn't taken them for 4 days at that point. The diagnosis seemed to describe everything that was going on, so we rolled with it.

Dr. S was knowledgeable and helpful. We saw no reason to think anything else was going on with Jim's body. He had already been through so much, there couldn't possibly be anything else going on. Lord knows we weren't able to handle another emergency, right?

Wrong.

11

SINCE YOU INSIST

ABSURD.
If I had to choose only one word to describe our journey since Jim's diagnosis, I would select the word "absurd," hands down.

Webster's Dictionary defines absurd as "ridiculously unreasonable, unsound or incongruous, extremely silly or ridiculous." Synonyms for absurd are: bizarre, crazy, insane, nonsensical, preposterous, unreal, and wild.

Each of those descriptive words fits the crazy, non-stop situations we faced.

I've often joked that I need to order a large, custom-made wooden cutout for my fireplace mantle that says "Absurd" in a nice scripty font. It would fit nicely in my family room with the word cutouts that I have that say "Peace" and "Blessed," don't ya think? I'm still convinced that I need it.

With the bizarre situations we kept encountering every few weeks, it felt as if we were little kids on a merry-go-round that kept spinning around faster and faster. We were the ones in the middle of it hanging on for dear life, pleading for the bully to stop spinning it. But, instead of bringing it to a halt like we were begging for, the evil bully kept pushing it faster and faster, knowing we had no chance of jumping off without flinging ourselves halfway across the playground in the process.

And this is where we found ourselves at the beginning of March – on the merry-go-round, getting queasier by the minute. I was figuratively queasy. Jim was literally queasy. He had been feeling nauseous for 5-7 days, along with the other symptoms I described at the end of the last chapter. The poor guy was trying to do his best to deal with it and not be a complainer.

By March 5th, I thought Jim had turned a corner. That was a relief for me, because it had been a really rough week for him.

Saturday, March 5, 2016 - PM Update:
Yesterday was another rough day. Jim wasn't feeling well still and had a doctor appointment to be at in the afternoon. It was pretty much all he could do to take his shower, get ready, and go to his appointment. To make matters worse, he had to do blood work an hour before his appointment and THEN the doctor was running an hour behind schedule. (I told Jim I was going to go out to the waiting room and kick over the doctor's whiteboard that had a magnet placed in the "on-time" area of the board. Of course I was kidding, but I kinda wanted to do it!)

Since Jim has had so much trouble with tapering off of the steroid he was taking, the doctor decided to put him back on an extremely low dose for another week, then wants him to taper to every other day with that dose until we see him again. Although we don't want him to have to take the steroids, tapering off of them has been a harsh adjustment for his body, so this compromise is ok. The doctor also changed his anti-nausea medicine, because the other one wasn't as effective as it needed to be.

Jim has eaten less than half of his normal meals for the last week. Yesterday he barely ate at all. It's wearing to watch someone feel so lousy like that and not be able to do something to help them. It sure has taken a toll on me this week. It feels like someone is slowly whittling away at my soul, taking small chunks with each challenge.

Jim asked the doctor to hold off on the chemo scheduled to start last night. He didn't feel like he had any strength to add one more stresser on his body. The doctor was a little reluctant, but understood the situation. He wants to see him back in 2 weeks.

My mom offered to pick the kids up from Jim's mom's house late yesterday and take them to her house for dinner and a movie. I eagerly agreed to accept the help because there was nothing fun planned for our house for Friday night. In fact, Jim came home from his doctor appointment and slept for 2 hours before the kids arrived home.

I think we turned another corner again this morning. Jim woke up feeling a little better, a little stronger. He even ate a decent amount of breakfast and lunch, then offered to take us out for dinner. I can't even tell you how relieved I am to see this change! It's nice to see him eat! He's tired this evening, but that's ok because he only napped for a little bit today, unlike other days this week and last week when he slept most of the day.

I have had thank you notes ready to mail out for almost 2 weeks now, but ran out of stamps. Ugh!!! Who does that?!?!?! I finally got some tonight, so I can get the thank you notes out of my car. If any of you are impatiently waiting at your mailbox each day for our thank you note, I'm sincerely sorry. (Yes. This is a little sarcasm. I know people aren't tapping on their mailboxes wondering where our note is.) So many people have told me to stop writing thank you notes and save my time, but I just have to say that my momma raised me to thank people who have helped me or given me a gift. It's important to ME to acknowledge it. But, sadly, while we're on this topic, I do have to admit that I'm sure that I've forgotten MANY thank you notes, too. If I have missed sending one to any of you I cannot tell you enough how sorry I am. It was not intentional by any means! My brain has holes in it. It doesn't function like it used to. I'm trying to remember everyone who needs to be thanked, but some things leak through the holes in my brain and get forgotten when I sit down to write notes. In fact, I still have yet to figure out if I did or did not send a note to a specific person. How do you figure that out with a leaky brain? I'm trying, but I'm human. I'm giving myself room for mistakes (at times!). Most days I'm just trying hard to just keep existing.

Your prayers are needed and appreciated! Thank you for your love and support. We love you all so much!!!

ANXIOUSLY expecting a miracle!!! Very anxiously! ANY day will do!!!
♥ *Jim and Brenda*

On Sunday morning, we still thought Jim was on the mend. We had navigated our normal Sunday routine that day: the kids and I getting ready for church; going to worship team practice while Court stayed with Jim; then me going back to get Jim ready and take him to church. The afternoon was pretty typical; nothing seemed out of the normal except the fact that Jim was still working on regaining his strength.

Around 5:00ish, Jim decided he needed to go to the restroom, so he headed down the hall and into our master bathroom. I was carrying some items into our bedroom, and as I passed the bathroom door I could hear Jim say, "Oh no . . . Oh no . . . Ohhhh noooooo." Immediately, my ears perked up. My heart sank. I knew something was very wrong, so I stepped in to check on him.

Jim had his hand on his forehead and looked very obviously distressed. I walked over to where he was standing by the toilet and glanced inside, only to find that there was a massive amount of blood in his urine.

Once again my adrenaline kicked in. I was forced right back into battle mode. I knew something was very wrong and I needed to get him to the hospital right away to figure out what we were dealing with. This was a new challenge we hadn't experienced yet.

I had Jim sit down for a few minutes as I stopped to talk with him and calm him down. He was very distressed, knowing it had only been a month since his last hospitalization. It was all he could do to pull himself together and resign himself to get ready to go back to the hospital again. He dreaded going back.

I left him sitting in the bathroom, while I went to break the news to our teenagers. I took a deep breath and tried to put on a brave face as I walked out of our bedroom door, then down the hallway. I found the kids sitting in the living room, and I calmly explained that they would need to start packing a few items to spend the night with my parents (or whoever could come at a moment's notice for them that night). I tried to sound reassuring and calm, but I have no idea if I was successful in hiding the panic and dread I had in my heart. I really wanted to cry, but there was no time or space for that.

I made all the usual emergency calls to the usual people, feeling like I was reliving the same moments over and over and over again, feeling like I was stuck in the movie *Groundhog Day*.

Our kids bravely packed a few items for the night (and for school the next day). They were pros at it by this point. The fact that they had to be ready to pack at a moment's notice killed me. I can't even imagine the duress it caused them.

I packed what we needed for the trip to ER (and, more-than-likely, a hospital stay). Once again, the kids were covered, our items were packed, and we were on our way to the hospital. This time I drove Jim myself. At least THAT was a change from the experiences in January and February. We didn't need to call 911 and wait for emergency crews to arrive to help us.

We arrived in ER and checked in. They called Jim to go to the back for a quick blood test. I went with him. Then they handed him a cup to collect a urine sample. Although that may not sound like a big deal, I assure you that it was a huge challenge in itself. Because Jim still didn't have any use of his right arm/hand, he was barely able to navigate using the restroom by himself in normal circumstances. Trying to collect a urine sample in a cup was going to be impossible for him to do alone. I would have to go into the restroom with him, so I asked a nearby nurse for a restroom we could both enter, as I was not about to go into the public men's restroom with Jim. The nurse found a small restroom attached to the triage room and cleared it with other staff so we could use it.

Now, I knew Jim had blood in his urine – that was obvious because I had already seen it when we were at home – but when I handed over a urine sample to the lab that looked more like a blood test in a urine cup I was shocked. It was a horrible sight.

We sat in the waiting room for a few minutes and in a bit Jim's name was called by a member of the ER staff. They had a bed ready for him. I helped him change into his hospital garb and neatly folded his clothes to place them in the plastic bag provided. I hung my light blue backpack on the back handles of Jim's wheelchair, then settled myself in his wheelchair, deciding that it would be much more comfortable than the hard, plastic chairs I had become accustomed to in ER (the ones I attempted to sleep on overnight during his previous ER visit).

As usual, my hospital companion Courtney arrived and joined us in waiting for the doctor. (That young lady blessed me by standing by my side every time we rushed to the hospital!) She settled into one of the hard, plastic chairs on the opposite side of Jim's bed. I placed my feet on the floor and rolled myself back and forth slightly in the wheelchair, trying to find something to help me pass the time. Jim had a private room in ER this time, so no one was yelling about flat-lining. Although that's super entertaining, we were happy to have the peace and quiet.

The doctor arrived and reviewed Jim's case.

By this point in our journey, I could almost spout off any tidbit of information one needed about Jim's medical history - list of prescription meds, milligrams, and when he took them; the dates of his most recent round of chemo, current weight (as it fluctuated a lot during this time), dates and length of hospitalizations. You name it. I either had it stored away in my ever-expanding brain and could give specific info at the drop of a hat, or it was easily accessible to refer back to in the medical notebook I kept for all of Jim's appointments and hospitalizations. I didn't flinch when it came to reviewing this data, as I knew my documentation was solid. I knew Jim's medical history well. It was the most important job in my life at that moment, and his life depended on me tracking everything as accurately as I possibly could.

I answered all of the pertinent questions regarding Jim's health with the doctor. She said she was waiting for some of Jim's first test results and needed to run additional tests. She stated that Jim would be there for the night (at least), then left the room. We notified friends and family that Jim would be admitted and we would be staying the night.

I wasn't sure how Jim felt about me sharing information about his urinary tract, so I tried to be discreet and kept social media posts very vague, stating only that we were at the hospital again. After a few hours it occurred to me that some people would be concerned that he had fallen again or had another seizure. In my next update I simply stated that neither had happened, and we were waiting for tests to come back.

A bit later, the doctor came back in to talk, only this time her tune had changed and she was telling us that the supervising doctor had made the decision to discharge Jim, send him home, and have him see his primary care doctor the next day.

I was about to flip out. This was absurd!

By this stage in our journey, I had already firmly decided that no matter how idiotic the person I was dealing with was acting, I would choose to maintain MY integrity and speak as calmly and politely as I possibly could, That's a very difficult task when you are upset by their words and actions. Extremely difficult. But, that had been my goal while advocating for Jim every time we were at the hospital. I knew that every member of Jim's medical care team would flag me as the crazy, irrational wife who was ignorantly advocating for her husband. I needed them to see me as a team player, but one who was able to put her foot down when they were being unreasonable.

I choked back my fear and tried to reign in my anger as I asked the doctor to explain how they thought it was safe to discharge Jim at that moment. I pointed over to his monitor and asked about his high blood pressure and heart rate readings, stating that I was not comfortable with him going home under those circumstances. Something had to be wrong with him for his vitals to be so high. I explained to her that I wouldn't be able to sleep all night if she sent him home, adding that I would have to check his blood pressure and heart rate repeatedly throughout the night to be sure he was alright. Then I reminded her that Jim was no longer capable of running a fever to show that something was wrong in his body – a condition that we believe was caused by his chemo and radiation treatments. If that was the only thing missing that prevented them from being alarmed, I firmly urged her to reconsider their assessment.

Courtney was upset, too. She asked the doctor, "Soooo, you'd like to send us home so we can come back by ambulance in a few hours???" I nodded in agreement.

I pleaded with the doctor to go back to the supervising doctor and ask him to reconsider, pointing out that it was not safe to discharge him with that much blood in his urine and his vitals reading so high. She agreed that she would present our plea to him, but couldn't guarantee the result we were asking for. Then she left the room. I prayed.

She returned a few minutes later to relay the information from the supervising doctor. She said, "The doctor said since you insist on having him stay here, he will move him to the observation unit for the night." Nothing was mentioned about the fact that he found that this was necessary.

Although I was relieved to hear that they would be keeping Jim overnight, I was seething with anger over her choice of words "since you insist." I'm sure at that very moment I could have burned a hole through the wall with the fire in my eyes. I turned my head and body toward Jim and Courtney, telling them under my breath that they would need to finish the conversation with her. I was not going to be able to maintain my integrity and finish talking to her. I literally bit down on my tongue, looked toward Jim's monitor (away from the doctor), and did my best not to rip her apart with the words that were sitting on the tip of my tongue . . . or to karate chop her (because that sounded like a good solution, too). . . . No good could come from expressing those fiery thoughts at that moment (or karate chopping her), so I restrained myself to keep them from slipping out. I could feel my blood boiling.

The doctor finished giving Jim and Courtney the information we needed, then scooted out the door. I waited. I carefully listened for her footsteps down the hallway and around the corner, waiting for her to be out of earshot. Once I ascertained that she was far enough down the hallway that she wouldn't hear me, I opened my mouth and let it spew like a volcano. (Not cussing, mind you. I'll clear that up right away in case you thought that might be what spewed from my mouth. Hahaha!) "SINCE I INSIST?!?!?!?!? ARE YOU KIDDING ME?!?!?!? SINCE I INSIST? YOU HAVE GOT TO BE KIDDING ME!!! I'M NOT TRAINED IN THE MEDICAL FIELD, BUT EVEN I CAN LOOK AT YOUR VITALS AND SEE THAT SOMETHING ISN'T RIGHT! . . . SINCE I INSIST!!! . . . REALLY??? . . ." The volcano continued spewing for a few minutes before I could calm myself down and stop angrily repeating the phrase "since you insist." She made me feel foolish for advocating for Jim. She made me feel like I was wasting their time and resources by asking for them to reassess his condition before making the rash decision to send him home. I could see his vitals displayed on the monitor very clearly with my own eyes and I was NOT comfortable with their first decision.

I get angry all over again just typing these words to tell you the story. No joke.

Eventually the hospital staff located a room for Jim and he was transported to the observation unit. Courtney headed home once she knew we were ok. We had no idea what the plan of care was. I prayed that the hospitalist assigned to Jim the next day would see the urgency of his situation, and not rush to discharge him before finding the cause of his bleeding and determining if it was serious or not.

I texted my cousin Sheri the next morning to see if I was being over-the-top in asking for them to reconsider their assessment of Jim. She assured me that if I felt things were not right it was perfectly fine for me to push more to get Jim the care that was needed. I needed that reassurance. I was thankful that she was available to help me.

The hospitalist came in on Monday morning. She scheduled Jim for a few tests and determined that Jim needed to see a specialist. Due to the pending tests and consultation with a specialist, Jim's status was changed from "observation" to "in-patient." The idea was thrown around that Jim possibly had a urinary tract infection and it was complicated by his blood thinner. When I stated that I was concerned that she might send him home immediately, she quickly replied that there was definitely something wrong with Jim and they needed to get to the bottom of it before they discharged him. That put my mind at ease. She was not going to approach this the way the ER staff had approached it. I could sit back for a bit and relax, knowing that they were searching for answers.

I talked to Jim about the updates I was posting for friends and family, explaining that I hadn't wanted to share private information without his approval. We talked it through and he agreed that it would be better to openly state the symptoms that had brought him to ER in the first place and allow our friends and family to pray specifically for this current medical dilemma, rather than be left in the dark and worrying about all the "what ifs." With his permission, I posted an update giving basic details.

Enter Dr. W.

Our first encounter with Dr. W was pleasant. He was an average-sized man with reddish hair and he seemed to have a good personality. He took the time to chat with Jim a bit and tell us about his wife, children, and grandchildren. It put our minds at ease that we might actually be dealing with a real live human who cared about people.

Dr. W said the results from Jim's CT scan showed that he had 4 kidney stones: 5 mm, 3 mm, and two 2 mm stones. He explained that they would start him on some medicine to help open things up for him so they could pass easily. He told us that he would reevaluate Jim on Tuesday to see if his status had changed at all. If necessary, he said he would put Jim on the procedure schedule for Wednesday (and if not Wednesday, then Friday) to remove the stones. He preferred to wait to see how things progressed. He wanted to leave surgery as the last option.

Kidney stones... THAT would describe the nausea, lack of appetite, and fatigue Jim had been experiencing for a week! We were finally getting somewhere with this!

Tuesday came and went. We sat in Jim's hospital room waiting for new news, but didn't receive any.

Wednesday, March 9, 2016 - AM Update:
Yes. We're still at the hospital. Jim was scheduled to have a procedure done today, but the urologist was called in for jury duty. The procedure is marked as postponed (not cancelled) in the computer, so we don't quite know what that means regarding when Jim can go home. He has a new hospitalist today. We haven't seen him/her yet. Maybe we'll have more answers after we meet with them.

Jim had a migraine last night. Cara stayed with him while I went home to shower around 5:00. When I came back she said he had a headache. By bedtime it was a full migraine. They had just given him his migraine medicine and he had settled down to get some rest, when they decided at 9:00 that he needed to be moved to another floor. Needless to say, I was livid. I'll leave it at that.

His head feels better today, but he is still complaining of back pain and kidney pain. His back pain is chronic. Since he is used to always being in pain, it's hard for him to determine if pain is coming from other areas near his back. When I rubbed his back early this morning, while he was waiting for pain meds, I ran my hand across his side, and he realized a lot of his pain was coming from the kidney area on his right side.

Jim keeps saying he wants to go home today. Since he hasn't passed any kidney stones yet, I'm not sure how I feel about that. I fear that we could go home and have to come right back if his pain is unbearable. And then, there's the confusion about the plan for the procedure. So, although home sounds great, I'm not sure what's best right now. I guess we'll get this sorted out and know better later on today.

Thanks for your prayers!

Expecting a miracle! ANY day will do!!!
❤ *Jim and Brenda*

Wednesday, March 9, 2016 - Afternoon Update:
So, it looks like Jim will be here at least until the end of the week.

I decided to run downstairs for a late lunch and almost missed both doctors (hospitalist and urologist). I saw the hospitalist in the hall and asked if Jim was on his list. Surprise - he was! So I went back to Jim's room. After the hospitalist finished with all his evaluations and information for us, the urologist stepped in. And so, now we have all the info we need.

Jim is scheduled for a procedure on Friday (mid to late morning). Jim asked if he could go home in between time, but the hospitalist is concerned about his kidney being so swollen and tender. He said it's too risky to send him home right now. Because of the swelling it could become completely blocked and that wouldn't be a good situation without medical care available. He wants to play it safe and keep him monitored, give him an antibiotic, and continue with his pain meds to assist him. Although Jim isn't thrilled with that answer, he understands.

He's been sleeping a good part of the day (partly from the pain meds). The doctor would like him to get up and walk a little more to prevent blood clots, since he can't take his blood thinner right now. We've requested a hemi-walker or cane to assist him, so hopefully that will be up in the next hour.

That's about all I can think of for now. Hope I didn't forget anything.

What I failed to include in my Wednesday afternoon update, was something that Dr. W mentioned when he told us about his day at jury duty. He said that he had to explain to the judge that he was needed for some surgeries that had to be postponed due to his jury summons, adding that he had a couple of patients in renal failure who needed his care. When he told us this little detail, I remember feeling horrible for that patient (and their family) who was waiting for a surgical procedure because they were currently in renal failure . . . . Unbeknownst to me, Jim was one of those patients and I was one of those family members.

So, we waited . . . for Friday to arrive . . . for Jim's first cystoscopy to remove the stones. Yes, you can probably see my eyes roll as you read that sentence. The whole situation was absurd.

And here's a good place to insert certain details about Dr. W that we had discovered up to that point: Dr. W was one of five urologists in an area where there should be twelve. He had many patients waiting for him each day. In fact, I quickly learned that he loved to spout off these statistics every time that we saw him. Every. Time. He would often tell us how many patients he had already seen before he came to see Jim, then he would be sure to tell us how many people were still waiting to see him. And, if that wasn't enough, Dr. W would then proceed to tell us if it was actually his scheduled day off or not. It was apparent that he wanted us to know that he was very important and for him to remind us that many people were waiting for and counting on him.

Can you see the turn of events slowly unfolding?

Thursday, March 10th, arrived and departed. Jim felt horrible. He slept most of the day, complaining of a lot of pain and nausea. He couldn't eat. No kidney stones had passed yet. His procedure was scheduled for the next day.

Finally, on Friday morning, he was transferred to pre-op and prepped for surgery. I was able to stay with him until they moved him to the operating room. He was nervous, but was comforted by the fact that I could stay with him while he waited. He loved for me to hold his hand, place my hand on his chest, or even hold on to the top of his feet through his blanket when he felt apprehensive.

Soon the anesthesiologist and Dr. W made their rounds through the pre-op room and completed their checklists. Jim was ready to go. The nurse allowed me to walk down the hallway with her, alongside Jim's bed until they made the turn toward the operating room. Then I was excused to the waiting room.

I chose to sit in the hallway across from the unit housing the operating room and recovery area. Jim had taught me how to be a good people watcher, so this was the perfect spot to observe people entering and leaving the hospital at that entrance. My friend, Dana, arrived shortly after Jim was taken back, bearing a cup of peppermint hot chocolate to help me pass the time. We sat and visited while we waited, even taking time to talk about the difficult journey Jim and I were on and where it might eventually lead us. Conversations like that were hard, but necessary in situations like we had been experiencing the previous months. Dana sat patiently and let me share what I needed to express, without judging, only offering her input as needed.

Dr. W exited the unit housing the operating room and came directly to talk to me. He explained that he was able to insert a stent and that when he did so, a lot of pus drained immediately from Jim's kidney, indicating that it was fully blocked and none of the urine that had been collected in the previous days was from his right kidney. He said he would have tried to scope into his kidney to retrieve the kidney stones, but with the infection he saw it wasn't wise to proceed until the infection had cleared. He indicated that another procedure would be needed in a week or so, then quickly explained that he needed to run because he had other procedures waiting for him at another local hospital. And that was the end of that.

Can you say "Absurd"?

Can you say, "Yes! I insist!"?

Oh, how I wanted to find those ER doctors and tell them how right I was about Jim's assessment in ER on Sunday night. I'm not gonna lie, a nice karate chop would have been fulfilling at that moment, too. Hahaha!

Jim was wheeled out the door and into the hallway in his hospital bed about 30 minutes after Dr. W left. Dana and I walked alongside his bed as he was transported back to his room. He introduced me as his wife to the person in charge of transporting him, then he introduced Dana as his "other wife." Dana and I laughed and let him have his moment of humor. It was refreshing to see him in a mood for joking after such a long week in the hospital. He was obviously not feeling the pain from the procedure yet. Dana followed us to the room, stayed briefly, then said her goodbyes and headed home.

Jim actually ate a good portion of his dinner that night, which was a good sign after watching him pick at his food for days.

His nursing staff checked for orders from the urologist in the computer, but didn't find anything. Everything was left up in the air as to when Jim could be discharged from the hospital – maybe a day, maybe two. The nurses didn't even know the outcome of the surgery or the fact that Dr. W couldn't retrieve the stones because of the infection that had completely blocked his kidney. The hospitalist was left trying to make decisions for Jim with the same absence of information.

Saturday, March 12th, arrived – my 44th birthday. It felt like a repeat of Christmas: "And here we sat in Jim's hospital room." Jim didn't feel well that day. He battled the pain from his procedure from the day before and wasn't up for having much conversation.

The hospitalist, Dr. G, didn't round until later in the afternoon, and the nurse warned me that before the hospitalist even assessed Jim, he was already talking about discharging him. Whaaaat??? Looking at Jim lying in the bed in extreme pain and checking the color of his urine in his catheter bag, I was very concerned that the hospitalist had decided to send him home before even talking to him. I camped out in Jim's room and was dead set that I wouldn't leave to grab my lunch until he made his rounds. I had lots of questions and concerns.

This same hospitalist had been very chatty the previous two days, but when he entered Jim's room on Saturday, I could clearly tell that he was all business and was ready to be done with his rounds as quickly as possible. He talked over Jim. He talked over me. He was very rude and unprofessional that day compared to the other days we had dealt with him. When he stopped long enough to assess Jim and realize that I knew no information was left in Jim's chart regarding his urology procedure, he backed down a bit and decided that Jim should be discharged the following day. We were good with that. We wanted to go home as soon as possible, but not at the expense of Jim's health.

The rest of the day was sprinkled with short visits from my family, bringing birthday wishes and cards. My parents brought Hanna, Americis, and Christopher to visit, along with the gift of a new pair of tennis shoes I needed. Cara and Courtney each stopped by briefly as well. Our sister-in-law, Jennifer, stopped by later in the afternoon and brought me a container of chocolate eclairs – one of the highlights of a very depressing day in the hospital. And soon my birthday was over and done with for 2016. After dinner, I curled up on the couch-bed in Jim's room and watched a few episodes of a show on Netflix while Jim snoozed in his hospital bed beside me.

I stewed a little that night and the next morning. I was upset that the hospitalist had drawn conclusions before seeing Jim the day before, but was bothered even more by the fact that he seemed rushed and talked over Jim that day. The next morning, before I left to go to church, I wrote a note to the hospitalist and handed it to the nurse, urging her to have him read it before he dared to step foot in Jim's room. I was not taking any chances on having Dr. G treat Jim disrespectfully while I was away for a couple of hours! With Jim's speech being such a challenge, it was hard for him to speak up for himself fast enough.

With that, I finished getting ready for church, kissed Jim goodbye, and headed off to worship team practice at 7:30 AM – It was one of the few reasons I ever broke away from the hospital, other than going home to shower and wash my clothes.

I returned to the hospital a few minutes after 11:00, as I had left church soon after I finished leading worship that morning. The nurse saw me return and handed back my note for the hospitalist. She informed me that Dr. G hadn't been in yet for the day and that I could talk to him myself when he arrived. I changed my clothes and settled in on the couch-bed once again, chatting with Jim. He seemed to be a lot perkier and willing to have conversation, so I was content.

Jim's brother, John, stopped by for a short visit that afternoon. That helped to break up the monotony of just waiting around for the hospitalist to make his rounds.

Soon after he left, Dr. G entered the room. I sat up straight, took a deep breath, and prepared myself to address him calmly. He greeted us and was ready to review Jim's case. I jumped into the conversation as quickly and cautiously as I could, asking if I could have a brief moment to address some concerns before he continued. He agreed, so I proceeded. I thanked him for the first few days he had cared for Jim and how thoughtful and professional he had been. Then I proceeded to tell him how disappointed we were that he had come to conclusions long before he had assessed Jim the day before, and how he spoke to Jim (and over him). I kept my comments as brief as I could and tried to acknowledge both the good and the bad things we had encountered with him. To my surprise, he backed off slightly (physically, as well as in the tone of his voice), then apologized for his rushed, rude behavior the day before. Once I realized that he had reset to the doctor we had first encountered, I was content to let him continue with his review of Jim's case.

Dr. G felt that it was safe for Jim to be discharged, so he could continue recuperating at home. Jim and I both agreed that he was at a point that he could handle going home. Jim was actually ready for it on that day, as opposed to how awful he felt the previous day. Dr. G left the room on good terms and wished us the best.

And with that, we packed up our stuff, waited for discharge paperwork to be processed, then headed home.

It had been one full week since Jim entered the doors of ER, and we were hoping not to return anytime soon. We always held on to hope. Many times it turned out to be false hope. Once again that was the case. More absurd situations were lurking around the corner.

12

ROUND TWO!

Monday, March 14, 2016
So far today we have accomplished 2 things:
    1. sleep 2. shower
    Now, that's an accomplishment, people!!! I know you're wondering how we did so much.
    If I could only get back up to brush my teeth and dry my hair that would be great. I've gotta pick up medicine and get us some lunch. That might put me in over-achiever status! Woohoo!

WE EXPERIENCED HOSPITAL hangover after almost every one of Jim's hospitalizations. Monday, March 14th, was no exception, especially after a week-long hospitalization.
    What is hospital hangover? Extreme fatigue – mentally, emotionally, and physically. Trying to catch up on lost sleep from the days we were

in the hospital, as well as dealing with the newest trauma we had both endured – for me, emotionally; for Jim, emotionally and physically.

On Monday afternoon, I searched for Dr. W's office information in Jim's discharge paperwork then called to schedule an appointment with him. I explained to the receptionist that Dr. W had done a procedure for Jim at the hospital and wanted him to schedule another procedure. The receptionist quickly took the message and said she'd pass it along.

On Tuesday afternoon, I still had not heard back from Dr. W or his office staff, so I called again. I tried to have a pleasant voice and explain that I had called the day before, but hadn't received a phone call back. In a snippy tone, the receptionist told me that he hadn't had time to check his messages yet. Well, alright then.

On Wednesday, I still hadn't heard back from Dr. W or his office staff, so I called again, trying to talk in a professional, cheery voice to explain that I still hadn't heard back from anyone, and that Dr. W had told me Jim's next procedure should be in about a week. As I started off by saying, "Hi! This is Brenda Davis. I'm calling about my husband, James Davis, Jr. . . ." the receptionist cut me off and said, "Yes. You called yesterday."

Ummmmm, excuse me? Did you just say what I think you said? I was taken aback. I was instantly angry, but was trying to hide it in the tone of my voice. I said, "Uhhhh, yeeeah. I'm calling back because no one has returned my calls the last two days." She gave some snippy reply (I honestly can't remember exactly what she said, but it was dripping with sass), then quickly wrapped up our conversation and hung up.

Absurd.

Is it too much to call a doctor's office (at their request) and expect that they will call you back in a day or two? I couldn't believe it. Why did EVERYTHING in my life have to be such a huge challenge? I was so done with having to deal with difficult situations every time I turned around!

Early on Thursday morning, I still hadn't heard back from Dr. W or his office staff. I decided a different course of action was required that morning. I picked up the phone and dialed his office number. When the receptionist answered the phone I started off with my usual, calm greeting and information, "Hi! This is Brenda Davis. I'm calling about my husband, James

Davis, Jr." She recognized me from the previous days' calls and indicated that she didn't have any new information for me. But, then I got bold and said, "You know, we haven't heard anything back from Dr. W or your office all week. My husband still isn't doing well and I was hoping to get him in to see Dr. W. I really don't want to have to do this, buuuuut I will be calling you back every hour today until you have some answers for me."

She fumbled around a bit and sounded very ticked off. She explained that I'd need to wait to hear from Dr. W. I confirmed that I understood that, then stopped to remind her again that I would STILL be calling back in an hour if I didn't hear from them. My voice was quivering and I was hoping she couldn't hear it on her end of the call. I was stressed out and couldn't believe how ridiculous it was that I had to go these lengths just to get information from the doctor's office. She was not happy at all. Her attitude jumped through the phone as she tried to bring the call to an end and hang up.

I called back one hour later and went through the whole scenario all over again, still trying to watch the tone in my voice.

Soon after my second call on Thursday, a person from Dr. W's office called me back and said that he had ordered a new x-ray for Jim. She instructed me to pick up the order at their office and take him in for the x-ray. Thankfully, we were already on our way to see Dr. S (Jim's local oncologist) that morning and he could have the x-ray done right across the hallway from Dr. S's office. We hopped in the car and drove to Dr. W's office. It was all that I could do to walk in and hold my tongue as I requested his orders. They handed me the paperwork, but made no effort to smooth the situation over. They were happy to see me leave. I was happy to be leaving.

The x-ray and appointment with Dr. S went smoothly. Soon we were heading back home.

Thursday, March 16, 2016 - PM Update:
Jim is doing ok. He still hasn't passed his kidney stones. His pain in his right side has been bothering him a lot today. Another procedure is needed, but we haven't heard anything about when that will happen.

His appetite is still decreased, although I did manage to get him to eat McDonald's after his oncologist appointment today. (His request!) He hasn't eaten dinner the last few nights. He drinks a Glucerna (similar to Ensure, but less sugar) before bedtime to keep his glucose levels high enough for the night. If he doesn't do that they drop too low in the morning. (Not to mention that he still needs nutrients!)

His oncology appointment went well today. Pretty basic. Because his body is so overloaded with everything else going on, his oncologists (yes, both of them) don't feel comfortable with doing the next rounds of chemo. It's just too much for his body to handle. They want to wait until he stabilizes better.

We REALLY need your prayers tonight concerning some challenges I'm experiencing in contacting doctors and keeping things moving for Jim. I'd prefer not to go into it at length, but I'll just say I'm at my wits' end. I'm tired of fighting for what Jim needs. I'm tired of feeling like I have to be pushy for things that are necessary. I don't want to be the witchy wife no one wants to talk to regarding her husband's medical needs. That's just not my style! I'm just extremely frustrated and would like to run screaming down my street right now with my arms flailing about. . . . Yes! Again. It sounds silly, but when you are so worked up and are getting nowhere, it sounds like the best thing to do to ease the stress. . . . But, seriously, pleeeeease pray that God will open the right doors for us; that He will go before us and prepare the way so that I don't have to karate chop people; and that He will speak to the right people to help us. I'm exhausted over this. I just want what's best for my husband.

And then, there's always my usual prayer request: Pray for Jim's COMPLETE healing. We know God is able!!! Pray for complete restoration of everything this disease has stolen from him and our family. Pray for our entire family as they navigate these crazy days along with us. It's wearing for our WHOLE family.

WE ARE EXPECTING A MIRACLE.
ANY DAY WILL DO!!!
WE WANT THIS MIRACLE TO COME SOON. We're tired.
Anxiously expecting,
♥ *Jim and Brenda*

Saturday, March 18, 2016 - PM Update:

This week was exhausting. Emotionally and physically exhausting. I spent most of the week trying to contact one of Jim's doctors to get information on what their plan of care is for Jim. I seriously called every day to ask to talk to the doctor. Yesterday I finally had to resort to telling the office staff I would call back every hour if I didn't hear back from the doctor. I kept things very polite and respectful, but I was really at my wits' end trying to get the information we needed. It's just unacceptable for a doctor's office to keep you hanging all week long and not return your calls. They finally called back late yesterday afternoon (to schedule his next procedure). By the end of the day I was just a pile of mush. . . . Some days . . . .

ROUND TWO!

It's hard to adequately explain all of the frustrations of this kind of journey to people who have never experienced it. It's overwhelming on so many levels: tons of uncertainty; tons of stress; juggling regular life responsibilities amidst the craziness of life; relying on people you don't know to care for your loved one with the same care and respect you would; dealing with the huge disappointment that life has changed - and quite possibly has changed forever; keeping your head up and your hands/feet moving; staying strong in your faith in the Lord and continuing to speak His truth to yourself, even when you don't FEEL it; managing your own feelings and, at times, knowing that how you manage your feelings determines how well others will manage theirs; and so, so many other aspects that rear their ugly heads frequently. It's just overwhelming. There's no other way to explain it. It is seriously like entering an alternate universe. You can still see people in your previous universe who continue on with normal lives, while you sit still or operate in slow-motion. . . . And even with that description it doesn't quite summarize the whole of it. It's heart-breaking. It's torture. It's nothing you would wish on your worst enemy.

It definitely is an eye-opening experience to the pain and grief people are feeling around us every day . . . and some of those people have no hope in the Lord. Some of those people have no stable family/friends to help them through. I can't imagine how we would survive this without Jesus and without soooo many who pray for us and help us every day!!! How many people do each of us run into every day who are struggling to just keep breathing? If we could only see inside of them to meet their needs and bring them hope. If only . . . . God, help us to be sensitive to Your Spirit's leading to reach out to others and SEE their needs.

Today was a little more tolerable for me. I was able to catch up on some office work that has been waiting for me all week. Hopefully I can finish some more this next week. (My to-do list keeps growing.). Hanna spent a few hours working at the baseball snack bar for church today. Christopher and Americis found some games to play, then played outside for a while. Cara and Marcus came over for dinner and spent some time with us. (I can't believe they'll be married in less than 4 months!) We saw Court last night, but she was busy today.

Jim has had another difficult week. He continues to have pain in his right side and back, around his kidney. He feels bloated and nauseous off and on every day. His appetite comes and goes. He's just tired of feeling lousy for the last 3 weeks (one week before the hospital, one week in the hospital, and now this week). He seems to be having more pain today than in previous days. He is scheduled for another procedure in 2 weeks - if he can wait that long! Goodness!!! They need to remove the stent they put in between the kidney and bladder, and hopefully they can remove the 4 kidney stones. His pre-op appointment is next week.

Annnnd, while we're on the subject of those kidney stones, we've decided to name them. Say hello to Ed, Slinky, Itchy, and Scratchy! We've decided that Ed and Slinky must be in his right kidney because they have caused much too much ruckus and made Jim's kidney swell and become infected. Ed and Slinky strike again!!! Dun-Dun!!! Itchy and Scratchy have thankfully remained somewhat calm in the left kidney. We just need these "babies" to "be born" and stop wreaking havoc on my husband.

We seriously can't thank you all enough for holding us in prayer daily (or even weekly!). We are ONLY surviving by your prayers and the grace of God. Even though I feel like He has abandoned us at times, I know that is NOT truth. I really have to overcome those feelings with God's Word. It's not an easy task on dark days. It's an impossible task without your continued prayers, that's what it is! But through your prayers we are sustained and held. Through your prayers we find encouragement to keep going. Through your prayers God blesses us and holds us in our times of need. Thanks, friends!!! Thanks!

Once again, I remind myself that we are anxiously expecting a miracle for my Love. We know God is more than able, and ANY day will do!!!
♥ *Jim and Brenda*

By Monday, Jim wasn't feeling any better. In fact, his pain had increased significantly. I took the kids to school, then came home to assess what was going on with Jim. I called Dr. One-Of-Five-Urologists-In-An-Area-Where-There-Should-Be-Twelve, only to be told by his office staff that he would not be back in the office until the next day. They told me that if Jim was having that much pain, he should go to ER to get evaluated. We had only been home for a week, so the thought of making another trip to the hospital . . . the FOURTH trip in THREE months . . . was almost unbearable. By afternoon, Jim decided that we were delaying the inevitable and agreed to let me take him. I called to make arrangements for our kids, then started packing a bag (again).

We arrived at ER around 3:45 PM and had to wait for Jim to be seen. They evaluated him briefly, but didn't have an ER room open for him yet. They started an IV, but didn't give him any IV pain meds right away. He took some oral meds, but they still weren't easing the discomfort. We were sent back to the waiting room.

Jim sat in his wheelchair slumped over, with his head resting in his left hand. He didn't want to talk, so we sat in silence for most of the time. At times I stood in front of him and allowed him to rest his head on my stomach while I rubbed his back to ease the pain. Other times I sat next to him and held his hand or ran my hand across his shoulders to bring some comfort.

Six hours. We waited for six full hours before Jim was taken to a room in ER. I guess by this point the staff had seen us so frequently that they must have thought we were permanent fixtures at the hospital.

Tuesday, March 22, 2016 – Early AM Update:
So, to bring you up to date if you missed my post earlier:

We brought Jim in to ER yesterday (Monday) around 3:45 PM. He was not able to manage the pain in his side/back with oral meds at home. The pain has been increasing since Saturday and he felt he needed to be seen by the doctor. We called his urologist, but he was out of the office until today (Tuesday) and they said Jim should go to ER.

We waited in ER about 6 hours for Jim to be seen. They did a CT scan and ran some tests. They tried two initial doses of IV pain meds, then tried to switch back to oral pain meds. The oral meds still didn't touch the pain. They only made him drowsy and he was still in pain.

We just talked to the hospitalist. She will be admitting Jim for pain control since they weren't able to manage his pain with oral meds. They are starting him on antibiotics again because she thinks that his kidney infection has not cleared completely yet. Strangely, he never runs a fever anymore when he has an infection. It only shows with a high heart rate.

We are waiting for him to get a regular room. He's resting more comfortably now that his pain is under control.

Tonight has not been without excitement/entertainment in ER though. We had an unruly screamer again. And, yes, security was called in to restrain the guy. Thankfully, they were able to move the guy to a private room in ER to treat him there so other patients weren't disturbed.

Thanks for your never-ending prayers for us.

We are soooooooo anxious for a miracle! ANY day will do!
♥ *Jim and Brenda*

We had another extremely exhausting night in ER. We waited all night long as they attempted to get Jim's pain under control – first with IV meds, then with oral meds, then back to IV meds. Once the doctor realized that they couldn't manage his pain without IV meds, she felt he needed to be admitted to the hospital.

Jim was transported to his room in the telemetry unit at 5:45 AM the next morning (Tuesday). Although it was configured slightly differently, it was another tiny room like we had in September, and there wasn't much space to move about. Jim was connected to the monitoring devices to constantly track his heart rate and blood pressure, since both were high again. The nurse went through the ritual of asking every question known to mankind. I obliged by answering her questions, knowing they were necessary, but since I hadn't slept all night it seemed like a monumental task. The staff brought me a small loveseat that extended into a bed, but because the room was so tiny I wasn't able to extend it to bed-size without blocking the doorway to the room. By then it didn't matter. I finished the laundry list of questions, laid down, and slipped off into a short semi-coma, only stopping to post an update to friends and family and let them know that I wouldn't be answering texts or phone calls for a while.

After I awoke from my semi-coma nap, Jim and I met his nurses for the day. Karen was his assigned nurse, but Lawrence was a student nurse working with her for the week. We hit it off with both of them right away. They were kind, and both had a wonderful sense of humor. We had the privilege of having them as Jim's nurses three days in a row. They made their rounds to check on us frequently, often stopping to chat for a while over the next few days to hear more of our story – as they could see record of Jim's recent frequent flyer miles at the hospital. Karen was always sympathetic and offered encouraging words. You could tell that she was drawn to us. She mentioned a few times that she could see how much we loved each other by the way we navigated each day together in the difficult challenge we were facing. I stopped her and made sure to tell her that we definitely weren't perfect, but we always tried really hard to have a good relationship and work through the good and bad days.

As I think back to these moments, I still picture Karen perched on the top, left corner of my orange loveseat/bed, just to the right of the door to Jim's tiny room. She came to check in on us and took a few extra minutes to have a short conversation. Some tears were exchanged in those moments – some by her, some by us. I could see her genuine interest in Jim's well-being. This snapshot in time is one of those memories I tuck away in my heart and cherish. I thank God for the people who put life on hold for a few seconds to bring us some normalcy and tenderness. Karen and Lawrence were exceptional. They may never know the gift they gave us during that hospitalization.

By this point, you may have the false perception that I was the PERFECT wife/caregiver who did everything possible for Jim without grumbling or complaining, without snapping at him or getting frustrated. If that's the case, then I'm sorry. This is where I will be bursting your bubble. POP!

It's true that I did my best to accomplish each task for Jim with the best attitude possible. I tried very hard not to take out my frustrations on him or get short with him in my replies. He couldn't help the fact that he needed my assistance. He hated that I had to help him with so much, and often apologized for it. Many times I put my own feelings aside and just went about the task, knowing that he needed me. But, with all of that said, I DO have limitations – just like everyone else. I experienced them from time to time over the years that we dealt with Jim's challenges. This hospitalization is one of the times I can recount coming to the end of my rope with my patience for Jim.

We were both sleep deprived. We had already gone through a week-long hospitalization at the beginning of the month, then had a week at home where Jim still battled not feeling well. Then there was the night in ER with little to no sleep, followed by more days/nights of sporadic sleep.

I stayed busy every day. At meal times, I assisted Jim with cutting his food. Sometimes I had to feed him because it was too difficult for him to use his left hand (the only good one) with the IV stuck in it. When he needed more pain meds or had a question for the nurse, I tracked them down and got what he needed - always acting as the translator between him and his nurses because of his speech challenges. I stayed all day, every day, with the exception of quick trips home to shower and wash clothes or when I went to church. Some showers were even coordinated at the hospital with the nursing staff so I didn't have to leave Jim to go home. I brought office work to the hospital with me to keep up with my job responsibilities as much as I was able.

Yup. I stayed busy. And when I wasn't busy, I was trying to catch up on a few minutes of sleep.

If Jim needed to use the urinal or go to the bathroom, I went through the whole hoopla of putting his hospital socks on his feet; releasing the side rail to his bed; helping him scoot to the edge of the bed; adjusting his monitor leads and IV tubing to keep it from getting squished; then helping him to stand up and make sure he was stable. Then I would assist him with the task at hand; help him sit down and swivel around to lay down, lifting his feet and setting them in a comfortable position at the end of the bed; repositioning the monitor feeds and tubing; resetting the bed rail (to give him something to hold on to when he needed to reposition himself); taking off his hospital socks; charting the volume of his urine on the whiteboard for the nurses; flushing the contents of said urinal; cleaning the urinal; washing my hands; then getting wet paper towels with soap in them to wash Jim's hands. All of it was quite a time-consuming task.

In the evening, Jim would usually go to sleep around 7:00 or 8:00. I knew that evening meds would still need to be administered and vitals would need to be charted before we would have peace and quiet in his room for any length of time at night.

Most nights I would sit in the corner of the room on my loveseat/bed and watch a few episodes of a show on Netflix using Jim's iPad, trying to pass the time until those tasks were completed so I could sleep without interruptions. Around 10:00 or 11:00, I would convince myself that it was time to go to sleep, so I curled up in the fetal position on the bed or laid on my back with my feet extending up and over the arm of the loveseat, slightly protruding out into the entrance of Jim's doorway, and drifted off to sleep: Remember? The loveseat/bed didn't extend without blocking the doorway. Annnnd, most nights Jim would call out to me around 12:00 or 1:00 AM, asking me to help him get up to go to the bathroom.

He would usually wake me from a dead sleep, so it took a few minutes to get my bearings before I could see (and walk) straight. I tried to hop up as fast as I could, but to be quite honest I definitely wasn't feeling all perky and delightful in the middle of the night.

One night in the middle of this hospital stay, my patience flew out the window. Jim needed me to help him up to use the bathroom. He called out to me and woke me up. I sat up and slipped on my flip flops as I tried to clear my head enough to get up and help him. As I went through the list of things I mentioned a few paragraphs ago, I noticed that Jim was getting impatient with me. I tried to hurry, but he – not feeling well – got grumpy with me and started complaining. I finished helping him, but I could tell he was still upset with me. I walked over to wash my hands and asked him another question. His reply was short and snippy.

Then I snapped and the volcano erupted!

I proceeded to hotly inform my husband that I did not HAVE to stay with him at the hospital every day, night and day. I did not HAVE to do the duties that the nurses were required to do. I did not HAVE to bathe him to help him maintain his dignity. I did not HAVE to cut his food for him and feed him. I was not REQUIRED to be the go-between between him and his nurses. I did not HAVE to help him use the urinal. . . . IN FACT, if he wanted to call the nurses' station and wait for them to come help him, he would more than likely be waiting a whole heck of a lot longer than he had just waited for me to stand up and walk the two steps to the side of his bed. I did all of these things to be helpful to him and I didn't gain anything from it. I further informed him that I could go home each night and get a good night's sleep while he stayed at the hospital alone.

Then I sat down on the loveseat and stewed in silence.

I don't remember exactly how long it took before Jim started talking. His whole attitude had changed by that point, and he apologized profusely. He realized that he had pushed me way past my limits, and that if he kept pushing I would probably be heading home and leaving him to navigate the terrors of the hospital alone for a number of hours each day. It wasn't what I wanted to do, but I couldn't keep up under this pressure if he was going to be upset with me, knowing I was giving every bit of energy I possibly could give. I hadn't held anything back. Not one ounce of energy.

We both acknowledged the fact that we were at our wits' end and were desperately sleep deprived. We had both been impatient. As we worked through our disagreement, we eventually laughed together and talked about how we were on the brink of losing our minds in this tiny little room under the present conditions. Then we resolved ourselves to start over and try to approach the challenging situations with a little more grace for each other.

So there. Now you know I'm not perfect. As stupid as that sounds, I feel like it's important to recount moments like these so you can get a full picture of our life at that moment. It's important for you to see our imperfections and the moments that pushed us to the edge, realizing that we navigated through them, and in spite of them, throughout our journey. It wasn't easy, but we gave it all we had.

Our fabulous nurse tracked down the urologist at the hospital. She updated him about what was going on with Jim. He scheduled the procedure for Thursday, March 24th – the same procedure that was supposed to happen at the end of the following week. The goal was to remove the stones and remove (or replace) the stent. At that point it looked like he wouldn't be able to go home until after the procedure was done. We weren't exactly sure when, but we assumed maybe Friday. The nurse said the urologist would come in to see Jim on Wednesday.

Jim was still in a lot of pain, but was tolerating it much better with the IV pain meds.

Dr. W did come by the next day to review the procedure details. The nurse made sure to warn us that he was on his way, knowing that we were frustrated with him. I sat up on the edge of the loveseat and resigned myself to TRY to be polite and say as little as possible. You could tell from the moment that Dr. W stepped into the room, he was trying to get through his spiel as quickly as he possibly could. I nodded as he ran through the list of items he was required to give us information for or ask about, only speaking when it was absolutely necessary. I'm pretty sure I was physically biting the tip of my tongue to keep myself in check. Soon enough he was done and walking out the door. I was happy that I had made it through without losing my cool.

But wait . . . .

Then he stepped back in to tell us, "Oh, yeah. I almost forgot. Same risks and possible side effects as last time." At which point, I had decided that I was finally able to state a few things calmly. I stood up and walked a few steps closer to the door to talk to him face to face, every part of me shaking.

Me: "You know, we called your office all last week asking for help."

Dr. W: "Yeah. They told me you called a lot."

Me (trying to remain calm, but my voice starting to sound upset . . . and the fire in my eyes had been lit): "Uhhhh, yeeeeeeah. I wouldn't have had to call so much if someone had just returned my call to help us. No one called us back."

Dr. W: "Well, you know, I'm one of five urologists in an area where there should be twelve. I've been busy."

I restrained my anger the best I could. Uhhhh, he didn't just spout off his same statistics again, did he? I wanted to punch him in the tooth. (Just one tooth. It didn't have to be all of them.) Please tell me you didn't, Doctor! Please tell me you didn't go there again.

Me: "Wellll, you know . . . (trying to search for words that were concise, but appropriate) . . . iiiit juuuust doesn't make you feel like you're in very good hands."

Dr. W: "Huh. Wellllllllll . . . " (and he walked out of the room again).

And that was that. We were not happy with the conversation, but decided that once surgery was completed the next day, Jim could go home and we would seek a referral to a urologist at UCSF. We only had to deal with him for one more procedure.

Thursday, March 24, 2016 - Morning:
Our newest yeller must be a pirate:
    "Yo Ho!!!! What's going on out there? I need some help!"

I must admit he's my favorite yeller so far. But at 3 AM, I'll opt to close Jim's hospital door for more sleep and less entertainment. At least he sounds laid back and non-aggressive. Improvement!!!

Yo Ho, Facebook peeps! What's going on out there? Haha.

I like to include little excerpts from my updates to friends and family to add a little humor in our story. It was moments like these that gave us a good laugh and helped us endure the ugly predicaments we constantly found ourselves in. We needed the good laugh on Thursday morning, but we needed sleep even more. So I notified the nurse that our pirate friend needed help and then quietly closed the door to Jim's room to keep the noise out.

We waited around most of the day on Thursday. Jim's procedure was on the schedule for the afternoon. Eventually he was transported to the pre-op room and we went through the same order of events we had just encountered nearly two weeks before. Before long Jim was wheeled to the operating room and I was excused to the same hallway to wait for him, only this time I waited alone.

I'm quite certain that Dr. W did a procedure on another patient before coming out to talk to me about the outcome of Jim's surgery. I waited much longer than I had the last time. I watched the screen that listed the patient's numbers and indicated their current surgery status. Jim's had changed, but no one had come looking for me to give me an update. The surgery waiting room around the corner was empty by then. No one was waiting. No staff members were there to answer questions. I finally located a phone on the wall to ask someone to give me some information. I was assured that someone would come talk to me in a minute. I hung up the phone and looked across the hallway. Dr. W was on his way to talk to me. Grrreeaaaaaaaat! (You can safely assume that I just rolled my eyes as I typed that.)

Dr. W was rushed, as usual. He indicated that we could step inside the conference room just off the waiting room entrance and started walking in that direction. And, although I didn't understand the need for stepping into a conference room when no one else was around, I followed him. As he walked into the room, still facing away from me, he started his short little update . . . only it was hard to hear him because he was talking away from me, into the conference room, and I was still walking into the room behind him. I asked him to repeat what he said. He obliged, but talked very fast. He whipped out a picture he had snapped mid-surgery, revealing a kidney stone that he later removed during surgery. Then he said he removed the stent, there were more stones, and Jim would have to have another procedure to take care of them. And just like that, he was done with his update and he exited the room - in and out of the room in probably a minute or two, at most.

Jim was transported back to his room about 15 minutes after Dr. W left, confirming my suspicions that the doctor had purposely waited to come talk to me. Whatever. It didn't matter at this point.

Thursday, March 24, 2016 – Evening Update:
Jim's procedure went ok today. He wasn't scheduled until this afternoon, so he just got back to his room a little after 5:00. He got settled in, ate dinner, and received some pain meds. He's really tired now. It's been a long day for him just waiting.

I'm happy to report that "Ed" was born today. He was the kidney stone that got stuck in the ureter (between the kidney and bladder). The urologist even gave us a nice during-procedure photo of Ed. (Not strange at all! Haha. But please note that Ed is NOT going home with us. No baby shower is required.) The stent was able to be removed during the procedure as well.

And here's where the good news from the procedure ends.

The bad news from the procedure is that there are still other stones that were not removed today. Originally we were told there were stones in both kidneys - 4 stones total. If I understood the urologist today, it sounded like there are more stones than that. I don't know. He was kind of mumbling. But, either way, he said Jim will have to come back for a lithotripsy procedure to break up the remaining stones. Because the schedule is packed, it's quite possible it won't happen until May.

Jim might be discharged from the hospital tomorrow. It all depends on how he does tonight and tomorrow morning. His day nurse just came in to say goodbye and told Jim she hopes he never has to come back to the hospital again, and he's no longer welcome here. Lol!!! She has been a great nurse for the last 2 days. She has been so kind and compassionate to Jim. It's those kinds of nurses that make Jim's hospital stays more tolerable.

I guess that's everything I needed to include in tonight's update. If not . . . wellllll . . . it'll just have to wait until next time.

Expecting that miracle!!! ANY day will do!!!
♥ *Jim and Brenda*

We saw Jim's hospitalist when she made her rounds on Friday morning, March 25th. Jim really liked her because she was easy to talk to. That wasn't something we had the luxury of when it came to most of the doctors we encountered. After assessing Jim, she said she wasn't comfortable with discharging Jim yet. His pain levels were still too high after his procedure, and she said they needed to be able to switch him over to oral pain meds before thinking about discharging him.

By Saturday evening he was doing much better. He was finally eating well again – after 3 weeks of just nibbling on little bits of food here and there. His blood pressure and heart rate were back to normal. He was still dealing with pain from the cystoscopy and had some aching in his side. The hospitalist came by to review his case and decided to wait to discharge him until the next day.

We had the opportunity to visit with our three youngest kids on Saturday afternoon. My parents brought them to the hospital. It was nice to finally see them! Jim had been in so much pain all week, any lengthy visits would have been difficult for him. The next day was Easter, but didn't feel much like it. We enjoyed the visit with the kids and assured them we would see them at home the next afternoon.

Sunday, March 27, 2016 - PM Update:
Happy Easter!

Jim was released from the hospital this morning right when I got back from church. I snuck out of church a bit early because I thought they'd probably be quick today. I was right! Courtney stayed with him while I was gone. When

I returned, they had everything ready except the discharge paperwork, so I gathered all of our stuff, helped him get dressed, and out the door we all went!

Why did you not know about this yet? Well, it's simple. We came home and both took "comas" immediately. It's hard to post on Facebook when you're in a coma. Neither of us have slept well all week at the hospital, so the nap was super necessary. We still feel wiped out, but are happy to be home.

That's it for now. Hopefully our little monkeys will be home soon. Until then, I think I'm going to sleep some more!

Expecting a miracle! ANY day will do!!!
❤ *Jim and Brenda*

Wednesday, March 30, 2016 - PM Update:

I haven't posted for a few days, so I guess it's time. Sorry for the delay.

Jim came home from the hospital on Sunday afternoon (Easter). We've decided that it was an appropriate day since he came home from his brain surgery at UCSF on Christmas Day. At least we can be consistent with something here! . . . . We slept for a few hours when we got home, then our kiddos arrived.

Monday we pretty much stayed in a "coma" all day. I could barely get off the couch, but did muster enough strength to help Jim get cleaned up. Thennnnnn, I decided there was not enough strength left over to take a shower myself, soooo . . . I didn't! (Gasp! Shock!!! Ewwwww! You might have to unfriend me now that you know this.)

The kids seemed content to just be at home and rest, watch movies, and play on their electronic devices. So, Monday ended up being our "catch up on rest day."

Yesterday, we cleaned up the house a little; the kids practiced their instruments; they read; we did some chores; ran laundry; and then the kids had a little free time. Jim stayed awake most of the day. His appetite wasn't very good, but better than it has been for the last month.

This morning I ran errands and went to work briefly to drop off some things. I was supposed to pick up some music files, but totally blanked on that. Thankfully I have a sweet neighbor who works at the church and was thoughtful enough to bring me the files tonight. Uhhh, guess I need to work on those next!

Jim, Hanna, Americis, and I took a quick trip to Modesto this afternoon. Hanna got her passport pics taken for the missions trip she wants to participate in this summer. We grabbed lunch together before we headed home. Jim was tired by the time we returned, so he napped while I took care of some computer work and finished paying bills.

But here's my BIG NEWS of the day . . . I made a real-life homemade dinner in my own kitchen tonight! Bammmm!!! That just happened! I don't even remember the last time I made a dinner that didn't consist of heating up leftovers; cooking a dish that someone blessed us with; or was just a super quick dinner. And tonight's dinner was delicious!!! Jim even ate almost everything on his plate, so that's worth it! . . . Ok. I gotta say it one more time. Bammmmm!!!!

I had a little situation this afternoon that made me super angry. I've been stewing about it throughout the evening. Without going into all the details, for people to think they need to give well-meaning advice, I'll just say this . . . I try sooooo stinkin' hard to be polite (but firm, if needed) when contacting doctor's offices. Today I was trying to resolve an ongoing situation by phone. I reminded the office staff member that I've been very polite when I've contacted them . . . and mid-sentence she did this quick, clear-your-throat, I-don't-agree, half-chuckle at me!!!! . . . I couldn't even believe it! I felt like I was talking to a sassy child. I told her that she could make those noises at me if she'd like, but that it was very rude and unprofessional, and that I didn't appreciate it! I have tried EXTREMELY hard to not raise my voice, to choose my words wisely, and to keep myself calm when contacting Jim's doctors' offices - even when I was frustrated. I HAVE been persistent in contacting this particular office - I'll admit that - but that was only because they would never call me back! Soooo, I guess being persistent equals being rude. I don't know. I'm just livid over it. I'm almost more upset about that than the other challenges I've had with their rude office staff. I felt like it was an attack on my integrity and character. I'm really hoping I don't have to contact them about another single solitary thing for the rest of my life.

Ok. Rant over. . . . Well, kind of. I'm working through it.

I don't pretend to understand all of the things we have encountered along the way during this journey. Some things just seem so random and useless. But, I'm reminded that God can use ALL things for His glory . . . even when I have discarded them as useless junk. How He does this, I'll never know. It's ironic. It's mind-blowing. I know that through these challenges He is shaping me into the person He needs me to be, chipping away at my rough edges. Lately, the following verse comes to my mind frequently:

"And I am certain that God, who began the good work within you, will continue His work until it is finally finished on the day when Christ Jesus returns."
Philippians 1:6 NLT

I'm a work in progress. You're a work in progress. Yep, we all are! We're totally not perfect, but hopefully we're trying to improve ourselves and draw closer to our Savior each day. Some days we take 3 steps backwards. Some days we move forward. It's a little thing called "being human." Maybe you've heard of it? God isn't finished with us yet. He hasn't thrown down His tools and declared, "There's no hope left with this one!!! Take her away!" No, for those who are willing to stay under the steady pressure of His hand, we'll continue seeing bits of progress . . . "until it is finally finished."

And, once again I've gone completely off the topic I thought I had for this post. Yes. Again!!! I intended to give an update of the last few days and then rant a little. Hmmmm. Well, I don't know where to go from here . . . .

Expecting a complete miracle for my Love! ANY day will do!!!! Seriously!
❤ *Jim and Brenda*

And, that was the last update I posted for March 2016.

We were happy to finally be home again, recovering, and settling back into our routine. The first three months of the year had been an unrelenting nightmare for us and our family. At that point, I seriously felt like I needed a month-long vacation to lay on the beach and not be responsible for one single solitary thing. Jim felt like he had endured a full-on war. We needed a break. We needed a reprieve. We needed something besides more hospital visits and procedures!

There would be more challenges in the coming months. They would be difficult, but thankfully - although we didn't know it at the time - the worst of them for that year were behind us.

13

TO THE "MUSTARD" STATION!

THE THEATER IN front of us was massive. It spanned the entire width of the cruise ship and boasted an impressively tall ceiling decorated with ornate fixtures. Multiple rows of long, teal, neatly curved lines of couch-like seating hugged the stage area. Small, asymmetrical coffee tables were anchored every few feet in front of each row of couches. Balcony seating hovered above us.

We had been ushered in and asked to sit in one of the areas behind the curved rows of seating. In this cozy, lounge-looking area, the semicircle couches scalloped the back of the theater. Each couch had a coffee table placed in the center of the semicircle for easy reach.

One would naturally assume that we were anxiously waiting for a wonderful show to start. Oh sure, there would be some very entertaining shows over the weekend, but the first stop on our trip was not for entertainment. THIS was our muster station for the cruise!

For years, Jim and I had called the muster station the "mustard" station. We giggled over it every time we went through the whole muster station rigmarole on the cruises we took together. This trip was no different, and our stupid humor was still funny to us, so we continued using our endearing title and joked about it on our way to the "mustard" station.

We sat down in the area we were instructed to go to. We were the first ones, so we watched as other individuals and couples were sorted out and asked to join us. Each person in our "select group" had some sort of disability that would require extra help from a crew member in the event of an emergency. Some had wheelchairs. Others had canes. Some huffed and puffed as they rounded the corner and searched for an empty seat, because the distance they had just walked was a challenge for them.

The other people – those healthy enough to make it to the lifeboats without assistance – filed into the theater and sat in the long, neatly curved lines of couch-like seating that hugged the stage area. Once it was determined that they had accounted for everyone, the crew assigned to this area excused those people by groups to climb the stairs and assemble near the lifeboats. There they would receive special instruction about life vests, how to board the lifeboats, and other pertinent information.

Soon the theater was empty, leaving only our "select group" at the back, huddled in a small seating area. Most of the crew members disappeared to the lifeboats with the others. A few remained stationed at the entrance to the theater just a few feet away from us. We sat in silence, staring blankly at those seated across from us.

Nothing was said to our group. No instruction was given. No information was provided. And so we sat. Tick tock. Tick tock.

I asked Jim what we were supposed to expect in the event of an emergency. I wasn't really expecting that he'd have the answer I needed at the moment. I was just talking out loud to myself and wondering how this whole thing would go down if a real-life emergency forced us to evacuate our rooms and meet at the muster station in an orderly fashion - more accurately known as "mass chaos" in an emergency situation.

We sat a few more minutes, expecting that the remaining crew members would come over and explain any emergency procedures we needed to be aware of, expecting them to put our minds at ease. Still nothing.

After the previous months of ongoing, incessant emergency situations Jim and I had faced, their lack of information at this moment was not comforting to me. Every step I made, every corner I took, I had learned to be on high alert for whatever situation was lying in wait to catch us off guard. This non-information deal was not gonna work for me. My job was to protect Jim, and without adequate information I couldn't do that. I stood up and walked a few steps over to the crew standing near the doorway and politely asked, "Soooooo, in the event of a reeeeeeal emergency, what exactly will happen with all of us here?" circling the group of people next to me with my pointer finger as I asked. "How will we get to the lifeboats? Can you explain the procedure to us?"

And, after experiencing the previous months of ongoing, incessant absurdity, I should have totally expected to receive the vague answer I got from the crew member who decided to field my question: "Oh! Don't worry. We have people assigned to be on the lookout for you. They will find you and assist you."

And that was it. No explanation of exactly HOW that would happen.

This empty promise of "someone will find you and help you" seemed all too familiar to me. We had heard promises that paralleled this one many times since Jim's diagnosis. "Call if you have any questions." "Let us know if we can help you with anything." "Don't worry. We're here to assist you. You're not alone." All of these proved to be empty promises once another emergency situation came our way. No matter what the situation was, when the chips were down and Jim needed someone to walk us through the next challenge we were facing, I was the one left holding the ball and wondering where to go to get the medical help Jim needed and how to navigate our new challenge. I was the one left to firmly advocate for every single solitary thing. I was the one standing alone and wondering where to turn to next. We had LIVED at this figurative "mustard" station for almost a year. Why would we expect anything better at this point? And yet, I held out hope for something different.

So, you can safely assume that the crew member's answer to "What exactly will happen?" left me feeling alone, holding the ball once again. I had another mini panic attack at that moment.

Within a few minutes, they received the "all clear" signal and notified us that we were free to leave the theater and head to dinner or wherever else we wanted to go.

We exited the theater and rounded the corner. Our room wasn't far away – first room on the left after we cleared the entrance area to the theater and a bar not far from it. We stopped in to briefly grab a few items, then received a phone call from Arney and Dana to let us know they would meet us in the dining room. They were going to get in line and get a table reserved for all of us.

Yes. Our best friends had joined us on this weekend excursion. It was the ONLY way we were able to journey out of town at this point. I had learned back in November, on a brief trip to Monterey alone with Jim, that I was not capable of transporting luggage to/from the car and in/out of our room; checking on Jim; pushing him in his wheelchair; checking in/out of the hotel; parking our car; and everything else I had to cover on my own without running myself ragged. Most of that took multiple trips back and forth while Jim sat and felt awful about the fact that he couldn't help me. The purpose of this specific trip was to get away to have a short reprieve, not to kill myself trying to manage it. Lord knows that the previous months had already taken every ounce of my energy I had in reserve.

Once we had the items from our room we needed, we navigated the route to the dining room, waited a long time for the elevator to come to our floor, then passed on many of them because there wasn't enough room for me and Jim's wheelchair in the remaining space in the elevator. Eventually we made it up one entire floor and joined Arney and Dana in line for our table. We talked about our experience at the muster station (which the Corbins also called the "mustard" station) and the "great comfort" that it brought us to know the crew would "handle everything we needed" even though they didn't offer details of how that would happen. Yes, you hear sarcasm again. Sorry.

Arney, always being VERY protective of me and Jim after Jim's diagnosis, immediately offered the solution we needed. He firmly instructed us that in the event of an emergency while we were on the ship, we didn't need to worry because HE WOULD FIND US. He would not leave and go to his mustard station without knowing that we were ok first. He further assured Jim that he would strap a life vest to Jim and throw him over the ship rail FIRST and make sure I had jumped too, before he would jump over the rail and join us. As crazy funny as that sounded – and we laughed about it a lot - it brought much more peace to us than the brief "We will find you and assist you" explanation that the crew member had offered with no details. We KNEW The Amazing Arney Corbin would move heaven and earth searching for us if we were separated in an emergency. He wouldn't stop until he found us and knew we were safe. THAT was the assurance we needed, and our friend provided it.

As the cruise ship pulled out of port on Friday night and began our short weekend journey, we sat down to the first meal of our cruise together. We made it! We had finally made it out of town after four hard, grueling months of crushing events. It was the breath of fresh air we needed. It was the break in perpetual trauma that every part of our bodies screamed for at that moment. The first meal was an active sigh of relief that we had climbed out of the pits of the living hell we had just survived.

We laughed on that trip. We laughed a lot. It was good to hear/feel laughter escaping our own lips. It almost seemed foreign to us by this point. It had been many months since we had experienced good belly-aching laughter. It felt good to reset. It felt good to spend time with our friends and not have to talk about medical stuff every moment. And, I have to say, as we went through our weekend together, our friends never treated us any differently than they had in the past. We were not less-than. We were not damaged goods. They did not tread lightly with their conversations for fear of offending or insulting us. They just fell right back into normal friendship conversation as if that day was as typical as any other day we had spent with them. Did they step up to the plate and assist me with everything I needed for Jim? Why, yes they did. They offered help with <u>every</u> step, but allowed us to make the decision of if we needed the help they offered. (I'm forever indebted to these incredible souls. You just don't know the half of it.)

At this meal, as with every other meal on our trip, we found that Dana and Jim ordered every foreign, bizarre item they could find - appetizers, main course, and dessert. They were game to try anything new and exciting. Arney and I always ordered the tried-and-true selections on the menu, at times ordering multiple appetizers to make up for the main course we couldn't find to suit us. Dana and Jim enjoyed their fun, new selections, and Arney and I were happy with our mundane, everyday-meal selections. Annnd, if worse came to worst and we didn't like the meal we were served, we found our way to the burger joint by the pool to order burgers. . . you know, lest we starve on our weekend excursion.

We spent most of the weekend together, but did things alone as couples here and there. We saw a few comedy shows and joined the crowd in the theater to watch the humorous game shows the crew put together with a cast selected randomly from those vacationing. But, one of the highlights of our trip was sitting in a lounge area at night in the walkway of the ship, near the casino, and watching intoxicated people dance. . . . Well, I guess that's what you'd call it. Dancing, that is. Some of them never lifted their feet off the floor for fear they would fall over, while others flailed all over the place. This was our prized entertainment. Arney recounted to me recently that he thought we should've strapped Jim into his wheelchair that night because we all laughed so hard while watching drunk passengers dancing that he thought Jim was going to fall out of his wheelchair.

When our cruise ship took port in Ensenada, we knew that most of the organized excursions wouldn't be accessible for us. We went into this vacation knowing that, and we were perfectly fine with it. Jim felt well enough on this day that he wanted to go into town with us, so we took a walk into town. It sounds easy enough, but it ended up being a bumpy ride for Jim in his wheelchair because the cobblestone brick/cement path from the cruise ship into town was anything but flat and even. He was NOT happy with me about that and grumbled quite a bit to me about it quietly, but I had no way of changing the path we were on. We encountered many challenging twists and turns navigating the broken sidewalks on the way to Starbucks, but we enjoyed conversation between all of us along the way and eventually made it there. We sat and enjoyed our coffee/hot chocolate together, then Arney and Dana left us in search of some souvenirs from the trip (even helping us pick up a few things for our kids because we couldn't continue on the uneven walkways further into town with Jim's wheelchair). They returned with a few bags of souvenirs in hand, including two extremely large sombreros I had asked for them to get for my Missions Week stash I continually collected. They had also purchased two tiny sombreros for the babies of two friends.

We started on our journey back to the ship, but made sure to stop for the perfect picture with the cruise ship behind us: Jim and I in our obscenely large sombreros, and Arney and Dana wearing the teeny tiny sombreros. It was the Kodak moment of the trip that is now a treasured memory for all of us.

The weekend was not without its share of pain. The realization that I had switched from Jim's treasured, protected wife into a caregiver who was in charge of protecting him was ever present on this vacation. It was a punch to the gut. I still navigated the daily routine of helping him shower and get dressed/ready each morning. There was never a vacation from that. And then there were his trips to the restroom when the two of us were out and about on the ship without Arney and Dana. At those moments, I wheeled him as close to the public restroom door as I could, helped him out of his chair, gave him his cane, and assisted him through the door as far as I could go. Then I anxiously stationed myself directly outside of the men's restroom and waited for his return. At times, when he took longer than I expected, I found myself being the pervert wife glancing into the men's restroom every time a man would leave. That must have been a sight! Most of them had seen Jim in the restroom and sweetly recognized that I must be concerned about him, offering information that he was on his way and assuring me that everything was alright. Some even paused long enough so they could stop and hold the heavy restroom door for him so he could exit the restroom easier.

We rolled into port early on Monday morning, April 11th, and before long we were collecting our luggage, going through customs, and rolling

Jim and our luggage out to the car in the parking garage. Once we got to the car, I took the time to post a few pics and information about our weekend on social media. Up until that point we had chosen not to share news about our trip with many people, because we knew they would worry about us the entire time we were gone. We had been through so much with Jim's medical challenges in the months before that many of our friends and family were panicked, distraught, and extremely protective of us. We didn't want them to be overly concerned, so we waited until we were headed home to share that we had the opportunity to ditch town for a few days.

We enjoyed more fun conversation on the road home, stopping occasionally for coffee, to use the restroom, or for a meal. Around six or seven hours later we were home. Arney grabbed our luggage and carried it into our house. I helped Jim get out of their Suburban and, if I remember correctly, Arney wheeled Jim up the two stairs on our porch and into our house.

Vacation complete, we were back to reality again.

Sombreros All Around! (April 2016)

14

MELTED CHEESE ON THE SIDEWALK OF LIFE

WE JUMPED BACK into our normal routine immediately upon returning from our cruise. There was much to do that had been on hold for months. So much. On one hand, the time away had rejuvenated me just enough to start tackling these necessary tasks. On the other hand, I had an unexpected dagger that had pierced my heart while we were away – a new realization that cut me to the core.

I find myself struggling to write this chapter. This one, as well as the last one and the one to come. The content of these chapters doesn't bother me as much as the question of how to wrestle them into submission and put them into words. I feel as if the events of December through March were ready to write themselves because the details were solid and concise: "And then . . . . And then . . . . And then . . . ." All I had to do with those chapters was to retell the story and add the description of our emotions during those challenging moments. There was a precise order to follow in the turn of events I recorded. With this chapter specifically, I feel more as if I'm trying to sum up a month of five million other chronological events that each one has nothing to do one with the others. There is no linear motion of one subject.

At this point in time, it felt as if we had just spent many grueling months climbing Mount Everest; finally arriving at the top peak; and then dropping straight into a lower crevice, onto a flat trail. The exhausting climb was behind us, and we were soooo grateful, but we still felt the intense effects of it on our bodies. The trail in front of us was relatively flat terrain, but we knew all too well that at any point we would be climbing or descending again without a moment's notice.

As I scramble to find adequate words to describe the rest of April, May, and June 2016, I guess I have to say it was a "lull" in time. But in the same moment, looking back at the events that were happening, I realize that there was so much still going on that kept me hopping every minute of every day, that I would have to say there was a lot of chaos as well. But, this was the chaos I could handle. It was the type that could be somewhat planned out on my calendar and/or my to-do lists. I COULDN'T handle more emergency situations at this point, but I COULD handle "The Chaotic Lull" we were dropped into for the time being.

Wednesday, April 13, 2016 - PM Update:
Just poppin' in to let you know that we had another good day. Jim is feeling good!

We "toured" Escalon together this morning: went through Starbucks drive-thru; stopped at the Escalon Youth Center to admire all of the great progress going on there (and Jim peeked inside for the first time - eeeeek!); went to work at the church office for a couple of hours; then stopped at Pizza Plus for lunch. By the time we got home, Jim was ready for a nap.

This afternoon/evening I was able to take care of a little more office work from home, then I started sorting/organizing tons of paperwork that should have been organized months ago. There just hasn't been time to get to it, so it sat and sat and sat. There's still much more to be done, but I was able to accomplish so much today. It felt good! If I didn't have any other responsibilities for the day/night, I probably would've organized and cleaned the whole house! I was just in one of those "get it done" moods. Hopefully that will continue!

We have a couple of appointments tomorrow, and again on Friday. That makes for chopped up days that are difficult to accomplish very much. But the appointments are necessary, so we just plug along.

Oh!!! Almost forgot! Jim DID get the referral to a urologist at UCSF. He has an appointment for the first week of May. Thanks for your prayers regarding that. He seems to be doing very well. I'm praying that by the time he gets there they won't need to do anything at all.

I'm waiting for that beautifully complete miracle for Jim every single day. Yes, it can be discouraging waiting so long, buuuuut sometimes I just look at that long journey behind us and remind myself that we're THAT MUCH CLOSER to Miracle Day. I can't wait!!!! God has been so faithful to us during this journey. We are grateful that He never leaves us.

Until that anxiously anticipated day . . . .

We are expecting a miracle! ANY day will do!!! Soon, Lord; please soon!
❤ *Jim and Brenda*

Friday, April 15, 2016 - PM Update:

We've had 2 very productive days. Jim had speech therapy yesterday morning. We applied for Hanna's passport yesterday afternoon. (She wants to go on the church's missions trip to Mexico in June.) Jim had an appointment with his local oncologist this morning. Annnnd, we finally completed our taxes with our tax preparer tonight! I'm super excited about that! There just hasn't been any time until now to get it done. . . In case you didn't notice, life has been slightly insane lately! LOL . . . I'm feeling quite accomplished with these 4 things marked off my list. I've been stressing a bit over the passport and taxes. So here's my victory dance now that they are done.

In between all of these appointments, I've continued to organize/file more paperwork at home (ugh), and work on projects for work. I still have things I'll have to finish tomorrow, but that's ok. Just keep swimming. Just keep swimming.

Jim had a good appointment with his local oncologist this morning. His BP looks good. The doctor said he can start the next level to taper off of his steroid. He had done this once before, but because of complications he had to resume a low dose. Now he's working to taper off of that dose.

No chemo for now. The local oncologist wants to wait to see results from: Jim's oral surgeon follow up (from the abscessed opening left in his gum); the UCSF urologist appointment (to see what still needs to happen treatment-wise); and the follow-up with Jim's UCSF neuro-oncologist. We have to be sure his body is able to tolerate the chemo and not tank him. All of the upcoming appointments are at the beginning of May, so that's a good plan. We're happy with it.

Jim walked into his doctor appointment today, instead of using the wheelchair. And when we got home he seemed to have an easier time getting up the 2 steps into the laundry room. He has been taking short trips around the house without his cane, too! You know that means he's more steady on his feet. That makes me worry less! Woohoo!!! He's getting a little stronger each day. I'm so grateful for that. We'll take every bit of the progress we are seeing!!!

Jim gets tired really easily. He has to nap in between appointments to keep up his strength. We're also trying to watch how much he does so he doesn't overdo it and exhaust himself. It's a difficult balancing act.

As for his kidney stones, we think he passed 2 tiny ones a couple of days ago. Maybe Itchy and Scratchy have been "born!" The last conversation I had with the local urologist left me confused about the count of kidney stones that remained in Jim's kidneys. He made it sound like there were more than what he originally said. Not to mention that a conversation with Jim's primary care physician gave us new info that 2 stones were removed during the last procedure, not 1. Soooo, apparently Ed and Slinky were "born" together. . . . The huge dilemma we have now is that IF there are more kidney stone babies we have not named them yet! What are we gonna do??? . . . Yes, I'm being silly again.

Jim still has some discomfort in his side, near his kidney area. We hope to have more answers about all of this once we see his new urologist.

That's all I have for tonight. My brain needs a rest. Sorry if you find typos. You'll just have to deal with it tonight. Ha!

Sending our love to each of you! Thanks for your continued prayers.

Expecting a MIRACLE! Any day will do!!!
♥ *Jim and Brenda*

Yes. We were back in full swing with things: Doctor appointments, taxes, filing paperwork, speech therapy, work, running my kids around for various activities, getting info for Jim's urology referral to UCSF, and finding our "new normal" all over again. We were getting really good at bouncing back.

I would reeeeeeeally like to just stay on the current course and continue walking you through the rest of April seamlessly. It would be much easier that way. Instead, we'll take an inconvenient detour and talk about events I'd rather keep hidden and discreet. Things I'd prefer not to share about myself in an effort to preserve my integrity. I've battled with the arguments in my head about "sharing versus not sharing" and have decided that I'll keep to my original conversation/agreement with God – to share the good, the bad, and the ugly; to be vulnerable and real, no matter the cost to me personally. I feel there is value in that.

I ended the first paragraph of this chapter with something along the lines of "On the other hand, I had an unexpected dagger that had pierced my heart while we were away – a new realization that cut me to the core." That unexpected dagger was the fact that with each day in our present battle, I was moving closer to being a caregiver to Jim and farther away from being the treasured, protected wife. It hurt. It hurt deeply. I felt like I was losing him one piece at a time. I truly was. Each new challenging situation brought with it more realization that my life had forever changed. That cut into me a little deeper with each step.

On top of this deep hurt, my subconscious mind was already starting to count down the events of the previous year that led up to Jim's diagnosis. It was starting to brace itself for the threat of repeat trauma. I started to see it in my emotions, but didn't recognize/understand it at the time. I was able to keep up with the day to day routine on the outside, but I was spiraling emotionally on the inside. My body was recognizing the road signs and bracing for another enormous pothole in the road ahead. A pastor friend of mine, Jim Uhey, privately messaged me and pointed it out, as he deals with people in crisis situations frequently and knows how the body works in this area.

I will say that this whole topic of your body remembering traumatic situations and bracing for the possibility of it returning in future years is something that blows my mind and intrigues me at the same moment. Now that I've experienced it to the degree that I have, I can definitely say it's a real thing. Before this point, I would have told you it was a bunch of nonsense.

Although I haven't shared much about my emotional breakdowns yet, since the news of Jim's diagnosis I had many days when I was drowning in deep grief over the loss of life as we once knew it, the loss of Jim as I once knew him. I struggled to keep my head above water and just survive. I struggled to keep Jim and our family afloat. Some days I seriously felt like a piece of melting cheese on the hot, sundrenched sidewalk of life. I've used this analogy many times in the last few years because it speaks to me. You could take a spatula out to the burning hot sidewalk and try your best to scrape up the cheese, but there is truly no adequate way to recover every speck of cheese in that process once it's fully melted.

That was me. Cheese. Melted cheese. The days I fell apart, I felt like even when I tried to scrape myself up and put myself back together, the full damage was evident. I was losing parts of myself along the way, parts that were gruesomely left melted to the sidewalk of life and could never be recovered again.

On emotional days like this I hated it even more that I KNEW I would have to share them at some point and expose the ugliness of those moments. I dreaded having to share them, but felt compelled to be real and honest about the struggles we were facing and allow people to see firsthand that we were not perfect. At times I waited a few days to share it. Other times – times that it took longer to pull myself together and bring myself to write about it – I waited a week before I confessed that I had been scraping bottom. I just couldn't handle exposing myself in those raw moments. And, truthfully, I didn't want to hear platitudes, kind "you've got this" comments, or be coddled. As sweet as those things are (and the people behind those words/actions are), I couldn't gather up enough strength to even go there in those moments.

On this specific occasion, my official press release on April 23rd word-for-word was: "We started off the week kinda rough. Jim is fine. We just had a couple of rough days. We all experience these from time to time, right?" . . . and nothing more was ever shared about my actions.

In truth, there was MUCH more to that story.

I woke up on Tuesday, April 19, 2016, and jumped right into the normal swing of the day. I woke the kids up and they got ready. Soon we piled into the car and I drove them to school. When I returned home, I proceeded with my list of things to take care of like I usually did. At some point early in the morning Jim and I had a heated argument. I honestly can't remember the exact details of the argument, but I know it was about two completely unassociated things: his medication management and my needs. Given the months we had previously endured, I can look back at this argument with 20/20 hindsight and tell you that it probably didn't matter one iota what the topics of the heated discussion were that day. We were both fed up with all the crap that life had shoveled in our direction in great, heaping mounds. We were on massive overload emotionally, physically, mentally, and spiritually. There was bound to be a blow up of this proportion, and it's surprising that it didn't happen sooner.

I snapped, and I snapped good. This shattered soul couldn't handle one more thing. I had already been spiraling, but stubbornly refused to give in to it up to that point. Life had given me a first-hand look at how intensely cruel it could be to a person, no matter how hard they worked to keep their head above water.

Eventually the argument came to a halt and I decided to leave the house for about 30 minutes. When I returned, I had a full bottle of Bacardi in hand. I walked into the kitchen and put away the other groceries that I had picked up. I didn't talk to Jim, except to give him the meds that were due at the moment. I proceeded to grab a glass, a few cans of Pepsi, and my new liquid friend, then locked myself in our office. I was pretty successful in making a dent in that bottle that morning. I even surprised myself, as I can honestly say that I <u>very</u> rarely drink alcohol. If I've had one or two drinks in an entire year that's pretty unusual for me, so maybe that gives you a better stick to measure this occurrence.

Within a few hours I was hammered. To tell you the truth, at that moment I really didn't care. I needed something to numb the ongoing, torturous pain I had felt day in and day out. I needed something to help me forget the horrible nightmare I was living in every minute of the day, the heartbreak that I experienced every time a new challenge came our way and stole another chunk of my husband with it.

I prepared a nice bed of blankets on the office floor. I laid down and watched movies on the small television we had in that room. Buuuuut at one point, in my extremely intoxicated state, I made the error of deciding to message someone some information that I should not have given them.

Side Note: I know that my mother, kids, friends, and family will probably grill me incessantly about the exact content of this message and whom it was sent to. Although I have freely shared here that I made a poor decision in my distressed state, I will not divulge the exact content or reveal whom it was sent to. Don't ask me. What I will say, is that once I talked to Jim about it the next morning and told him what I had done, he graciously agreed to go with me so I could apologize and clear up the mess I had made. And days later, the person who received the message graciously accepted my apology and vowed to take it with them to their grave, never to be shared with another living soul.

For those of you who know me, I know you'll be shocked to read of such an occurrence in my life. You know how I operate in day to day living. You know that I am not typically a person you'll find drinking alcohol, because I choose not to. For others, I'm sure you'll read this and say, "I don't know how you kept yourself from grabbing a bottle up to that point! Your life had been completely messed up for months! You were bound to snap at some point." Either way, I'm including this information here in this chapter in an effort to show you what took place during that time. By keeping it to myself, and not sharing moments like this, it actually leaves you trying to fill in parts of my story on your own . . . even assuming that moments like this happened more frequently (or worse things happened) and I chose not to expose my actions completely. Whichever side of the fence you find yourself on in the full disclosure of these events, I can't help that at this point. I'm choosing to be an open book and show that even people with the best of intentions, those trying to follow Christ and have good integrity, are still human. And when life beats you up repeatedly, sometimes you snap . . . and regret it later.

It may not sound like much to some of you, but I assure you it was a crushingly embarrassing moment for me.

Now that we have navigated that detour in this chapter, we will get back on the main road and continue forward to our destination – the chaotic lull we were experiencing in April and May.

The rest of my update to friends and family on Saturday, April 23rd, shared that we continued to have a jam-packed schedule of all the things I listed earlier. I continually scrambled to juggle these aspects of life and still keep up with laundry, making dinner, and running errands. Multiple appointments for the beginning of May were written in on the calendar – two of which would be at UCSF within a few days of each other.

We were able to join the RV Maps team for dinner at our friends' home in Ripon that night. This organization organizes volunteers (many who are retired and own RVs) to work on special building projects for churches across the United States. Some of those who attended the yearly convention that night had been working diligently on the Escalon Youth Center our church was building! Many of the workers from this organization were retired from specific trades and used their talents for the Lord. Annnnd, they worked for . . . you guessed it . . . FREE. They did such a fabulous job at the youth center. We were blessed as a church and community to have them come and do top-notch work. (Again, I'll hit more on the subject of the Escalon Youth Center in another chapter soon.)

The next big event on our calendar was the Assemblies of God District Council in Sacramento. This is an annual meeting of all the pastors in our district. We had been planning for it for months, but as always there were a lot of things that had to be covered before we could leave: office work that had to be done in advance; arrangements for our 3 teenagers and dogs; then packing/loading everything needed for Jim while we were away; and driving to Sacramento, about an hour and twenty minutes away.

Cara, being a licensed pastor, was planning to go to District Council. She would stay at the same hotel with us. At this particular District Council, she would be recognized as an ordained pastor in a special ceremony of one of the evening services, so it was extremely important to be able to be there with her.

When we arrived at our hotel, Cara checked into her room first. I followed behind her to ask if we could be on the same floor, in the same area. Cara walked off to head to her room, and then the hotel clerk made my day! She said, "Oh! Are you two sisters?" I laughed as I explained to her that she was our oldest daughter. Her eyes got very big and she looked slightly embarrassed as she replied, "Ohhhh! I didn't think you looked old enough to be her mom." I thanked her kindly for the nice compliment and giggled as I collected Jim in his wheelchair (sitting a few feet away) and entered the elevator. I'm pretty sure that made my entire year!

We arrived at District Council services/business meetings the next morning. We took time to sit and relax in the car to rest a bit between events and after lunch. We tried very hard to manage Jim's energy levels and not overdo it. That was a difficult task.

The ordination ceremony was beautiful. Courtney and my parents are able to join us. We took multiple pictures before, during, and after the service. At the end of the ceremony, all of the ordination candidates were lined up in a long row in front of the stage, and presbyters/leaders were able to pray with them. Jim had the privilege of being able to pray with Cara during this moment. My eyes leak a little as I think of the sweet moments I was able to capture with my phone camera – Jim sitting in his wheelchair in front of Cara, gently holding her hand, and praying over her. It was a touching moment.

We returned home on Thursday, April 29th. The rest of the day was filled with unpacking our car; starting laundry; picking up our youngest kids' stuff from the various houses of our friends they had stayed with while we were away; reclaiming our dogs; and then, in the evening, running off to two award ceremonies and a school open house for our three youngest. Hanna and Americis had each earned a perfect attendance award. Christopher had earned a perfect attendance award and a high honor roll award. We were very proud of all of them. We knew even if they didn't earn honor roll awards that they were working hard to improve their grades. It only mattered that they were working to the best of their abilities.

And here's where I pat myself on the back again (along with a pat on the back for everyone else who helped me with our kids): How awesome is it that my kids received perfect attendance awards during a time of complete upheaval and trauma? They pushed through each day just like we had. They were warriors. They still are!

Jim had his first physical therapy (PT) appointment on Friday morning, the day after the award ceremony. The therapist made appointments for him for the next six weeks, and started helping Jim build the strength in his right arm – the arm that had been floppy and lacked any muscle tone at this point. He liked his therapist and found him very friendly and easy to work with, so that was helpful.

By Saturday the 30th, I was more than exhausted, but we had scheduled an appointment for Hanna to take photos for her upcoming 8th grade graduation. Her cousin, Nicollette, helped her do her hair and makeup beautifully, then she dressed in her pretty, lacy, burgundy dress. I drove her out to the park to meet our photographer, and snuck in a few pics on my phone while she positioned Hanna and snapped away. The photos she took turned out amazing!

And that was the end of April 2016.

15

WELCOME TO OUR CRAZY LIFE – EPISODE #342

IT WAS A rainy day. We all crossed the street together. Me – tucked under the umbrella, pushing Jim's wheelchair and trying to navigate the transitions between the street and the sidewalk safely. Jim – holding the umbrella over my head with his left hand, sitting back in his wheelchair to keep from flipping it forward while I navigated the bumpy transitions. Our 5 kids followed us. Cara was carrying my trusty medical folder that held all things important regarding Jim's medical history.

Courtney snapped a picture of Jim and me as we arrived on the other side of the street and headed up the walkway to the front of the building. It was the perfect glimpse of our combined effort to take care of each other. If you knew Jim, you knew that even in his diminished state he always looked for ways to take care of me. He wanted nothing less than the best for me at all times. And on that day, he was dead set that I would not walk in the rain just because I was pushing his wheelchair. He didn't care if his arm hurt from holding the umbrella so high. He was happy that he could keep me out of the rain . . . . You know, it really was the little things that made our marriage so amazing. I never doubted Jim's enormous love for me.

On this day, we were back at UCSF for another brain MRI and an appointment with Dr. B (Jim's neuro-oncologist). It was our second trip to UCSF that week.

All 5 of our kids joined us on that day. The next day was Mother's Day, so we had purposely planned to spend the day together and have a family meal on the way home. We always tried to make the best of our circumstances, even though life was stealing chunks of our hearts at every turn. We had all piled into our Expedition that morning and started the drive to San Francisco. Our wildly hilarious kids brought us much joy on this trip. They were extremely entertaining, even though most of their jokes were at my expense. We arrived at UCSF and ate our sack lunches in the cafeteria area by Panda Express. Once lunch was finished, we headed to Jim's MRI appointment across the street at the hospital, on the 3rd floor.

As usual, immediately after his MRI, I helped Jim get changed, then we gathered all of our belongings (including our kids this time) and headed downstairs, back across the street to the medical building to see Dr. B. His office was on the 6th floor and gave a spectacular view of San Francisco. On beautiful, clear days you could see all the way to the Golden Gate Bridge.

Dr. B's staff was always prompt to take us back to a room. In fact, if we waited too long in the waiting room, Dr. B would get very upset. He was remarkably kind and sensitive to the needs of his patients. Usually by the time we finished completing the health update form (which asked about changes with senses, capabilities, and other medical issues), the nurse would take us back to update his medicine list and get his temperature and blood pressure readings. Sometimes we were escorted back to the waiting room to wait for Dr. B, but usually we were asked to wait in the room the nurse brought us to until he popped in, greeted us, and moved us to another room to review the MRI results.

This time Cara and Courtney joined us in the tiny exam room to discuss the MRI results, while Hanna, Americis, and Christopher waited in the waiting room. The scan looked good. Dr. B fielded our questions about specific items, and we were on the road in no time, making sure to stop for a nice family dinner in Tracy on the way home.

Saturday, May 7, 2016 – PM Update:
We are in such loving, capable hands. We give God all the glory for the wonderful report we received from Jim's neuro-oncologist at UCSF today. We know that God is in control of our lives and we are so grateful!

I'll just give you an update, point by point. My brain works better that way. (As if you didn't know this already!)

- The neuro-oncologist says that what Jim is experiencing with pain in all of his joints is perfectly normal when stopping a steroid one has been on for a while. We knew this, but it's good to have confirmation. Hopefully he'll start feeling better in a couple more weeks. It just takes the body a while to adjust.
- The doctor is happy to hear that Jim's mouth has healed well from his oral surgery and that his kidney stones are stable. He gave Jim some suggestions on how to KEEP the stones stable and avoid additional problems with them.
- Jim's MRI from today looks great! The cavity in his brain (that was left when the surgeon resected the tumor) has now collapsed/compressed, and the space is much smaller. There is a little bit of fluid that shows on the scan, but the doctor didn't seem concerned with it at all. He said sometimes it gets trapped after surgery.
- Dr. B said his MRI looks stable and he gave Jim 2 options:
  1. Start chemo within the next couple of weeks, or
  2. Wait a couple of months to do another MRI, then reevaluate if chemo is needed at that time.

The doctor said he was comfortable with either decision Jim made. Jim opted to wait for re-imaging in a few months. The doctor said that was probably the better option since things have been so crazy with hospital visits, and now with the steroid withdrawal Jim is experiencing. It will give his body a chance to rest and get stronger. . . . And it gives Jim a chance to feel good for Cara and Marcus' upcoming wedding! . . . So, to clarify: no chemo for now.

- Buuuuuuut, the best news of all is . . . THERE IS NO NEW GROWTH that shows on the MRI!!!! Did you hear that? No. New. Growth!

This is amazing because he hasn't had any chemo since before his surgery in December! They had planned multiple times to start chemo, but Jim had many other medical challenges that prevented it. I truly believe God has His hand in this! I believe He is keeping that tumor from growing.

Many times since Jim's surgery, I've sat and worried because chemo couldn't be started as planned. I worried that they wouldn't be able to keep the cancer controlled without chemo. But, every time this happened, I felt a gentle reassurance from God reminding me that HE has things under control and that there is purpose in it.

We may not have "the news" we've been anxiously waiting for - news of complete healing. Sure, we'd love to hear that! But we'll definitely take the news we heard today, "No new growth!" I believe God is showing His faithfulness, power, and ever-loving care. He doesn't stop! Every day He carries us and helps us through. Today, we just get EXTRA encouragement in our journey! Little steps. Big steps. Sometimes a few steps back. And yet, every step we take GOD is right with us - good, bad, ugly, and exciting, He is there!

We still believe that complete healing is coming for Jim. Our faith is in our God - the God of the IMPOSSIBLE!

Thank you for your prayers for us! Thank you specifically for holding us in prayer for safe travels this week, going back and forth to UCSF. I know God has been with us and protected us along the way. Isn't He amazing?!?!?!

Expecting a MIRACLE! We are seeing lots of "small" miracles along the way!
♥ *Jim and Brenda*

Soooo, backing up a few days . . . .

May had started out with a bang! We had five appointments in the first week. Yaaaaay, us!

Monday, May 2nd, Jim began the week as normal, visiting Jim S. for speech therapy. That was the usual Monday routine unless another appointment took its place or Jim wasn't feeling well. Once speech therapy was complete, we headed home. Jim rested up while I took care of work emails and started some laundry.

After a late lunch, we went to Jim's follow-up appointment with his oral surgeon. We received great news that the opening from his mouth into his sinus cavity had finally closed. It took a long time for the gap the abscess had created to heal and close completely. This was fabulous news because this was one of the things holding Jim back from receiving his next round of chemo as planned. (After Dr. B gave Jim the option of holding out on chemo for a few months, he decided that it would actually be the better choice. His chemo regimen in Fall of 2015 tanked his body pretty horribly, and with the memory of that, Jim chose to hold off on it again if he had the option to do so.)

On the down side of things, Jim had two really tough days physically. He was feeling very fatigued. We were noticing a little change in his speech and his bones were aching. Knowing that he had started the final taper off of his extremely low dose of steroids, we chalked it up to this. You wouldn't think that the body would notice the change and revolt so drastically, but it did. It was the only thing in his routine that had changed that we could pinpoint it to, and it fit the symptoms one would have when tapering off such a medication.

As I've expressed multiple times so far, I felt stretched to my utmost capacity on most days. This week was no different.

Excerpts from Monday, May 2, 2016:
. . . Some days I wonder how long I can last with the craziness of our life, and still keep a little sanity. I know it's only by the grace of God that it's possible. I'm thankful that "He gives power to the weak and strength to the powerless." (Isaiah 40:29). Without God there's no way I could make it through a single hour of this journey. Seriously, I would've fallen apart *permanently* on day one!

Speaking of our journey, it occurred to me last night, as I was trying to go to sleep, that exactly one year ago (sometime between May 1st and May 2nd) is when Jim first started noticing symptoms. A week or so later the doctor thought it was possibly Bell's Palsy. And then, a few weeks after that (on June 4th), we received the news no one wants to hear: "You have a mass in your brain." So much has happened in a year. So much has changed in a year. It all STILL seems surreal. There aren't many things that are the same as they used to be. WE have changed. It's good to know that God's Word says, "And we know that God causes everything to work together for the good of those who love God and are called according to His purpose for them." (Romans 8:28). I'm banking on the fact that God can use this journey of ours and work it for His good and ours.

I'm exhausted now. I hate to cut this off when I feel like there's more to say, but I have a few things to cover before I head to bed. Good night!

Expecting a miracle!!! NOW is a good time! I'm so ready!!!
♥ *Jim and Brenda*

On Tuesday, May 3rd, Jim was scheduled for PT for his right arm/shoulder. I sat a little way away from him and watched carefully as he moved from station to station to work on building the strength in his arm. Since I wasn't close enough to follow the conversation he and his physical therapist were having, it made Jim have to work extra hard on continuing the conversation and answering the questions on his own. Although it made me a little panicky, it was a good thing for him to work on his speech during his physical therapy appointment. I knew his therapist would be extremely patient in waiting for Jim's replies. If he had a question on something specific and Jim was struggling to answer it for him, he would pop over and run it past me to be sure he had the correct information. Jim did really well at working hard on his workout AND having conversation alone, without my help.

After his physical therapy, we had two meetings at our house to cover church business. I sat in on the meetings with Jim to help him when he got tripped up on his words. It also helped me to stay in the loop and keep track of anything that needed to be taken care of in the future.

Business complete, I needed to run multiple errands and take care of other things for our home. And, as if that wasn't enough, I still had office work to complete from home that night and needed to sit down to complete a guardianship report for Hanna and Americis, which had to be mailed off the following morning. If what I submitted to the county was satisfactory, then it meant we wouldn't have to appear in court to review our guardianship.

Jim was still feeling achy and fatigued that day, but on top of that, he started feeling nauseous off and on and noticed some tenderness in his right side. It hurt when I gently pressed on his flank area. On any other day I would've been freaking out more than I cared to admit, but knowing that he was scheduled to see his new urologist at UCSF the next day I just pushed through the day and focused on the enormous stack of to-dos that were piled right in front of me at that moment.

Enter Dr. S (the urologist from UCSF) – not to be confused with Dr. S (Jim's local oncologist). He was a tall, thin, distinguished-looking man with thinning white hair. Jim didn't like to have the door closed to his teeny tiny patient room, so we witnessed Dr. S (from UCSF) rushing through the hallway from room to room with his entourage of residents, trying to manage his packed schedule to see patients. I half expected that he would be rude, rushed, and not friendly at all, but was delightfully surprised when this important doctor entered our room, introduced himself and his staff, asked multiple questions about Jim's medical challenges, actually listened to the answers, annnnnd took time to offer his sympathy for all we had endured to the present date, stopping to acknowledge that it had been a very rough road for both of us. He was a very well-known urologist with a crazy busy schedule, but this man, unlike "Dr. One-In-Five-Urologists-In-An-Area-Where-There-Should-Be-Twelve," did not have one bit of arrogance in him. It was very refreshing to meet this doctor and be assured that Jim would be well cared for by him.

Wednesday, May 4, 2016 - PM Update:
We met with the urologist at UCSF late this morning. He and his team were EXTREMELY kind to us and listened well.

He sent Jim downstairs (same building) for labs, but wanted to do a CT scan today as well. Labs were supposed to be quick and effortless, but we had a couple of delays with the orders in the computer.

They couldn't fit us in at this UCSF location for the CT, so they sent Jim to UCSF China Basin to get that done. We made it there and got the CT scan done. They asked us to come back to the Parnassus location and get the CT results, so back to the first location we went.

We just walked out of the 2nd visit with the urologist for today. The CT scan shows a total of 7 stones (3 in one kidney, 4 in the other). The urologist says they all look stable right now. He gave Jim the option to do a procedure and remove them all now, or to wait. Jim opted to wait. They want to see him back in 5 months. If anything comes up between now and then, the urologist said to call him.

We've toured a lot of San Francisco today! MY FAVE!!! . . . Not! . . . But, it's a good thing I wore my Wonder Woman shirt today, 'cause it was a Wonder-Woman-Needed Day. . . . Seriously though, God really helped me navigate around SF and get us back and forth safely. I'm soooo thankful for that.

I'm sitting in the medical building lobby, delaying heading for home. We're both tired and I'm dreading the traffic. But, I guess I'd better load Jim up one more time and get on the road.

Expecting a miracle! Today's a good day for one!!!
♥ *Jim and Brenda*

Wednesday, May 4, 2016 - Additional Update:
Two very important (not really) things I forgot to share with my update earlier:

1. I don't have 7 names selected for Jim's 7 kidney stone babies. Since we think that Ed, Slinky, Itchy, and Scratchy have already been "born," we can't include them in the "unborn batch of babies." Maybe we'll have to go with the names of the 7 dwarfs. Hmmm. Food for thought.
2. I may or may not have eaten my Panda Express chow mein and orange chicken for lunch with my fingers today. If it did happen, it would've been because we were stressed, in a hurry, and I forgot to grab a fork and napkins before heading to the car to cram 1/2 of my lunch down my throat and search for our next medical care destination.

Remember: It may or may not have happened. Innocent until proven guilty, people!!! (It could've been worse with fried rice, instead of chow mein.)

With the Wednesday appointment at UCSF complete, that brings us back to where we started in this chapter – back at UCSF on Saturday, May 7th.

Our tiny victories of "the kidney stones look stable" and "no new growth (for Jim's brain cancer)" were tucked away safely in our pockets. We were so happy to have good news and be able to look forward to celebrating Marcus and Cara's wedding in July without having to navigate the terrors of chemo slowing Jim down in between time. Even though the next few days were busy and chaotic, I had already learned to focus on each of the tasks that were laid in front of me, tackling them one by one, eventually checking them off of my list as I continued trudging forward.

That is, until the next dramatic episode of our crazy life . . . . Oh yes, there's more!

Wednesday, May 11, 2016 – PM Update:
"Welcome To Our Crazy Life" Episode 342

Although I had hoped that today would be a little less chaotic and stressful, things didn't quite turn out that way. In fact, I think we ended up with as much craziness, if not more, today.

We spent part of the morning discussing what to do with our Expedition and the needed repairs. I made arrangements to drop it off at the shop to be fixed. And Jim and I attempted to charge the battery in his Cadillac together, but never got it started. We were going to let it charge for a while, but got a phone call regarding his mom.

His mom was admitted to the hospital this morning. She has an infection in her foot and may need surgery. We appreciate your prayers for her right now, as it's very painful.

On our way to the hospital, we got news that our dear, sweet friend Ruth, a lady from our congregation, passed away peacefully in the middle of the night. We are sad to hear of our loss and her family's loss, but we know she is rejoicing with her Savior now and is pain free. I just have to say again what a sweet, sweet spirit this lady had. She'll be truly missed.

After visiting Jim's mom, we went home and shuffled cars around with family members and friends. I think we're set for now for transportation for a few days. We're so grateful!!! I hate having to rely on others to help us, but it's so nice to have people who are willing to help.

I'm at the hospital with Jim's mom for a while this evening. I think I'll sign off for now and get some studying done while she's asleep . . . Oops! She's awake now.

Although the previous update sounds like I am very nonchalant that Jim's mom was now in the hospital and facing a serious surgery on her foot, in fact I was pretty much panicking.

Jim's mom, Becky . . . well, "Mom" . . . and I have a good relationship. She has always treated me like a daughter, not a daughter-in-law. She has especially made a point to remind me of that many times in the past few years. We worked in the church office together for a number of years. She was our church bookkeeper. During those years she and I grew even closer than we had been in the past. She endured my silly antics and laughed at my absurd behavior. I think I was her free entertainment most of the time and I loved to make her laugh. On stressful days in the church office, she sat in her office quietly and offered a few sweet words when we bumped into each other. On bad days after Jim's diagnosis, when I stopped by the church office to take care of my work, she searched my face for telltale signs of what was really going on – things I preferred not to share because they hurt too bad to acknowledge out loud.

Now that she was in the hospital, I took on her duties for the church bookkeeping. I wasn't able to do the whole job, but I kept us afloat by doing deposits, payroll, and accounts payable . . . for 7 months . . . . You know, ummmmm, because I had nothing else to do.

I know that you're probably scratching your head at this point. I can hear you saying, "Whaaaat??? Brenda, why did you take on one more thing? How was that possible?"

There are various reasons for my choice to take on that responsibility. The first would be the fact that the person she had trained to take her place, in the event of an emergency, had just had a baby. She was on maternity leave from her full-time job and trying to find her "new normal" with her firstborn son. She was slated to start back to work within a week, so having her come in to start helping with the books, after working all day and taking care of her son in the evenings, just wasn't gonna work. The second reason would be that any other person we brought in would have to be completely trained on the ENTIRE computer program we were using in the office. Since it was a church management program that paired with an accounting system, it wasn't a program that was well-known by many people. I was the next-most-knowledgeable person in our resource pool that knew a little of both aspects of the program. Even as the next-most-knowledgeable person, I still had a lot to learn about her job that I didn't have reason to know before this point in time. Annnnnd, the third reason that I considered covering Becky's job was the fact that I knew someone would have to account to her for everything that had been done. If I did her job and we didn't switch off to multiple people during that time, the mistakes that were made in the accounting program would be the SAME mistakes over and over again.

There wouldn't be different mistakes from different people, causing a lot more havoc and stress to fix. I knew I could stand before her, taking all the blame for whatever went awry during that time, and she would know I had done my absolute best. I made sure to write notes along the way to let her know how each thing was handled while she was gone.

I was preparing for her to come back to her job. I was keeping things going until she was able to return. Every note I left, every item I added to the file for her to review when she returned, showed that I was anxiously anticipating her coming back to work. Only, that's not how this story ended, either. (Refer back to the end of my chapter "Whatever You Do, Don't Fall" and you'll be reminded of my warning that this indeed followed along with the Series of Unfortunate Events quote I referenced.)

Days turned into months. The months started stacking up one after another. But, Becky wasn't able to return to her job at the church office. After a couple of surgeries and many medical setbacks - being moved from the hospital, to a rest home, to home, back and forth – she was finally admitted to a care facility because her mobility had greatly diminished.

As much as the task of filling her role in the office pushed me to my limits while doing my own job, caring for Jim, performing some of Jim's job, parenting my squirrely teenagers, and still keeping my house in order, I continued in this capacity until December, when we were able to find and train a permanent replacement for Becky in the church finance office. Our new bookkeeper, Gwen, has been a huge blessing to me since she stepped into that role.

It's a good thing that I have Facebook to remind me of all the insane things I recorded in May 2016! In my mind, as I think back through specific events in that year, I have never thought of May as being a "hoppin' month." But as I access my posts to help me remember what was happening during this month, I'm floored by the incessant motion of crazy events. I'm sitting here wondering when I ever slept during the month of May. SERIOUSLY, LIKE WHEN DID I SLEEP??? I'm tired just reading about it . . . so tired that I might just need a nap right now. We're only halfway through the month and there are a few more main events I haven't even hit yet. Sigh!!!

The second half of May we were busy winding up the school year for Hanna, Americis, and Christopher. Hanna's 8th Grade Graduation was scheduled in a couple of weeks, so we had started preparing for her graduation party and ceremony. I sent out invitations with beautiful pictures from her photo shoot we did in April. All of the planning was coming together pretty well considering all of the other tornadoes spinning around us.

Cara's wedding was scheduled for July, so a bridal shower was planned by one of her best friends for Saturday, May 14th. I spent most of the day Friday helping her and her friends set up for the shower. Her friend, Lexi, purposely planned the bridal shower for Cara knowing that our family's free time had been consumed with caring for Jim's needs. She wanted to help us in this situation, so she did most of the party planning and set-up on her own. We spent the day celebrating Cara and taking lots of pictures together. Friends and family showered her with generous gifts for their upcoming wedding. It was a beautiful day and I enjoyed having something more upbeat and uplifting to focus on for that brief moment in time.

A few days later, on Monday, May 16th, Becky had her first foot surgery.

By this point in time, I had started attending Church Board Meetings with Jim. He liked to have me there so I could explain the details of specific agenda items when he got tripped up with his speech. Days before the meeting, we would begin discussing the agenda items. I would talk through what I thought he wanted to highlight for each item, then I'd ask what he wanted changed, added, or deleted. Sometimes he wanted me to approach it from a different angle. Sometimes he found specific information was unnecessary and would waste time. Sometimes he decided he wanted more information given on the topic. So, we'd discuss each item, until we finished them all. I went to great lengths to sit patiently and wait for him to be able to express everything he needed to say. On the night of the board meetings, the church board graciously allowed me to attend the meetings and assist Jim in this capacity, and they treated me with much dignity and respect.

Every direction I turned in these years gave me the feeling I was enrolled in multiple internships, unbeknownst to me: nursing, bookkeeping, pastoral, caregiving . . . the list kept growing. Who had enrolled me in these programs without my knowledge? Apparently God needed me to be well-rounded for something he planned/plans for my future. I don't know. I still don't quite understand it.

At Jim's PT appointment on Wednesday, May 25th, his therapist noticed some swelling in Jim's right shoulder. Jim had been experiencing pain in it for months, but with the swelling, the therapist felt that it was necessary to have it checked. Up to this point, no one thought it was necessary to check it when we asked. It was assumed that it only hurt because of his lack of use of that arm. He started having sharp shooting pains in it when he moved it the wrong way. At the therapist's suggestion, our primary care physician, Ken, sent in the MRI request to insurance.

I had another rough emotional day on Thursday. Although I cannot remember exactly what happened that day, I can definitely tell you that if I mentioned it in my update (like I see now that I did), it must have been another day when I cried through most of the day, attempting to scrape myself off of the sidewalk again before picking myself back up to keep moving forward. I shared these kinds of moments (sometimes briefly, sometimes in detail) to be open about the fact that our ever-changing, and yet never-changing, lives took a huge toll on us. I wanted to be upfront and real about it so I didn't give the false impression that we were running along on this journey, singing, and tossing lollipops and roses along the road every day. That wasn't real.

Friday, May 26th, we found ourselves back in ER. There was no extreme emergency, but Jim was experiencing excruciating pain in his shoulder and we just couldn't get the pain under control for him. He couldn't even move it without having sharp, excruciating pain.

I'll let my posts from that experience tell the rest of this fun story for me.

Friday, May 27, 2016:
We're still waiting at the hospital for an MRI. They did an X-ray and didn't find anything (as we suspected, since it's more than likely a muscle/tendon issue,

not bone). Loooooong story, but the doctor that took over Jim's case a bit ago sent orders for an MRI and he's waiting to be taken back for that.

I've come to the decision that one's spouse must emotionally fall apart before someone advocates for you. Mind you, he's in a "hall bed," so I'm sure that was a pretty sight to behold.

Saturday, May 28, 2016 – AM Update:
We got home at 12:00 last night. I don't have much time this morning to go through all the details of our experience in ER yesterday. I have to finish prepping for Hanna's graduation party this afternoon.

They did give Jim a sort-of, "we think" diagnosis after his MRI was complete. He couldn't do all of the imaging because of the amount of pain some of the positioning caused him. He couldn't hold his arm still in those positions for as long as it required. He came back shaking in pain on the gurney.

I have LOTS of thoughts and feelings about this recent trip. Some I probably won't share on Facebook. We'll see. I need time to process my thoughts and be sure to filter my words/thoughts/emotions appropriately and avoid sounding inappropriate or offensive. Pretty much I just want to cry.

Saturday, May 28, 2016 – PM Update:
I survived Hanna's graduation party. Sure, my house wasn't completely clean like I wanted it to be, and I was finishing making dessert after guests arrived, but it's just gonna have to be good enough. We had a great time with family and friends. Hanna was thrilled. That makes it all worthwhile.

Back to Jim's ER trip yesterday . . . . They think his shoulder is frozen. He has some movement, but the muscles are squeezing the shoulder and causing more pain when he tries to move it any further. And it's possible it could get worse. We will need to look into options for how to resolve this. We have a friend who has contacted us already with some info.

I'm thankful that we decided to go to ER for the imaging, because there's no way Jim could've tolerated the imaging without the pain meds they gave him. As it was, he came back from the MRI shaking in pain on the gurney. It took some calming down and more pain meds before he could get settled again.

As for the other part of our ER experience that had me in tears and makes my stomach sick, it's kind of a 2-part deal. I know some may have a difference of opinion on these topics, but I'm begging you to please be kind if you comment on this. I'm feeling very . . . I guess the descriptive words needed here would be "crushed" and "stripped of dignity."

First of all, I always feel upon entering ER that we have to "prove" a need to be there. They never take into account that Jim has been diagnosed with brain cancer and that we have had a roller coaster journey that has included more trips to the hospital than we'd ever hoped for. Visiting the hospital isn't our idea of fun. But they always want to push us out the door before resolving the current issue, and they never look past the current issue to see that Jim's body has been run through the mill this last year. Usually what they see as simple, turns out to be complicated. Usually.

Last night, after feeling like we were being shoved out the door with no answers once again, I just broke down. Not only was I crying in the hallway (Jim's "ER room for the night"), but I was just done with the whole process. When the nurse came to give us final paperwork, I had to tell her to give Jim the info, not me. She prodded me to find out what was wrong and in my squeaky, crying voice I shared the above info and much more. She said to give her a minute, but I couldn't stay. I had to ask Cara or Courtney to step in and replace me because I was crying too much. After I was requested to return, I was informed an MRI was ordered because the nurse advocated for us. . . . Soooo, my question is: why does one have to fall apart before anyone listens? We ask politely for everything Jim needs, but it seems like we are only heard if we are furious or crying.

I thanked the nurse for advocating for us when I saw her later. But her response brings me to my second issue, which seriously cuts me to the core. She said, "When I saw you earlier I recognized you and thought to myself, 'They shouldn't be OUT THERE.'" Then she apologized for not advocating for us sooner, like she felt she should have. It struck me kinda weird at first, but I wasn't sure why. As I thought through it (with the many hours of time to think and evaluate our surroundings), I have seriously come to believe that Jim was labeled as "drug-seeking" or something similar. The only other people in the hallway beds were extremely intoxicated; trying to escape; calling out to every person who walked by; disrobing themselves (no joke!); pulling out their IV lines; slurring their words; and/or complaining to the nurses every 3-5 minutes. . . . The fact that the nurse didn't think we belonged "out there" gives me the indication that someone else thought we did belong there. So niiiiiice to have our integrity stolen with the rest of our existence! I think back to all the medical personnel who passed us in the hallway last night and made eye contact with us, and feel shame and embarrassment that they would possibly think that of us. I'm convinced that we sat in the Hallway of Shame all night and never had a clue! I feel stripped of dignity and integrity. That's an awful feeling. That cuts deep.

I don't need "poor you" comments. Please know I'm not fishing for that. I'm just sharing the hurtful stuff that I alluded to earlier. I'm not even sure WHY it's necessary to share, but maybe it will help someone along the way. You know, that special way God has of making beauty from ashes? That's the way I'm referring to.

I don't understand all of these things we have experienced. I don't know what purpose they serve in our lives. All I know is that everything in life feels stripped away. Some people refer to things being "stripped away" to find the important things in life. Right now I just feel like *everything* has been stripped, stolen, removed - even the important things. I'm not quite sure what to do with this. All I can say is I don't see much more left that CAN be taken (and I say that with fear and trembling). I can only console myself with Romans 8:28: ". . . all things work together for our good." I believe God's Word! I do. It's just hard to LIVE IT and not lose heart.

So there's a fresh slice of vulnerability served up hot. I hate it. I sooooo hate it. I resist sharing the ugly stuff, but I'm continually reminded by God that our journey has no validity if I only share the good and sorta ok times. Our testimony loses weight without filleting our lives open to be read like an open book. (I kinda hate that book right now. Just sayin'.)

Ughhh!!! I dread hitting "post" for this one, but here goes. . . .

. . . Still expecting a miracle. Any day will do (still!)
♥ *Jim and Brenda*

And if that situation doesn't just punch you in the gut, I don't know what will.

We had endured another stupid trip to the hospital and had to fight to have someone help us get the answers we needed. And, yes, after fighting another battle on Friday, I had to get up on Saturday morning to finish cleaning my house and preparing food for Hanna's graduation party. That's hard to do. Everything in my body screamed that I just wanted to lay in bed for the rest of the day and only be responsible for breathing, but there wasn't time for that. So, I held my breath.

I survived the party and was successful in getting everything cleaned up and back in order. The next day was Sunday, so we were off to church early in the morning. Little did I know that we would be experiencing a miracle we needed that day.

Sunday, May 29, 2016:
You'll wanna read this post.

Expecting a miracle! ANY day will do! Today's a good day for a miracle!!! . . . Why yes, today's the perfect day for a miracle, AND WE HAVE EXPERIENCED ONE!

Jim was in a lot of pain from his shoulder this morning. As we drove up to the church for service, he asked me to get the wheelchair out because walking up the handicap ramp and into the sanctuary would have been too much movement for his shoulder. So, I did.

During worship service he continued sitting in his wheelchair. I was on stage on the worship team and I kept watching him to be sure he was alright. . . . And, quite honestly, I watch him every week waiting for his complete miracle. I don't want to miss witnessing it! . . . He seemed to be ok and I continued singing.

When I got done playing the offertory on the piano, I headed his direction to sit with him. It was fellowship time and someone was visiting with me briefly. I heard someone talking to him, asking about his shoulder. He told them it was good, doing better. I thought to myself, "That's a lie! Why didn't he just tell them it's hurting today?" As I sat down, I asked how he was doing. Instead of replying, he used his left hand to grab his right arm AND LIFTED HIS RIGHT ARM ALMOST COMPLETELY ABOVE HIS HEAD!!!!!! And then he just teared up.

He told me that at the end of worship he asked Pastor Arney (our associate pastor and good friend) to pray for him. And after he prayed and walked away, Jim was able to lift his arm!

Just Friday night he could barely situate his arm to do the MRI without excruciating pain (with pain meds). The doctor said he had a frozen shoulder and gave him muscle relaxers and new pain meds (which he's only used one pill of since then). Guess we can get rid of that now!

We just got home a little bit ago. As I helped Jim get changed, he said his arm/shoulder has very little pain and it has a crackling noise in the shoulder like tissue is still breaking up as he moves it. . . . And to that I say PRAISE GOD!!!!!! We know where this miracle comes from and we give HIM glory for it. It is so amazing that Jim and I just tear up every time we start talking about it with each other.

I told him that I'll wait for healing of his entire arm and hand by the end of today! . . . You know, ummm, because God's able to do that if He chooses!!! . . . My friend, Dana, said she's gonna start singing/praying "Head and shoulders, knees and toes" when she prays for Jim. I told her we need to add kidneys and back to that as well. Maybe a few more things.

I had a few people share with me after church regarding their experience during service right before/during Jim's miracle healing of his shoulder. Pretty cool. If you want to share what you experienced in the comments I'm perfectly fine with that. "They overcame him by the blood of the Lamb and the word of their testimony." Revelation 12:11a

Join us in giving God praise for what He has done for Jim. But don't forget to praise Him for the miracle that's coming too!

. . . And joy comes in the morning!

Expecting a complete miracle! Thankful for the one we experienced today!!! (This is real stuff, people!)
♥ *Jim and Brenda*

Hanna graduated from 8th grade on Thursday, June 2nd. She looked beautiful and we took lots of pictures of her on her special night. We enjoyed watching her ceremony, but getting Jim to/from the football field was quite a challenge for me. Although there are many details to this, in an effort to condense my story I'll tell you that I've already written about a similar situation in a future chapter when I tell about Americis and Christopher's 8th grade graduation. That chapter will give you a full, panoramic view of the challenge that nights like this posed. Thanks for being patient with me until then.

16

I SURVIVED . . .

"I SURVIVED __(FILL IN the blank)__!"

You see them everywhere - at amusement park souvenir shops, national parks, thrill-seeking experiences, after a family reunion, or possibly another special event where you may encounter crazy, fun-loving people. They come in T-shirts, keychains, coffee mugs, bottle openers, bumper stickers . . . you name it, you can have it! "I Survived the Tower of Terror." "I Survived Half Dome." "I Survived the Coburn Family Reunion." These souvenirs could symbolize a great feat you just overcame, or maybe just a silly moment. You can choose. And yet, we purchase them as a way to remember the moments we "survived," keeping them as mementos for years to come.

We had survived ONE FULL YEAR of battling GBM. Moments of sheer terror. Moments when we could barely catch half of a breath. Moments of pushing our fears down deep so we could just survive the challenge we were facing at that very minute. . . . Moments TOGETHER.

Yes. At this one-year milestone, the fact that we had survived a full year side-by-side was a priceless, cherished treasure. They had been grueling months. They had stolen everything they could possibly steal from us

. . . and yet Jim was still here! That gave us every reason to celebrate and continue the treacherous battle! That gave us purpose to push through on the hardest of days. This journey had taken us through the unthinkable, but God walked the path with us – before us, behind us, beside us. Sometimes I felt like He had truly abandoned us, but thankfully, my feelings didn't dictate God's faithfulness. His Word had promised He'd never leave us or forsake us. Whether I felt Him or not, He was present and working on our behalf.

I was fighting for the best care and treatments for Jim. I was managing everything I could to keep him going, and as healthy as possible: keeping detailed records of his appointments, dispensing his meds at appropriate times, helping him with tasks that he couldn't do alone, getting him to therapy/doctor appointments, and the like. Just when I felt like I had mastered the new, latest-and-greatest daily routine, I was forced to learn a new one because the most recent battle threw us into a routine that required additional steps, and additional work. The rules were changed time and time again, making it a frustrating task to conquer and feel any satisfaction in it. I battled each day with the never-ending list of to-dos that ran through my head. Sometimes I forgot things. Most of the time I didn't give myself the space to forget them. I was in robot mode. There was no other option.

Jim . . . well, he was in battle mode. He was busy each day fighting for more time with me. There. I said it. Truth be told, I know that he fought for more time with all of our family and friends, but he was mostly concerned for my well-being . . . as always. He didn't want me facing life alone. He didn't want me to carry the pain alone. It was the one thing that seared a hole right through his heart every time he thought about it. He knew the pain he would feel if he lost me, and he couldn't bear to know the pain I would endure once he was gone. He fought every single day so he could prevent/delay that from becoming my new reality. He gave all he had trying to protect me from it.

I remember sitting and pondering this one-year milestone when it rolled around. I struggled to grasp what it meant. Obviously, I knew it was a good thing that we made it this far, and I was elated that we had, given the circumstances we endured in one whole year's time. But, on the other hand, all I could hear screaming bloody murder in the back of my head was "18-month median survival!!!" If we had made it one full year, and 18 months was the median survival rate . . . ummmm . . . do the math. . . . That meant it was possible that we only had more or less than 6 months left with Jim, unless God chose to heal him.

It was crushing. It was traumatizing. My body and emotions were already in high gear, bracing for repeat trauma – trauma like we had endured at this time the year before. I had no control over it. Ohhh, I wanted control, but the control panel was out of my reach. My subconscious mind had hijacked my body and emotions. It started yelling commands to prepare for impact. It reasoned that because this horrific, traumatic event had occurred once, it was very likely that it was coming again. It made no sense to me. I ignorantly battled it, not understanding why it had kicked into high gear to brace for me and protect me. And now, on top of this PTSD reaction, I was consciously realizing that I may be facing the reality of the death of my husband within a few months. It was a battle for my mind. It was a battle of my will to push past it the best I could every single day.

The unknown was still dangling out in front of us. There was no final date to gauge how much energy to spend daily. Were we preparing for a short sprint or a marathon? Having this vital information would have been helpful to pace myself in the event of a lengthier journey, or would have allowed me to exert more energy in a shorter amount of time.

Nothing. No answers. No closure to anything. Only repeat emergency situations and the tedious daily management of a terminal illness for one year.

Where were our "I Survived" T-shirts? Where was the souvenir shop that could help us celebrate the monumental feat we had just accomplished? And yet, somehow we'd need to leave the hanging ". . ." because if we kept these T-shirts longer than we had expected, we'd have to adjust the timeframe indicated. Little did we know that we would eventually round back to this milestone anniversary two more times. Our final T-shirts would read "I Survived . . . 3 Years, 3 Months, 2 Weeks, and 2 Days of Battling GBM."

It was a difficult journey. The cruelest torture. And yet, we were staring it in the face every morning when we woke up, every night when we closed our weary eyes from another exhausting day.

The day after our 1-year milestone anniversary, June 5th, Hanna left for Mexico on a missions trip with our church. She had been anxiously anticipating the trip and we were excited that she was able to participate in it. She enjoyed her trip and had many stories to tell us when she returned home.

By June 9th, the 7 Dwarfs (Jim's kidney stones) were wreaking havoc again. We weighed our options carefully, knowing that a trip to our local hospital would land Jim in the hands of Dr. One-In-Five-Urologists-In-An-Area-Where-There-Should-Be-Twelve. A trip to San Francisco, although much farther away, would place Jim in the hands of kind Dr. S (from UCSF) if specific treatment/surgery was needed. Jim opted to endure the ride to UCSF, roughly 1 ½ to 2 hours away, depending on traffic. Courtney rode with us. Cara stayed with our dogs. My parents already had Christopher and Americis because my mom had requested to do a fun stay-cation with them.

It may sound crazy to you to go so far, but we were desperate after the previous experiences at our local ER. After waiting to be seen for a few hours, the physician's assistant that was assigned to triage Jim was super kind to him . . . and get this! . . . he even read through Jim's medical history before talking to him. It was amazing to see how much a small detail like that made such a big difference in the way he responded to Jim. He had adequate knowledge that THIS was not the only thing Jim had been dealing with in the last year, and it showed in the way he approached Jim (and me).

The staff started running tests and giving Jim meds for pain management. We stayed in ER most of the night before Jim was transferred to the observation unit around 4:00 or 5:00 the next morning. After that, we finally slept a little bit. Courtney had retired to our car, in the parking lot, around midnight to catch a few Zs.

The urology department couldn't find a specific reason for Jim's kidney pain, even though they definitely witnessed it when they started pressing on his right flank. No infection. No blockages. Nothing to point to. They could only surmise the stone he had passed at the beginning of the week caused inflammation. They said we should follow up with his urologist if the pain persisted or worsened.

Although Jim was being discharged to go home without any real answers, we had experienced a complete shift from what we usually got in our local ER. That was a huge plus for us! It was nice to witness the difference! The staff was very compassionate and easy to work with.

Five days later, we started noticing a slight turn-around . . . for the good this time (with an occasional bad day). These moments are conveyed best through my update posts to family and friends:

Tuesday, June 14, 2016 - PM Update:
Just stopping in to let you know we're plugging along. Everything is going ok.

Jim is doing well overall. He still has some unexplained kidney pain. It doesn't seem to be severe like it was, but it is still lingering. His shoulder was hurting after physical therapy today. Some soreness is to be expected when building muscle. I'm not sure if it's just from that or if he possibly hurt it while working out today. He tires quickly each day and by the time the kids are ready for bed, he's either on his way out or ready to crash.

He is trying hard to build strength and do little things by himself, instead of asking for help: walking around the house more frequently without the assistance of his cane; making himself hold his yogurt containers with his right hand (the one that doesn't work so well) - a HUGE deal even though it doesn't seem like it to you; doing small laps around the house; setting up his own toothbrush and razor without my help; and other things like that. Obviously this isn't an exhaustive list, but you get the point. He's doing really great with it and it's nice to have a couple of tiny things off my list that have to be done for him every day. It's a good feeling for him to not need the help, too! I can't even imagine.

Our days for the last month or so pretty much seem like a race to get through it all. Things that don't get done are quickly moved to the next day's list. Jim has physical therapy and speech therapy each week, sometimes twice a week for PT. The kids have lots of places to be, mostly at different times and different locations (of course!). I'm still trying to cover for Jim's mom for some of the bookkeeping duties at the church, plus my own work and part of Jim's. I've given up trying to count how many times I leave/return from/to our house each day. It's a revolving door most of the time. I'm definitely tired by bedtime.

Some nights it's hard to go to sleep because my brain won't shut down. Other nights I barely close my eyes and I'm out like a light.

Tonight, at dinner, I decided I must REALLY be tired when Jim said he was going to pray over dinner. In my mind I went directly to a funny thing I always repeat to my kids when I drop them off someplace, "Make good choices. Don't do drugs. Look both ways before you cross the street. Love your momma. Brush your teeth. . ." and so on. It's a good thing he didn't ask me to pray because that's what would've come outta my mouth at that very moment! . . . You know, because I've lost my ever lovin' mind. Hahaha!

We'll be gearing up for Cara and Marcus' wedding over the next few weeks. Cara has taken care of most of the details because she's being very careful not to overload me. She's very thoughtful with that, but a big part of me wishes it didn't have to be that way for her and Marcus' big day. I should be able to do so much more for all of it! I WANT to be able to do more. But I'm focusing on what I can do. For now, I think I have wedding clothing for everyone in the family. I have to double check Jim's stuff to be sure we're not missing anything. . . . I'm getting really excited about the wedding. I'm so happy for them. They are both so practical and easy to please.

My eyes are closing, so I'm gonna scoot. Tomorrow will be here waaaaay too soon with its long to-do list.

Thanks for your continued prayers for us! We love each of you!!!

Expecting a miracle! ANY day will do!!!
♥ *Jim and Brenda*

Thursday, June 16, 2016:
Some days are just rougher than others. I'm glad today finally turned around before dinner. I think I scraped bottom.

I wonder A LOT about how much God thinks we're able to handle. I would've said I was at my breaking point last year at this time. And that was BEFORE experiencing much more than just Jim's diagnosis and starting the first steps of treatment! My body feels broken. I can't even imagine how Jim's feels.

. . . Just keeping it real, friends. It's not pretty, but it's truth. Sorry!

Excerpts from Tuesday, June 21, 2016 - PM Update:
I went home to help Jim get ready for church on Sunday morning after I finished worship practice. When I got there he was completely dressed, had brushed his teeth, had shaved, and was sitting waiting for me to come in and help him with a few buttons on his shirt and to help him put on his shoes! Talk about surprised!!! He said it took him about 30 minutes to do it all by himself and he was pretty tired by the time he finished. Buuuuut, he did it!!! Pretty impressive with one hand, especially for buttons, zippers, and a belt!

He passed another kidney stone on Sunday afternoon. We're not sure which of the 7 Dwarfs exited this time. Maybe Sleepy? Jim hasn't mentioned any problems since then, though.

Today he was able to use the hand bicycle (I don't know what its real name is) during physical therapy. I think that's the first time I've seen such a great range of motion (forward and around) in his shoulder for a long time. They use a special glove for his right hand to help him keep a grip on the handle. Otherwise his hand would get too tired trying to hold the handle.

Annnnd, tonight he tried to use his right hand for a little while to feed himself during dinner. It was a little shaky, but he was able to make it happen. He's been using his left hand for everything and is able to do quite a bit with it, but it will be nice when his right hand can be in full use again.

His right arm looks like a normal arm again!!! For so long it looked like it didn't belong on his body because it was floppy, droopy, and super skinny.

He continues to cruise around the house without his cane most of the time (with the exception of first thing in the morning). He's been helping to load the dishwasher and keep the kids on track with what they are supposed to be doing while I run errands or go to the office to work. And, he's been sitting at the table for meals again for the last few days! (The kids love that!)

There are probably a few other things I'm forgetting, but you get the picture. We're seeing some IMPROVEMENT, and that's great!!!

Our days still seem to run together, and sometimes my energy runs out before the day is over. I'm not gonna lie; some days I have to take a little nap just to keep things going. When I have the chance, I definitely take it! With my emotions all over the place any given day (seriously!) and the run-run-run schedule, I just have to compensate in some way. So I do.

Laundry is waiting to be folded, so I've gotta scoot.

Expecting a miracle! ANY day will do!!!
❤ *Jim and Brenda*

Friday, June 24, 2016 – PM Update:

We have a little bit of exciting news for Jim today. I hope I can explain this adequately . . .

Jim had physical therapy for his shoulder this morning. He's been doing really well. The therapist even noted how much gained movement he had today. The improvement in it seems to be much more evident in the last couple of weeks. (I have to add here that we've noticed this improvement since the day our friend prayed for Jim's arm and the frozen shoulder encapsulation started breaking up. Thank you, God!)

Because of the way referrals work for physical therapy, the physical therapist only focuses on one body part at a time. They sign off on that part and then they're able to start working with the referral for the next body part. Jim has about 3-4 areas that need physical therapy.

Well, Jim has been anxious to start working his right hand and to get use of it again. With the way the referral system is set up we thought he'd have to wait until the shoulder was completely done, or ask them to sign off on the shoulder before they felt it was at maximum capacity. Today, the therapist started talking to him and said what he really needs for his hand is occupational therapy (for fine motor skills). Annnnd that, my friends, can take place simultaneously with the physical therapy referral. Jim doesn't have to wait another month or two before he starts it! Woohooooooo!!!!! And the doctor sent the OT referral this afternoon!

The downside? There always seems to be a little downside, right? But it's not too bad. The downside is that occupational therapy and physical therapy will be different appointments at different locations. So, basically we're adding an appointment (or more; IDK yet) each week. . . . For restored use of a previously dominant hand, I think we'll bite the bullet and make it happen.

Jim continues to try using his right hand and doing small exercises with it each day. I can't wait to see the progress he has once he has a hand specialist assisting him with occupational therapy! It's exciting!!!!!

We're so thankful for all of the improvements we are seeing. We know God is working on Jim's behalf and restoring his body bit by bit. I'd like to see a fast, immediate change for all of it, but apparently God has a different plan. It keeps us reliant on Him, that's for sure! Trust. Trust. Trust. It's not an easy lesson, but it sure is a long one . . . and lots of other lessons accompany it. Can I skip school today? Pleeeease?

Thanks for your continued prayers!!! You don't know how much your prayers carry us through each day. I can't stress this enough.

Expecting a miracle! ANY day will do!!!
♥ *Jim and Brenda*

Tuesday, June 28, 2016 - Afternoon Update:

Today we're waiting at Jim's physical therapy appointment. I'm just killing time again, so I'll give you a quick update on 2 exciting things:

1. Jim went IN the Escalon Youth Center for the very first time today!!! Now that the cement walkways are poured, he can actually make it inside. Up until this point he had only peeked inside from the doorway. It. Looks. Amazing!!!!!!!! What a fabulous job everyone has done on this building! We are so grateful, and we give God praise for all that He is doing.
2. I talked to the new physical therapy place, and Jim starts occupational therapy on his right hand next Wednesday. He's very happy! . . . I did find out a new bit of info while scheduling it today. He can't schedule

OT and PT on the same day or insurance doesn't cover it. Kinda weird since it's 2 different body parts, but oh well.

That's it for now. Thanks for your continued prayers.

Expecting a Miracle! ANY day will do!!!
♥ *Jim and Brenda*

By the end of June, things were starting to look up. Sure, we still had difficult days and emotional moments, but the progress we were starting to see was encouraging. We could see a faint glimmer of light at the end of the long, dark tunnel. Hope was slowly being restored as we started to see Jim's strength building back up. We needed hope. We were starved for it after this long, arduous trek.

17

PREPARING FOR A MARRIAGE, NOT A WEDDING

SHE SAT ON the floor of our family room, legs criss crossed, anxiously peeling away the wrapping paper of her first Christmas present. Courtney sat across from her, ready to dig into hers. Jim and I stood a few feet away and wondered how she would respond to this odd present. It wasn't her real gift.

Cara was 8. Courtney was 5.

As she tore the last bit of paper and scrambled to open the box, I held my breath. Inside that fake gift was a pair of my old sandals – slip-on sandals with two brown, leather straps and a square heel. And then the words of my precious, oldest baby girl crushed my heart and filled it with pride all at the same moment: "Oh, thaaaaaank youuuu!!!! I will grow into them!"

What 8-year-old in their right mind says that???

It was nothing an 8-year-old girl would be excited to receive, but my sweet, practical daughter was gracious in receiving them. Little did she know that her REAL gift – a brand new bike – was sitting on the front porch a few feet away from where she sat on the floor. I felt like the worst mother in the world as we stood and watched her open the second gift, and she gratefully accepted it, too. Thankfully, the third gift had a note inside that told her to look on the front porch.

We have always made it a point to give our children three nice gifts for Christmas. Sometimes there were more than three gifts tucked inside the three boxes. We told them, "It's Jesus' birthday. He only got three gifts (gold, frankincense, and myrrh). Why should you get more than He did?" On this specific year, since we bought a large gift for Cara and knew it would be her only gift, we couldn't put three boxes for Courtney under the tree and have nothing for Cara. Being the smart kid she was, she would certainly put two and two together and realize that we bought her the bike she had been asking for the previous months.

Fast forward nine years . . . February 2010.

Jim sat on the large chair-and-a-half in the living room of our dream home. I sat across the room from him on the end of the matching couch. Tears filled our eyes and the lumps in our throats threatened to choke us. Our three children had just filed out of the living room and had headed to their bedrooms. Moments before, we had given them notice that we were losing our dream home and would have to move within a month. It was torture. Absolute torture. It was hard enough to be woken from a dead sleep every night for months in a full blown, I-can't-breath panic attack that came out of nowhere, because the fear of the pending situation gripped me so tightly. It was quite another to come to the point where all options had been exhausted and we were now forced to break the news to our children and allow them to feel the world crashing down around them. It was heart-breaking.

Jim had followed God's leading to step into full-time ministry and the result of that, as we well knew going into it, was that there was not enough income to cover our house payment. We had talked about it many times, but felt that God's call on Jim's life was much more important than preserving the "stuff" we had acquired. We chose to be obedient in his calling and let God decide what would be weeded out of our lives as a direct result of this obedience. We had held out hope for many months that He would sustain us and find a way to preserve our beloved home. Although that's a story I would LOVE to tell you, it's not how it happened.

As we sat across from each other and mutually agreed to send out text messages to family members to notify them, we could hear rustling in Cara's room. We could tell she was very focused on whatever it was she was doing, but we were so crushed at the moment we didn't get up to check on her.

About 15-20 minutes later, as we still sat bewildered, Cara popped back into the living room. She was 17 at the time, almost 18. She announced, "Mom, I think I have everything in my room organized and it'll be easy to pack. If you need help packing the stuff in the house, just let me know. I'll help you." Touched by her soft-hearted response to this crushing news, I thanked her and apologized once again for the situation. Jim jumped in, in tears, and apologized for "failing" her. And, the response of that wise-beyond-her-years, tenderhearted soul floored us: "Dad ... God didn't say following Him would be easy. He just told us to be obedient."

And as I type this, I still feel the deep pain, shock, amazement, awe, and pride I felt in that very moment. This precious girl got it! She already knew it deep in her soul. Her words of wisdom and her gentle understanding of the predicament we faced as parents were a healing balm on our weary, hurting hearts.

Fast forward about six years . . . . Timeframe: October 2015 to June 2016.

Marcus had proposed to Cara, and she had gladly accepted. We were thrilled for them! The only problem was that we were now thrown into planning a wedding . . . you know, in the midst of all of the chaos that was thrown our way, without notice, during that time. As Cara and I discussed it, I told her my fears of not being able to afford much financially for wedding planning and not being a reliable source for helping with said plans. I wasn't sure how I would be able to be an active part of everything that needed to be done because, as you've already read about, I was going a million directions at a high rate of speed.

As we discussed her wish list for the wedding, in true Cara-fashion, she said, "Mom ... there are some specific things I want for the wedding, but the rest of it really doesn't matter. I'm not preparing for a wedding. I'm preparing for a marriage." And once again my heart swelled with pride as I realized that this sweet girl, knowing our limiting circumstances, was content to plan a very simple wedding and be just as happy about it as if she were planning the lavish wedding of her dreams. She saw the big picture – a marriage – and knew the value of it far outweighed the one-time event of their wedding day.

My practical, no-nonsense girl is quite a rare gem. I still have no idea why she is wired the way she is, but it's pretty amazing.

We talked about shopping for her wedding dress . . . you know, the way everyone else does - daughter, mom, and whoever else is invited go to a bridal shop together. The bride tries on dresses one at a time and the participants oooh and awhhh over them until they find the perfect dress. The mother of the bride gets emotional and sheds a few tears. Fun photos are taken. Yada yada yada. You know the drill. We talked about it and planned to do that, buuuut soon after Cara's engagement she started looking at dresses online. She found one she liked and asked how I would feel about NOT going wedding dress shopping together. I told her I was fine with whatever she wanted and acknowledged the fact that going out of the house (leaving Jim) for any period of time was going to be extremely difficult. She agreed.

We sat down together to look at the dress she had selected. It was beautiful! I could tell she was sold on it, so I gave my stamp of approval, but only after reminding her that the quality of the dress may not be everything she was expecting. To which she replied once again that her wedding day would be ONE DAY, and she was planning for a marriage, not a wedding. So, I placed the order for her dress . . . on Amazon . . . for $82 . . . including tax and $22 for shipping. True story! I can't even make this kinda stuff up.

Cara went into planning mode, asking her close friend to help her coordinate the wedding. Her focus was to take any pressure off of me to feel like I had to make things happen. She knew I was overextended and that even if I committed to help with any specific project for the wedding, I could quite possibly be taken out of the equation at any given moment because of the ongoing medical challenges Jim was facing. She didn't want me to add her wedding projects to my plate. She was adamant about it.

Throughout the months of October through June, Cara and her friend plugged away at the list of to-dos for the wedding. Many of those months I was taken out of commission because of the emergency situations we were managing. I helped with whatever I could, ordered supplies from Amazon as Cara let me know of the needs, and focused on purchasing clothes for the rest of our family for the special day.

Shopping. Yeah, that was a challenge. Since Jim's diagnosis the year before, most of my shopping had been done online. My favorite location . . . Amazon. From medical supplies to coffee k-cups, from slippers to wedding supplies, Amazon was my new, trusty, rusty shopping friend. It was the ONLY way I survived purchasing gifts for my 5 children for Christmas 2015. With Prime, I usually had our supplies within a couple of days, so we didn't have to wait long. If things didn't work out with what we had selected, their return policy was easy and hassle-free. It was brilliant! It was convenient for our extraordinary circumstances. I seriously don't know how I would have survived without this practical, everyday helper that was just a finger click away.

I started searching for clothes for the family. Christopher needed new dress shoes, a tie, and a button-up shirt. Jim needed a new tie, and I needed to assess the dress shirts he had to be sure they would fit him. (He actually needed a brand new suit that fit him properly because he had lost so much weight, but he was not in the mood for going out, enduring the measuring process, and selecting a new suit. He wasn't even interested in renting a tux for the wedding because his energy was nil.) Hanna and Americis needed dresses. I needed a mother-of-the- bride dress. All of these things were conveniently found on Amazon. No joke.

Americis' dress was too large, but she decided to keep it for her graduation the next year. I ordered another dress for her and it came within a few days. My dress didn't fit quite right, so it was sent back and replaced with another size. Truth be told, I really should have spent the time to find a seamstress to make alterations on my dress, but there wasn't time for that. Ongoing, real life emergency situations made that impossible.

Finally, the days and months to July 2016 clicked down, and the long-awaited wedding day arrived. Our house was abuzz that morning with bridesmaids joining us for breakfast, then taking over the office and family room with makeup, nail polish, dresses, shoes, hair supplies, and everything needed to make them beautiful for the day. The photographer arrived and snapped shots of Cara's dress, the rings, her shoes, and captured the moments of Cara and her bridesmaids getting ready.

I slipped into our bedroom/bathroom to assist Jim with showering, dressing, and getting spiffed up. Once he was ready, I took a few moments to get my dress on and finish final touches on my hair and makeup. Jim was not able to wear his wedding ring at this point, so I made sure to grab it and slip it on my thumb before we left that day. It meant something to me to have it with me for this occasion.

When we emerged from our bedroom again, the photographer caught a few snapshots of Cara stopping to help Jim tie his tie.

Most of the wedding photos were taken at my parents' neighbors' home before the wedding. It is a beautiful property out in the country, with a pasture area surrounding it. The natural wood house boasts a gorgeous wrap-around porch and was perfect for positioning the wedding party, friends, and family on the wide steps leading up to the front door. The owners weren't home that day, but had given permission to take whatever pictures we desired, even allowing Marcus and Cara to use their old cars and carriages for some special pictures of just the two of them.

Soon we were headed to the church - our home church, where my parents and Jim and I both held our wedding ceremonies many years before. Jim was tired by this point, but had the opportunity to sit and rest in the activity center while I finished preparing "the cake." Marcus doesn't like cake. In their wedding planning, he and Cara had decided to forego the tradition of it. They opted for root beer floats and a different type of cake. The cake they selected was actually multiple tiers of Oreo cookies stacked to look like a cake. While Jim rested and chatted with me, I tediously stacked the first 4-5 layers of Oreos in a circle to create the first cake tier, then proceeded to complete the next tiers, topping it off with a Lego couple cake topper and accenting it with a few yellow sunflowers to help it blend in with the rest of the décor.

I stopped to freshen up a bit, as it was an extremely hot day and taking wedding pictures outdoors made me look like a withered flower. As I finished up, I washed my hands and grabbed a few paper towels to dry them, tossing them in the trash can before I left the restroom.

Moments later I was preparing to help Jim get next door, into the sanctuary. As I grabbed a few items, I looked down at my hand and noticed Jim's wedding ring was no longer hanging from my thumb. IT WAS GONE! I frantically searched every place I could think that I had dropped it, as I KNEW that I had it when we arrived at the church. I even checked the restroom to see if I left it there. Nope, no ring. Time was ticking away, and the wedding was slated to start in 10-15 minutes. I needed to get Jim to the sanctuary and give him a chance to rest before taking the trip down the aisle with Cara. There was no more time to search for his treasured wedding ring.

I reluctantly gathered everything we needed, then assisted Jim with the journey to the sanctuary. As I stood in the foyer, waiting for the wedding to start, waiting for Christopher to escort me down the aisle to my seat, I choked back tears. And, only minutes before it started, my friend's daughter came searching for me, placing Jim's ring in the palm of my hand and explaining that she found it in the trash can in the restroom. Apparently, I had slipped it off of my thumb as I vigorously dried my hands and, not realizing that I had wrapped it in the paper towel, I threw it away. My mind was at ease and Christopher was ready to escort me down the aisle.

The ceremony was beautiful, but the highlight of the entire day was standing, turning around, and being able to watch Jim walk Cara down the aisle. In reality, SHE was walking HIM down the aisle, because he wasn't very stable on his feet and was still very weak. There wasn't a dry eye in the room. The incredibly precious moment was not lost on anyone in attendance. I struggled to keep from sobbing uncontrollably, stifling my cry the best I could.

Pastor Arney led Marcus and Cara through their vows, " . . . for better, for worse, for richer, for poorer, in sickness and in health." These words rang in my ears and stung my heart deeply. I choked back more tears. Pastor Arney tried desperately to reign in his emotions, but at "in sickness and in health" you could hear the quiver in his voice, because he knew his friends had been painfully living out those exact vows for months. He quickly regained his composure and finished out the ceremony smoothly.

Ceremony complete, guests were invited to the activity center while final photos were taken in the sanctuary. Before long, Marcus, Cara, and the wedding party joined their friends and family for the reception. Food. Speeches. More photos. Everything was simple, yet enjoyable.

Jim asked for the mic. He labored to get his words out correctly, but he desperately wanted to say a few things. He thanked friends and family for attending. He congratulated Marcus and Cara. And, in true Jim-fashion, he couldn't resist adding in a joke, so he continued by saying that he had 3 more daughters and was taking applications to select their future husbands. Each word was carefully thought out as he struggled to speak clearly. It was a great challenge for him, but he wasn't going to let the opportunity pass him by just because of the challenge.

Unbeknownst to Cara, we had asked our local fire department to escort Marcus and Cara from their reception. They had made special arrangements to have their post covered for a short period of time so they could be part of this special day for our family. (Remember? Jim was their volunteer fire chaplain. You have no idea how much we love these guys/ladies and treasure the compassion and friendship they offered us.) Marcus knew about the arrangements. He had dropped off his car at the fire station earlier in the day and had his brother pick him up.

At the end of the reception I received word that the fire crew had arrived in the fire engine. I let the happy couple finish visiting with their guests, then we made the announcement that their fancy ride was there to pick them up. Cara was somewhat surprised, but had an inkling that something was in the works. As they walked out to the fire engine, I tried to follow as fast as I could so I could get a few pictures. Jim was heading that direction, but was taking much longer to get there. They greeted the crew, checked out the inside of the fire engine, and were almost ready to go when Cara remembered that she hadn't hugged her daddy goodbye. She jumped back down and hurried to meet him as he finished his last steps to the fire engine. As she hugged him tightly and thanked him, I was able to capture another priceless moment in time.

We waved goodbye as Mr. and Mrs. Marcus Woodworth were whisked away in Engine 1-1 to start their honeymoon. The wedding day was complete. The new Mrs. Woodworth had prepared for this marriage and was entering a brand new chapter of her life with the man of her dreams.

Wedding Day - Cara Hugging Her Daddy Goodbye (July 2016)

18

THERAPY AND LOTS OF BABIES

"**L**ET'S TAKE A look at your hand!!! Show me what you can do."
Jim grasped his right wrist with his left hand, gently lifted it up, and placed his hand limply on the table in front of him.
"Can you tap your fingers like this? . . . Ok. Can you separate your fingers like this? . . . Alright. Let's test your gripping and pinching strength . . . Ok. I'm going to touch the end of your fingers with this special tool so we can test the sensation in your fingers."

Jolene was an amaaaaaazingly compassionate therapist. Her jolly laugh was contagious. Her blue eyes were bright and they sparkled when she talked. She was Jim's new therapist for Occupational Therapy (OT). She was a brilliant woman and you could tell she loved what she did. She was good at it!

Jim was excited about getting started on therapy for his right hand – his previously dominant hand. He was tired of doing everything with his left hand or asking for help. It was frustrating for him, but he had managed it very well up to this point. He wanted use of his right hand again. He wanted to rely less on my help every day. He wanted to be able to do things alone and not be a "burden."

We had walked into the physical therapy building, checked in, and waited in the lobby for Jim to be called. When they called him back to the therapy room there really wasn't space for me to sit with Jim. You could tell that made him extremely anxious. It was written all over his face. The staff identified the situation and quickly placed an extra chair at the end of the table for me, just next to Jim's. Meeting a new therapist would require answering a lot of questions, and that in itself was stressful for Jim. Many people didn't like to take the time to wait for him to finish his sentences. Usually, in an effort to help Jim, they finished his sentences for him – which only frustrated him more when they didn't fill in the blanks correctly, with what he truly intended to say. We weren't sure what to expect from this new set of therapists and assistants. We had never met them before.

The room was set up with two long sets of tables facing each other, one row on each side of the room. There were sets of chairs lining the outside of both rows of tables. Each chair was a spot for clients to sit during therapy. This line of tables and chairs was just steps away from a linoleum walkway on each side of the room. The walkway led to the doors that went out to the indoor pool for aquatic therapy – a place we would use in the future. Inside of these rows of tables you would always find occupational therapists and their assistants sitting on rolling chairs, moving back and forth between clients. Sitting directly in front of each patient made it convenient to assess their needs and help them through the variety of therapy exercises of each appointment.

On July 6, 2016 – three days before Marcus and Cara's wedding - this is where Jim and I were sitting and waiting for an assessment of his hand. This was the day that I was exposed to yet another medical field I had never had a reason to know about before this point. Over the years we attended Jim's therapy, I absorbed many fascinating facts about the intricate design and function of our hands – something we don't really stop to think about very often in life. It's intriguing and astounding to me when I pause to realize how intricately God designed every part of us.

I still remember this day like it was yesterday. I can still picture EXACTLY what it looked like when Jim picked up his right hand with his left and placed it on the table in front of him. I play that video in my head every time I think of this day. It is one of the moments that are forever engraved in the memories of my heart. He proceeded to place his floppy hand on the table and used his left hand to delicately move each finger of his right hand, individually spacing them out to a semi-normal position before he pressed down firmly on his right hand to get it to lay as flat as he could. His fingers had been curling due to muscle atrophy from not using his hand. There was no strength, barely any movement to it, and it looked like a hopeless situation to try to build strength in this hand.

I observed as Jolene walked through the steps of his assessment. I took notes in Jim's medical notebook as she went. When asked if he could tap his fingers "like this," I strained hard to see the teeny, tiny movement at the tip of each finger as he gave all of his effort to attempt the tapping motion. It was so minimal that if one wasn't specifically looking for the movement it would've been missed. When asked if he could separate his fingers "like this" (spreading them out on the table as if he were signaling the number 5), once again you could only see muscles and tendons twitching in an effort to move like they desperately wanted to move.

Jolene started assessing the strength in Jim's hands with tools from her kit. She measured the squeezing strength of both hands. His left hand measured at 32 pounds, his right at only 4 pounds. When she measured his pinching strength, the left hand was at 15 pounds and his right hand was at 5 pounds. I share these numbers hoping to accurately paint the picture of the extreme diminished function of his right hand – a hand that had previously been his dominant hand. He struggled every single day when he tried to use it in any capacity.

More tools were pulled from Jolene's handy, dandy toolbox. She jotted down specific measurements of his hand in different positions, giving them a baseline to compare to later to evaluate his improvement.

By the end of the appointment, Jolene had given Jim many helpful tips to reduce the swelling and spasticity in his hand/forearm, as well as a list of exercises for him to work on at home between appointments. She wanted him to stretch his hand and arm frequently by pressing on the countertop at home throughout the day. This would stretch his flexor muscle. Rolling an object across a surface with shelf liner (a rubbery mat) was also advised. Tapping on and lightly brushing the top of his forearm with the fingertips of his other hand throughout the day would help reduce the spasticity in that area. That was something I could help with when I was holding his hand or snuggling up close to him. (Smile!) Jolene also prescribed him a resting hand splint to wear at night, to stretch the tendon in his arm while he slept. It took a while to get this molded for Jim, but in no time at all he was complaining about how much he detested wearing it. He found it very uncomfortable and only wore it because he knew it would help him. I'll also add that there were nights that he "forgot" to remind me to help him put it on before climbing into bed. How convenient!

They scheduled Jim's OT appointments for twice a week. That added a new challenge for our already complicated schedule. We soon discovered that our insurance didn't allow for different therapy appointments to be held on the same day. Speech therapy, physical therapy, and occupational therapy all had to happen on different days. Although, we did find that sometimes it wasn't a problem to do speech therapy and OT/PT on the same day. I don't really know the reason for such an odd policy, but that's how it worked.

Why was this a challenge? Well, quite frankly, because it forced us into a schedule of 5 therapy days a week. Mondays were designated for speech therapy. Physical therapy and occupational therapy typically happened on Tuesday/Thursday and Wednesday/Friday, but due to scheduling conflicts between the two sometimes they were switched around.

Welcome to the newest change in our routine! Every weekday (usually in the morning) you would find us on our way to some sort of therapy appointment. The drive to/from these appointments usually averaged 15-20 minutes each way. Therapy time generally lasted an hour or two, depending on the skills the therapist was working on and how much energy Jim had for the day.

Throughout the years Jim did OT for his right hand, we spent a lot of time with the ladies in this department. Jolene, Anita, Rosemary, and Kayla were a joy to work with, and they loved working with Jim. At times I think the assistants, Kayla and Rosemary, were disappointed when they weren't assigned to him for the day. He kept them on their toes and enjoyed teasing them. Even with his broken speech he couldn't resist the opportunity to be funny and sassy. He rolled his eyes when certain therapy tools were brought out for him to use. Sometimes, when their backs were turned, he would prematurely wrap up the exercise he was working on, push the tool he was using over to the side (to indicate that he had finished with it), and move on to the next exercise before they noticed. Of course, he would give me The Look, quietly tell me, "Shhhhhh," and impishly grin at me.

Jim's therapy team learned very early on in the game that Jim didn't like to have me in the waiting room while he did hand therapy. They discovered that I was a key ingredient to his successful therapy sessions, because he couldn't concentrate when I was out of sight. If they had space at the end of a table, they would bring over an extra chair for me to use so I could be close by for him. If they had a vacant space at the therapy table and wouldn't need it anytime soon, they would place me there and allow me to work on my office work. In between work tasks, I talked with them and Jim and cheered him on in his progress. I seriously became his own private cheerleader. When he reached new milestones in his therapy exercises, I'd convey how proud I was of him and tell him I was pulling my pom poms out of my purse to do a cheer for him. He always laughed, got a little embarrassed, and then he'd tell me that my pom poms weren't needed. He pushed so hard every day to restore what had been stolen from him in his battle with GBM. I thought it was amazing. I still do!

Later on in his hand therapy, when Jim was more steady on his feet without using his cane, one of his exercises was carrying a serving tray around the room, balancing it on his right hand. Various objects were placed on the tray to add weight to it: boxes of cake mix or canned food from the "shelf therapy cabinet," other therapy tools, or whatever else was in the room that could be used. In true Jim-fashion, he walked around the room and pretended to offer treats to the therapists and other clients. He found himself wildly funny, and I honestly have to admit that he really was. The fact that he still had a smile on his face and was searching for ways to make other people laugh showed a lot about who Jim Davis was and strived to be every day. GBM was not going to suffocate his love for life.

Going back to July 6, 2016 again. What I failed to mention about this day – the day of his first OT appointment – was that Jim was battling kidney stone pain again. Those kidney stones were a constant problem for him. He had passed another stone two days before the appointment. That gave a count of 4 out of 7 kidney stone babies that had been "born" since his scan at UCSF at the beginning of May. He would have skipped his hand therapy assessment that morning, but was really anxious about starting the process of restoring use of his right hand. So, instead, he suffered through the pain for the entire appointment.

That week we noticed that he was very fatigued again. Along with that, we took note that his scalp and skin got very flaky during those tired times. It was evident that his body was going through cycles of trying to re-stabilize. We didn't know if it was from the steroids he was on for almost a year or if it was the remaining effect of chemo and radiation. Whatever it was, it definitely went through noticeable cycles. He napped frequently during those cycles of fatigue, especially after he got home from appointments and such. He would take a "coma" – what we have always called really long naps.

Three days after his OT appointment, we were celebrating Marcus and Cara's wedding. And, a few days after that Jim was "birthing more babies." The remainder of the Seven Dwarfs were finally arriving! . . . Yes. I named my husband's kidney stones. It gave us something to laugh about in the absurd situations we were facing. Funny enough, it also helped me to keep track of how many kidney stones he passed over the years.

Tuesday, July 12, 2016 – Update #1:
Dun, dun, dun . . . Another one bites the dust!!! Jim passed another kidney stone late this afternoon. Woohoo! By our count that would be #5 of the Seven Dwarfs. Because it started last week (when Jim's mom was released from the

rest home and Cara got married), I was going to name this one Happy. But since he waited until this week to be "born," his name is now Bashful.

We're hoping the urologist will choose to do another kidney CT scan when Jim has to go to UCSF at the end of the month for his brain MRI. That would give us a better idea of if our "baby" count is accurate.

Thanks for all of your prayers. Please continue praying that the remaining stones will pass quickly.

Expecting a miracle! ANY day will do!!!
♥ *Jim and Brenda*

Tuesday, July 12, 2016 – Update #2:
Annnnnnd, TA DA!!!! Jim thinks another kidney stone baby was born. This would be #6 by our count. Tiny baby Dopey arrived about 1/2 hour ago. Thank you, Jesus, that these stones are passing!!! Now I really think I'd like to push for the urologist to do a new scan soon. Please pray for wisdom for the urologist in this matter.

I'm reserving the name "Happy" for his 7th stone, since we think it's the last one. Hopefully Happy arrives on the scene soon.

Thanks for your continued prayers!

Expecting more miracles! ANY day will do!!!
♥ *Jim and Brenda*

By the evening of July 13th, Hanna, Americis, and Christopher were all packed and had headed to bed for an early departure the next morning with the girls' grandparents. We were so thankful that Buffalo and Laura were providing this special trip for them. They needed a good dose of fun, and they needed a chance to get out of the house. They were good sports about going to appointments with us or hanging out with my parents for a little bit, but they definitely needed a break from the "senior life" we were experiencing at home.

Buffalo and Laura would have the kids for about 10 days for their special trip. Cara and Marcus were on their honeymoon in Columbia. The only "kid" remaining in the area, Courtney, worked all the time and didn't live with us anymore. It was going to be a strange week and a half, but was probably needed by all of us.

Excerpts from Friday, July 15, 2016:
Well, it's day 2 of having a temporary empty nest. We've stayed busy the last 2 days, so it's hard to remember the kiddos are gone right now . . . you know, besides coming home to a creepy quiet house in the evening. It looks like all 4 kids (plus our son-in-law) are having a good time while they're away. The 3 youngest kiddos were at Universal Studios today with their grandparents and cousin. Cara and Marcus are posting honeymoon destination clues on FB, and I've received a couple of text updates that they are safe and arrived at specific destinations. I had to call Court at work this morning to be sure she was still alive. I haven't seen her or heard from her in a few days. Good news. She is!

Jim had occupational therapy for his right hand late this morning. His appointment lasted a little over 1 1/2 hours. He's working hard to get that hand moving again. And I still can't say enough how blessed we are to have a great therapist (who is also a Christian). She has been so good with Jim. . . . although I cringed when she made the lady next to me cry during her hand therapy. Not joking. These people hurt trying to just get the basic function of their hands again. It's hard to watch. I wanted to run over and give her a back rub to help ease the hand pain. Jim pushes through and tries to be a champ about each hand exercise or the muscle/tendon stretches.

Jim noticed some pain/discomfort again today from his kidney stone(s). He had/has small amounts of blood in his urine again. He thinks Happy (his 7th kidney stone of the 7 dwarfs family) is trying to pass. He's trying to determine if possibly it passed today and he just didn't see it. Some blood is normal when kidney stones move around, are passed, or have recently passed. I guess we'll know better in the next few days. He is doing well and hasn't complained about as much pain since the 2 stones passed on Wednesday. . . . Soooo, maaaaaybe a Happy birthday to Happy??? I dunno.

Thanks for praying for us! We love you all! God has been so good to us. We are blessed.

Expecting a miracle! ANY day will do!!!
♥ *Jim and Brenda*

Friday, July 22, 2016 - PM Update:
Jim did well at occupational therapy today (right hand). This was only his 5th appointment. The therapist did new measurements to check his progress since the first day and found that every assessment measurement shows improvement. Yahoooo!!! He still has so much farther to go before having full function of his hand, but the improvement is great! We'll take it. He's been working very hard on it.

After therapy today he was invited to have lunch at the fire department. He always enjoys that, and today was no exception. What a great crew of guys we have serving our community! We are blessed to call them our framily. Thanks EFD!!!

Jim has struggled all week. He hasn't felt well at all, but has pushed through and continued with his therapy appointments. He complained of having no energy and just feeling crummy. I noticed that his walking was much, much slower and he was back to using his cane for everything again - even short trips in the house. Today I contacted our local doctor's office and talked to his assistant. She offered to run a urinalysis for him this afternoon (even after their lab had closed). We had just returned home when I received her call, so we got back in the car and ran out to Ripon. Her call back a few hours later revealed that he has a urinary tract infection, just like we suspected. It's probably caused from the kidney stones he has been passing, but no matter the cause . . . POOR GUY!!! I'm sooooo thankful we found this before the weekend. We most certainly have saved ourselves from another weekend ER visit! Can I get a woot woot? God is good to give me the wisdom I need to call the right people. Thank you, God! (And a quick shout-out to Kat at Ripon Docs! She rocks!!!)

I picked up Jim's antibiotic and contacted his urologist at UCSF - just in case he wants something more done before we see him next week. Hopefully he'll be on the mend soon. We appreciate your prayers.

And now I say . . . I'M TIRED! We are physically and emotionally exhausted by this journey. I told my friend today that I feel like we've entered an alternate universe. This universe consists mainly of taking care of the urgent and important things. It's mostly about survival, not the fun things in life. It's about the struggle to regain normal functions again. (Side note: my eyes are opened to a whole new world of people's struggles and hard work to regain the normal functions we take for granted every day.) It's about battling the medical field and advocating for what is truly needed. There are no beautiful white beaches. There are no fruity drinks with cute umbrellas in them. There are no churros or Dole pineapple whip ice cream. (That was a Disneyland reference there, in case you missed it! Disneyland is calling me. Hello? I'm answering. Can you hear me? Disconnected.) And the only rides we get are in elevators and wheelchairs. And unless Arney Corbin is pushing the wheelchair there isn't much excitement. You're still banned from that, Arney. Sorry! Lol.

I told my friend that I'd like to go home now. I don't like this alternate universe anymore. In fact, I didn't like it the first day we arrived here. Nothing has changed, except that I dislike it even more now. Where are my red ruby slippers to click together? Where is Scotty to beam me up? Where is . . . well, ummmmm, I've run out of clever references. But you get the point. Right? . . . There's no place like home. There's no place like home. There's no place like home . . . . Nothing! Hmmm. Still here. Same alternate universe.

Well, tonight's plans are to lay low and allow Jim to rest. Since the week has been crazy busy with therapy appointments and work, I have to say I'm not too disappointed to have a quiet night. Hopefully I can find a good movie to watch while he sleeps.

Our 3 youngest kiddos come home tomorrow! We're excited to see them. By their reports so far, I'd say they've had a pretty terrific trip with Grandma and Grandpa Smith (Hanna and Americis' grandparents) and their cousin Nicollette. It will be good to have them home again and get lots of hugs and snuggles. I missed that this week. Although I haven't had time to prepare wonderful notes for their doors (like another wonderful mom I know has done for her kiddos - she's very thoughtful!), I hope they know they were missed and we're happy they are coming home.

I'm off to search for a good movie! My class I'm supposed to be working on is DEFINITELY not getting done tonight. My brain needs a break!

Thanks for keeping up on our journey. Thanks for your love and support. But, mostly, thank you for your continued prayers! We are forever indebted to all of you!!!

Expecting a miracle! ANY day will do!!!
♥ *Jim and Brenda*

Wednesday, July 27, 2016:

So, we're waiting for Jim's urology appointment right now. They said they're running behind, so that gives me a chance to update you on the news so far today.

Jim did his kidney ultrasound and x-ray this morning. After lunch he did his brain MRI. They were running behind and made us late for his appointment with the neuro-oncologist. But that's ok, because that appointment didn't take long. The neuro-oncologist says:

- The MRI looks stable
- No new growth
- It looks better than May's scan
- The cavity shrunk in size
- There is less fluid in the brain than last time
- No need for chemo
- Come back in 6-8 weeks
- And, best of all, the doctor had to look at the MRI multiple times to make sure it was the current scan! HA!!! (He seemed very happy about the good report, too.)

We are rejoicing at this incredible news! GOD IS SO GOOD!!! Like I said, we're waiting for the urologist right now. Unofficially, we were told Jim still has multiple kidney stones. We hope the urologist has a good plan of action for us to get rid of them. Jim is so ready for that. It's hard on his body to have problems with them off and on all the time.

Thank you for your prayers, friends! We serve a capable God and we are seeing our miracle day by day. It's not an easy journey, but we're never bored!

Expecting more miracles!!! Thankful for the ones we see today!
♥ *Jim and Brenda*

Thursday, July 28, 2016:
Here's the rest of the scoop from our day at UCSF. . . .

Jim's urology appointment was scheduled for 3:15 yesterday. Unfortunately, the urologist was running very late and didn't see Jim until 6:00. That was fun. That made for an even longer day than we had expected.

The results from his x-ray and ultrasound show at least 10 small stones in each kidney. Yes, you read that correctly. There are a total of at least 20 small stones. The doctor discussed a couple of options for him. Jim and I have differences of opinion on the plan of care, so Jim is going to think some more about what he'd like to do and go from there.

I'll just say, I have no clever names for 20 kidney babies. That's just craziness right there. The entertainment of choosing funny names must come to a screeching halt. Sorry!

We got home between 10:30 or 11:00 last night. We're both completely exhausted and I don't feel very good today, so we're taking it easy.

♥ *Jim and Brenda*

On Monday, August 1, 2016, Jim, Courtney, and I met Marcus and Cara at Starbucks in Escalon. We visited briefly, took a few pictures together, and said a very teary goodbye. Marcus and Cara were moving to their new home in Washington to start their life together. Courtney was traveling with them to help with a few things, then she planned to drive back home by herself. And Jim and I? Well, we were off to speech therapy, then hand therapy, for the next 3 hours.

My heart was broken. Not only was my oldest daughter married and now leaving the state, but we were losing part of our team – a family member who helped us keep things functioning when unexpected emergencies popped up. To make matters worse, I knew that once Cara was removed from the situation, it would be harder to keep her in the loop about Jim's day to day progress/decline. I knew that when the next emergency situation popped up, it would tear her apart that she couldn't just hop on the next plane to stay with us indefinitely. There would be moments she would have to experience from afar, without the comfort of family and friends who knew our journey well. The road was going to be a little rougher for all of us now that we were separated.

19

A STORY OF REDEMPTION: THE ESCALON YOUTH CENTER

AN ABBREVIATED TALE OF A MOTEL - C.R. WOODWORTH

She had had enough.

This woman had driven past the motel day after day; she drove past it to and from work, when she dropped her kids off at school or picked them up. She had to drive past it when she stopped to pick up hot chocolate and coffees at the Starbucks across the street. And every time she drove past it, she shook her head and prayed something along the lines of, "Lord, you know what happens there; shut that place down."

This motel had a reputation, and it wasn't a good reputation. It was a place of despair of the worst kinds: drugs, alcohol, unsavory interactions, just to name a few. In reality, it was a "motel" in name only: the people who rented rooms essentially took up residence there. The cops frequented the place because of the many, many calls that came in due to the illegal activities that happened. It was a haunt for the broken, the desperate, and the addicted. The Escalon Motel was a pit of darkness; and it sat directly across from the local high school.

Miraculously, just a couple of years later that woman's prayers were answered! And the motel was shut down and put up for sale. By this time, a dream had taken root in a local pastor's heart. He desired for this motel to be owned by the church he pastored and used as a safe refuge for students in the school district. He wanted there to be a spot that they could go to during lunch and after school and just hang out in a safe environment. It was prime location; it sat directly across from the local high school.

This local pastor began inquiring about how to buy the property- only to find that it had already been sold to someone else. So he went back to praying about the property again, as the passion for this dream had not yet diminished.

A few months later, the property went up for sale again. The pastor quickly began making calls about who owned it so he could talk to them about it. Then one day, he got a call from someone saying that the owner was currently on the property showing it to someone. He, quite literally, jumped in his car and raced down to the motel.

He introduced himself to the current owner of the motel and briefly laid out his vision of what he was going to do with the motel. Twenty minutes later, the owner called the pastor back and said that another person had offered more for the motel, but that he would sell it to the pastor for less because he believed in the vision of what the motel would do for the community. The owner even postponed the selling of the property until the pastor could get approval from the church to buy it.

The entire church voted yes.

Three years later, the Escalon Youth Center stands where the Escalon Motel used to. It is a fully volunteer run center that has gaming systems, a snack bar, and all sorts of bistro tables and couches- all for the purpose of giving the youth in the community a safe place to go. They have nights where kids can come and learn special skills (like how to change a flat tire, or how to repair drywall), have video game competitions, or just spend some time with friends. It is truly an incredible work of God, considering what the Escalon Motel used to be.

By the way, the woman who prayed for the motel to be shut down was actually the local pastor's wife. And these two incredible people are my parents.

I take the time to tell this rather long (and really condensed) story because it is an incredible story of God's redemption. As it was, the motel was a filthy and vile place filled with all sorts of unimaginable evils. And yet, today it is being used for God's glory.

It's a constant reminder to me that God can take what was messed up, mangled, and broken, and He can still make it beautiful and perfect for His use. I so need that reminder. Too often I feel like my dad's brain cancer has taken too much from us. It's marred us in a way that we can never escape from. It has been a thief of time and joy. And most of the time, I feel like this cancer has no purpose; it's just there to burden us and inflict us with suffering and pain. Never once have I thought that brain cancer was a glorious gift given to us. Never.

I don't know how, and I don't know when, and I definitely don't understand why, but I KNOW that all the pain and the suffering we endure now is for God's glory. Ultimately, He is the redeemer. He is the one who can take something that was life-sucking, like the Escalon Motel, and turn it into something that is life-giving and life-changing.

So while I wait for these years of brain cancer to be redeemed, I continually remind myself that there is absolutely nothing in the realm of earth that He cannot redeem; there is nothing and no one that is so far gone that He can no longer reach them.

(Note: the previous excerpt was written by our oldest daughter, Cara.)

I stood in front of the glass window, watching the taffy pulling machine twisting and turning the lavender-colored taffy over and over again. I could see my faint reflection in the window. It took me back immediately to the metaphor I had used multiple times to describe to my family what my life felt like – constantly being stretched and asked to step into areas where I didn't feel confident. I commented to Jim, once again, that this machine reflected my life . . . our lives. He agreed.

I stopped to take a picture of it because it struck me so deeply. The taffy was pulled over and over again. Twisted and turned. It had no choice of whether to be there or not, but there it was. Without the pulling process it wouldn't become the wonderful treat it was designed to be, so the creator loaded it onto the pulling mechanism and turned it on.

At this point in life, the struggles we had faced and the areas God had asked me to grow in made me feel like I had been stretched as much as I could be stretched. There had been some extremely rough roads and difficult decisions to be obedient and allow God to use our lives as He saw fit. I often commented to Jim that if I were the elastic in the top of some clothing, I soon would be stretched to such a capacity that I would lose my elasticity.

Little did I know that the stretching process I would endure . . . that Jim and I would endure together . . . would take me to the brink of my limits, and on certain days would push me over the edge, only to pick myself up again and force myself to keep trudging forward over, and over, and over again. Jim's diagnosis of Glioblastoma Multiforme, grade 4 cancer wouldn't happen for almost two more years. And yet, here I sat, feeling like God had stretched me enough already. I stared at that taffy pulling machine for a few minutes before I forced myself to walk away.

This was September of 2013. We were at a Ministers' Retreat in Seaside/Monterey, California. Arney and Dana, our associate pastors, were with us for the conference.

At the last service of Ministers' Retreat - on Saturday morning, September 13, 2013 – our guest speaker wrapped up his sermon and decided to close in prayer. As he began to close, he explained that he was going to start a prayer and that when he got to a specific part he would have us fill in the blank as we prayed with him. For example, he would start with, "God, I really need help in this area of ministry _____," then he'd say to fill in the blank. I followed along, but was stumped when he said something along the lines of believing for a specific property that God would need to provide for an area of ministry. I found it a little odd, as not everyone in the room would be in need of a specific property.

Let me backtrack briefly to the night before. After the Friday evening service of our conference, Jim, Arney, Dana, and I went to Denny's for a late dinner. As we sat and talked, Jim was excited to discuss new ways to reach people, unconventional ways that maybe those in ministry hadn't approached before . . . and if they had, it was a rare occurrence. He often liked to "spitball" – a phrase he absolutely loved to use – and dream about different ways to do things. If it were left up to me, I would always stick to the tried-and-true methods, but Jim was a dreamer. I can't remember all of the things we talked about that night, but I DO remember that Jim was searching for ways to reach our community that we hadn't accessed yet. It called to him from the depths of his heart. It was his passion.

Back to the prayer our speaker led us in together. I filled in all the blanks to this prayer as he encouraged us to do, but that one "fill in the blank" about the property left me a little baffled and stuck in my mind. And soon, the speaker closed the service, and we were dismissed. We loaded up the Corbins' Suburban with our luggage and began heading home.

On our drive home, Jim engaged in the conversation we had started the night before, but had a little tidbit to add to it. He told us as we prayed that prayer together with the speaker and got to the portion of the prayer that asked us to fill in the blank about a piece of property we were believing God to provide for us for ministry, God immediately showed him the old Escalon Motel and gave him the vision of turning it into a safe place for teenagers to go and hang out. He was excited to talk about the possibility with all of us, and immediately started dreaming about what that would look like for our small town. I <u>rode</u> home with the Corbins that day. I think Jim <u>floated</u> home, immersed in the vision God had placed on his heart.

The Escalon Motel was a place of ill-repute up until this time. It was no longer really a motel, but had become a permanent residence for many lower income families in our town. That wasn't a problem. The fact that it had become a well-known place for drugs and prostitution was, especially given that it was located on a corner just across from our town's high school. Any student leaving campus for lunch, would have to walk the sidewalk just across from these buildings. It was easy access to drugs for students, and many of them were taking advantage of the opportunity.

The funny thing about this property was that it was a location in our town that God laid on my heart to pray for some time before God had ever placed this vision on Jim's heart. No, I wasn't praying for the property to be available to purchase. I was praying for God to change the hearts of those who lived there. Although I can't remember an exact timeframe, it had to be sometime between March of 2010 and the beginning of 2013. I passed it one day, and was repulsed by the activity happening there. God stopped me and said, "Why don't you pray for something to change?" I agreed that it was a better plan than just being repulsed by it, so every time I drove by it on my way home I would pray, "God, you see what's happening there. Please change the hearts of those who live there. And if they don't choose to change, then I ask that you remove them."

Sometime around the beginning of 2013, the City of Escalon closed down the Escalon Motel due to violation of city housing regulations. Multiple repairs and adjustments needed to be made in order for them to stay open and rent the units for permanent occupancy. Once all of the tenants were evicted from the unsuitable dwelling places, the outside of the two buildings was boarded up and signs were posted. It was an ugly sight in the center of our little town.

Days upon our return from Ministers' Retreat, Jim started searching for information on the old Escalon Motel. He found that it was going to auction, but before he could jump at the chance to consider purchasing the property, he found that it had already been sold to the highest bidder. It wasn't a done deal for him yet, though. He still watched the property closely.

Later he saw that the new owner posted a sign on the property listing it for sale. He began calling around to get information, but found himself going in circles. Until the day our daughter, Courtney, called him at the church office.

Courtney worked a few doors down from the Escalon Motel. The owner stopped by asking to borrow some tools to pry off some of the plywood covering the entrances to the motel rooms. He said he had someone coming to look at the property that day, but didn't have the tools with him to manage the task of opening it up. Courtney, knowing that Jim was looking for information on the property, promptly called Jim's cell phone and told him the owner was on site. Jim ran into my office and announced that he'd be back soon, but he had to run to the motel property pronto.

Upon arrival, Jim saw that the owner had already opened a few units for the prospective buyers. He was allowing them to peruse the property by themselves, while he stood and watched from a distance. Jim approached the owner, Sammy, and introduced himself. He told him that he understood that he had prospective buyers on the property, but he wanted to pitch an idea to him. He described his vision to turn the property into a youth center for the students in our town. He backtracked a bit and said he didn't want to intrude on the offer that the prospective buyers might give him, but that if he was interested he would like to talk to him about it more. He thanked Sammy for his time, handed him his business card, then left the premises and returned to the church office.

Twenty minutes later Jim received a phone call from the property owner. Sammy began to tell him that he was interested in the vision Jim had pitched to him. Jim was astonished when Sammy told him the prospective buyers he had seen that morning offered him **full asking price** for the motel, but he turned them down on the spot. Not only did he turn them down, but he proceeded to tell Jim that he would take less for the property if it was going to be used for the purposes Jim described to him. He needed to make some profit on the property so he could purchase a vineyard he was looking at, but he would make his profit minimal so the property could be offered to the church for a fair price.

The wheels began turning that day.

On February 23, 2014, at our Annual Membership Meeting, the church membership voted UNANIMOUSLY to purchase the property for the purpose of renovating it for a youth center. Jim cautioned the congregation that it was going to be a money pit and we wouldn't be expecting to see a profit from this ministry. He told them that it would be an endeavor that we would all need to get behind financially to see succeed. No one batted an eye. They were all in for this new endeavor, excited about the possibility of changing the lives of students in Escalon.

Jim was excited to call Sammy and tell him the news of the unanimous decision that afternoon. He explained that we would need to request the funds from the church's investment account and that it would take 30 days to receive the funds. Sammy said he was happy to hear the news and he was comfortable with waiting for the funds to be available. He assured Jim that he would not sell the property to anyone else while we awaited the arrival of the funds.

On March 31, 2014, the Escalon Motel became the property of Trinity Church. Jim couldn't have been more elated. I think he floated through the entire day. He even had Courtney draw him some small signs that said, "Coming Soon . . . Escalon Youth Center" and requested that I go to the motel property with him the day before so I could take some pictures of him on the property. (Side note: as I write this chapter today – March 30, 2020 – I'm still smiling from seeing my Facebook memories pop up one of these pictures this morning. When I planned a couple of days ago to finish writing this chapter today, I didn't realize it would be one day before with the purchase date anniversary of the property. I'm sure God knew though.)

Plans for EYC (Escalon Youth Center) began immediately. An architect drew up plans for us and donated his labor. RV Maps, an organization through the Assemblies of God which helps churches with building projects, agreed to jump on board and help us renovate the property. Dana's father, George, had worked with RV Maps for years, so he had a little bit of pull with his friends to get them excited about joining us.

Conditional use permits and other legal paperwork tied up any work that could be started on the property for quite some time. Once everything was in order, we began implementing the plans that others had worked on tediously.

Of the two buildings on the motel site, one was deemed unfit for renovations and needed to be removed altogether – which left a nice lawn space for kids to use. The other building – a long, narrow building – was split. The portion that housed the property manager was left intact and renovated for an onsite manager. The other portion of the building was demolished and a new structure soon took form in its place.

There are many stories of donated labor and supplies to recount. I'd love to tell them all and give credit to those who donated them, but the truth is that by the time much of the construction began at EYC, Jim was already battling GBM, and I was distracted with everything that entailed (as described in my previous chapters).

Much of the project was supervised by Arney and Dana. They did an excellent job at the task that was thrust upon them – another reason we are forever indebted to our friends. They made most of the small decisions without bothering Jim, but were careful to run the big decisions past Jim and give him an opportunity to weigh in with his opinion. Dana's dad, George, was instrumental in completing the project and we appreciate all that he and his wife June sacrificed at that time. The RV Maps crew did a phenomenal job on building the youth center and adding the final touches to the inside.

Jim delighted in watching the progress of the youth center. Some days he'd ask to sit at Starbucks so he could look out the window, across the street, and watch the team work. Other days he'd request that I park on site and sit a few minutes so he could view the progress from our car before we headed off to one of his therapy appointments. But, until the sidewalk in front of the building doors was poured, he wasn't able to get inside to see anything that was happening there construction-wise.

After many months of planning, construction, and final touches, the Escalon Youth Center held its grand opening on Saturday, August 13, 2016. Jim was able to attend the ceremony and couldn't contain his excitement as he was asked to help cut the ribbon in the grand opening ceremony with the Escalon Chamber of Commerce.

Today, at the location in our town that was once known as a "filthy, vile place with all sorts of unimaginable evils" stands a beautiful building built with love. It's called the Escalon Youth Center. It is a place used for God's glory, a place designed specifically to minister to the young people in our town. And, like Cara penned, it is the perfect story of God's redemption.

The church leadership and team God has put in place to manage the daily activity there is incredible, and they love EYC dearly. I'm blessed to call these people my friends. Many of them hold this ministry dear to their heart because of their love for Jim and his vision to meet needs in our town. We have a large number of volunteers who come in to work the snack bar, help with projects, and supervise students. A good portion of this volunteer crew are seniors from our church and community looking for a way to serve. Other churches, clubs, and organizations in our tiny town have partnered with us, rallying around EYC and giving generous donations to help it operate. They love seeing their young people have a safe place to go during lunchtime or after school, a place where people will speak into their lives and encourage them to take a better road.

Oh! And, many people have a hard time believing that EYC is offered to the teenagers of our town free of charge, but it's totally true, I assure you! With the exception of the food in the snack bar and other special events, there is never a charge for their time there.

I love the Escalon Youth Center, but there is always a tinge of sadness in me every time I enter it or think of the beautiful things that happen there. I hurt that Jim didn't get to witness all the fruit of it. I hurt that he didn't see the number of students our church's youth group was able to take to winter camp this year – many of them with no connection to our church except through the youth center. I find that pill hard to swallow and very unfair.

But, in that same breath, I find the Escalon Youth Center to be another reminder of God's redemption to me. Sometimes I see the bitter brokenness of my current life and think there is no hope for restoration in those shattered pieces. When I see the youth center, I'm reminded that God loves to boast about how wonderful He is at taking the broken things and making them into something beautiful.

The last 5 years have been some of the most excruciating times I've endured. That taffy pulling machine that I took a picture of at Fisherman's Wharf in 2013 ... yeeeeeah ... that was a small one compared to the pulling machine I've been assigned to since then. This journey has stretched me in every possible way, and I've hated every step of the stretching process. It has taken me to my limits, and beyond, many times. Would I choose this horrible stretching process on my own? ABSOLUTELY NOT!!! The pain I've experienced has been grueling. Thankfully, God didn't give me a CHOICE of whether or not to grow and be stretched.

You see, I believe - even in my crushed, broken state - that God has used these circumstances to grow and strengthen me. I believe that many of the areas I've been stretched and grown in couldn't have happened any other way. I'm banking on the fact that God excels in making beauty from the ashes. I'm counting on the fact that He can use this for His glory someday. I'm counting on the REDEMPTION FACTOR. I just need to trust that He knows what He's doing and that He is certain of the results it will accomplish in the end ... before He ever begins.

Maybe you have some broken, crushed, trash-like parts of your life that you don't think can ever be used for your good ... or for God's glory, for that fact ... but I assure you that He has a plan. Don't give up! If He can turn an ol' broken down motel into something that brings light and ministers to a community, He most certainly can use YOU. You are more valuable to Him than you realize. Trust me!

Escalon Youth Center Grand Opening Celebration (August 2016)

Escalon Youth Center Ribbon Cutting Ceremony (August 2016)

20

WHEN NORMAL LOOKS EXTRAORDINARY

Excerpts from Friday, August 12, 2016 - PM Update:
I'm convinced this will be a long post. Beware! I just hope I can remember everything I wanted to update you on.

As always, I promise to keep you up on the bad, as well as the good. I try not to focus on it, but I acknowledge it is there. That way you get an accurate account of this journey we're on, not just lollipops and roses. I hope you're ok with that.

This week started out rough. Very rough. Some days are just too much. It's not any one thing. That's for sure. It's just the complicated mix of the life we live now. I don't know how to adequately explain it, but it wears on you in every possible way. It's exhausting. It's always there. It limits the way you WANT to live your life. It makes you wonder if normal will ever return in a way you will recognize. It forces you to surrender your identity and everything you ever knew about yourself. You have been forever warped and shaped into a new person who doesn't feel quite new. It turns your relationships inside out and upside down. Responsibilities and expectations in every area of life have now been redefined to urgent, necessary, and survival/existing mode. It's hard to balance all of the aspects of this journey . . . and eventually meltdowns come. Annnnd sometimes they hit like a tsunami. And so, that was kinda the beginning of our week - meltdowns. I wish I could say they don't happen, but they do. And they're not pretty. I sometimes feel like I'll never be able to scrape myself off the floor and continue moving on.

But, I'm happy to report that this meltdown only lasted for a day or so. The rest of this week was much better! Like, crazy better!!! Woot woot! And that's why this post will be so stinkin' long. . . . Sorry, not sorry.

Jim's PT on his right shoulder went well on Monday. The therapist felt comfortable with signing off on this therapy so he can start therapy on Jim's legs. Jim has really wanted this because his legs have been weak after his many hospitalizations and not feeling well for so long. The therapist will continue allowing him to do warmups at therapy that include his shoulder and will help Jim to know what exercises to do for his shoulder at home. That way he won't miss out on continuing to build the shoulder muscles and getting 100% range of motion in it. We're waiting for authorization to go through for leg therapy, so he only had one appointment for PT this week. Hopefully he'll get back on the PT schedule next week.

Speech therapy was also on Monday. This continues to be one of Jim's most frustrating challenges. He can speak and convey his thoughts, but it's much slower than he'd like it to be. He just never feels like he can express himself completely because it takes so long and takes so much effort. At times, people finish his sentences or appear to lose interest in what he's saying. That's difficult. Most people are thoughtful and patient, but the frustration for expressing himself still remains. We've been praying for healing in this area for some time now. Please join us!

Jim has been getting around sooooooo much better. Most days lately he barely uses his cane. I even noticed the last few mornings that he didn't use it when he first woke up. That's a big improvement for him! . . . This morning we had a meeting at Starbucks before his therapy appointment. He told me he forgot his backpack in the car. I was prepared to go get it for him, but he asked for the keys, walked out to the car, got his backpack, and walked all the way back without his cane. I was in shock. Part of me was ready to have a heart attack at any moment - ready to run out and rescue him if he needed help. The other part of me just beamed from ear to ear at his huge accomplishment.

Jim, Court, and I were talking last night about how weird it is to celebrate these "big accomplishments" that are really just normal tasks for most people's day. It's a strange feeling. And yet, WE see the huge difference. We know the hard work it has taken to get to this level of function back again. We know the struggle of him not wholly functioning. We know the heartbreak of bearing witness to all of it. And sooooo, WE celebrate the truly big milestones that to others seem trivial.

Let's talk more about these "trivial" "huge" accomplishments, because I'm dying to share these with you. I couldn't be more serious. Today was a HUGE day of Jim's hard work paying off. Eeeeeeeek!!!!!

Jim had hand therapy today AND HE ROCKED IT!!!!!! He had the most amazing, rewarding day of therapy so far. He so totally rocked it!!! Have I said that enough now? The therapists and aides were very impressed at how much progress they saw today. As they were working with other patients, they all watched him succeed in exercise after exercise. The looks of approval, excitement, and shock were awesome to witness. I sat and videoed as much as I could (without him knowing it at the time because I didn't want to redirect his focus). Most of the exercises are hard to explain here quickly, so I'll keep it basic. This isn't an extensive list. He used a soft peg board with large pegs, drew lines with a pen, and used a fork and knife to cut play dough. (These smaller items had special foam wrapped around them to make them easier to grip). He could hold his hand in front of him and spread out all 5 of his fingers and put them back together. He formed a fist better than any of the other days at therapy. Annnnd he even picked up a marble with his thumb and index finger - something he has NOT been able to do since he lost use of his hand. That thumb and index finger have had a grave aversion to working with each other up to this point.

The therapists sent him home with an arm splint to use at night. This helps to keep the tendons stretched out and prevent them from atrophying. He also got some foam stuff to use on a pen (to practice drawing lines) and another foamy thing to attach to utensils for eating. They are upping his exercise challenges, too. Is this the end of hard work? No, I wish. But it is a HUGE MILESTONE toward gaining full function of his right hand.

Jim has been working extremely hard towards all of these things, but we know that God is the one bringing healing and strength to his body. We give Him all the praise for these wonderful milestones we're seeing.

But wait! There's more!!! . . . For only $19.99 you can get 2 sets of. . . . Oops! I got carried away. Sorry. There really is more, though. Keep reading.

This week we received the check from the fundraiser my cousins coordinated during Escalon's Park Fete weekend. (Thank you to everyone who supported this fundraiser.) We are overjoyed to say that we were able to pay off ALL of Jim's current medical bills with the proceeds received from the fundraiser!!!!! I just wanted to cry as I wrote the checks out. It's crazy amazing. It's a very freeing feeling to know these bills aren't hanging over our heads as we chip away with little payments on them. I really didn't expect for all of the bills to be covered. God is so good to us!!! It's pretty unbelievable.

I think I've met my word limit now. . . . Like there's such a thing!!! Hahahaha! . . . But you've probably met your word limit for reading my updates. Sorry I'm wordy, but if I wasn't you wouldn't hear all these great testimonies of what GOD is doing.

One last thing before I close. Can't believe I almost forgot it! Tomorrow is an exciting and emotional day as we celebrate the accomplishment of a vision God placed on Jim's heart 3 years ago. The Escalon Youth Center's Grand Opening starts at 3:00. We'd love for you to join us in celebrating all that God has done in this project. He has paved the way and provided in countless ways.

With that I say:
Good night, friends! Rest well. Know that we serve a faithful, loving, capable God. Hold on!!! Hold on!!! Don't give up!

Expecting a miracle! ANY day will do!!!
♥ *Jim and Brenda*

Thursday, August 18, 2016 - PM Update:
I'll try to break things down for you by topic to update you on life this week:

Kidney Stones -

I'll start off with this one because it's kinda an exciting one. On August 7th, Jim passed a kidney stone. Yesterday he passed another one. And this morning he decided to be an overachiever and passed THREE stones at the same time! So, according to my old math skills (I didn't use Common Core. Sorry!) that's a count of 5 kidney stone babies that he has passed in the last week and a half. Only 15 more to go. Well, we think there are 15. Possibly more. ???

Therapy -

Jim had hand therapy (OT) on Monday and Wednesday this week. Yesterday was also his progress assessment, because his OT authorization has to be renewed. I'm happy to report that all of his measurements for strength and range of motion showed great improvement!!! There was only one measurement that stayed close to the same. That was when they asked him to touch all of his fingers to the palm of his hand, making a fist. His index finger still can't squeeze down to touch the inside of his palm yet. . . . Right now we're waiting for authorization to continue his OT and authorization to start PT on legs to strengthen them. That gave us a little extra time in the schedule this week. Although we like that therapy is helping Jim to get stronger, the break in the constant therapy appointments was nice.

Work -

Jim and I made it to work last Thursday morning. He made it through the whole morning (about 4 hours) before I took him home, and I made it through A WHOLE DAY AT WORK!!! It may not sound like much to you, but I was so thrilled to work straight through the day and be able to stay focused on the tasks at hand. Up until now I've completed my work via mobile office (taking stuff with me to Jim's appointments or working from home) and running in for quick segments of time to complete required tasks at the office. I can't tell you what a challenge that is for me to stay focused and not drop any of the tasks I'm juggling. It always feels chaotic and never seems to be enough time to follow through with a normal thought process for each task. Soooo, a whole day at work is more calming than one would think! . . . We also made it to work a little longer than half of a day on Tuesday morning (both of us) and I made it back to work for accounting duties for 2+ hours yesterday and almost 5 hours today. Yahoooo!!!!!!!

Back to School -

I survived Back to School night at high school last night and middle school tonight. Courtney was gracious enough to go and help me tonight since I had 2 kids' schedules to manage at the same time. She's a life-saver! I sure appreciate her!!!!

Separation Anxiety and Adjustment, Adjustment, Adjustment -

Jim had a board meeting tonight, so I took him to the church. It was hard for me to leave him because I've attended the last few board meetings with him. The board allows me to attend and help Jim with his speech when he gets tripped up. Tonight was a stretch for me to drive him to the meeting and drop him off so I could be at Back to School night. I was glad to hear his report that things went smoothly. It's weird to think that he did all these things without me before. It totally seems like a lifetime ago!!! We're learning that fine line of me giving him enough space to step out where he's feeling more comfortable and capable, but still sticking close enough to help where I'm still needed. It's an adjustment for sure!!! And this isn't the end of our adjustments. Over the last 15-16 months, we've slowly made the adjustment of going from fully-functioning to him needing help with most things. Now we'll need to work in the opposite direction. It sounds easy, but it's not. Finding the right healthy boundaries for Jim will be an adjustment for us every day. Please pray for us in this. Pray that God will give us wisdom and that the transition will go smoothly. I don't want to hinder his progress, but I definitely don't want to let go before he's ready for specific tasks and risk his safety or make him overly anxious. Finding a new balance is exciting and nerve-wracking at the same time.

I don't know if there is anything I missed for this update. If so, I guess I'll catch ya up on it later. I've gotta throw some clothes in the dryer before prepping a few things and heading to bed. These early school mornings are killing me. (Unfortunately, I'm soooo not an early morning person like my mom is.)

Expecting a miracle! ANY day will do!!!
❤ *Jim and Brenda*

Tuesday, August 23, 2016 - PM Update:
This should be a quick update! For reals this time. Truuuuust me!

Jim is doing well. He looks sooooo good lately and has had many comments from others about this. He just looks like he feels good and is so determined to regain his strength and function of his hand and such. I love it!!!

He had speech therapy yesterday morning, but no other therapy appointments this week (yet) because we're waiting for authorization for PT (legs) and re-authorization for OT (hand). He has been doing lots of speech homework and exercises at home - provided I remember to get everything out when I'm supposed to.

He passed another kidney stone this morning. It was unexpected because he hadn't had any pain like he usually does before one passes. That's a plus!!! 6 down. 14ish to go.

This week my taxi mom hat has reappeared. Besides school drop-offs and pick-ups, we have 2 soccer practices for 2 kids (different nights, of course); a girls' class at church that just resumed; piano lessons; youth night; another doctor appointment for Hanna (with more to come); along with all the unexpected trips each day. And, soccer games are just around the corner! . . . Organization is my friend. It's the only way these things are possible. And God is so gracious to give me strength for it!

Jim really can't wait until he can drive again. He mentions soooo often that he'd like to be able to help me with running the kids around. Provided he continues getting stronger and his next scan looks good, we'll be asking about this at his next UCSF appointment at the end of October.

That's it for tonight. (Applause!!!)

Blessings to you, my friends. We can't thank you enough for your love, encouragement, and prayers!

Expecting a miracle! ANY day will do!
♥ *Jim and Brenda*

Thursday, September 1, 2016 – PM Update:

I'm exhausted tonight, but I thought I should update you on Jim's status since it's been a while since I posted his last update. I'm hoping my thoughts will actually make sense as I type them out. No promises, though. Bear with me, friends. If you see typos, just pretend they say what they should.

Jim felt pretty good today. That's a good thing because the last few days he hadn't felt as well. He had felt more fatigued and didn't have as much motivation as he had the last few weeks. I think all the dust in the air from harvesting is one thing that has him feeling crummy. He also said he feels like another kidney stone is starting to move around. Maybe he'll birth another kidney stone baby soon. I'm glad today was better. We'll take "better" any day of the week!

He starts PT and OT again next week. He's been doing exercises at home to maintain the strength in his hand and shoulder. He also started riding the stationary bike we were given for him. He doesn't ride it very long, but he's trying hard to continue building himself up in every area he can without overdoing it. I'm so proud of his determination and hard work!

The last 2 weeks Jim has made a huge effort to help me with small things around the house and with cooking dinner. His main job for dinner is browning hamburger meat - which is a big accomplishment since he has to hold the pan handle with his right hand (his very weak hand) while chopping up the meat with the spoon in his left hand. It may not sound like big stuff to you, but I assure you it takes much effort and he's doing FABULOUS!!!

He hasn't used his wheelchair for any outings since the end of July when we went to UCSF. Annnnd, most days he has been leaving his cane in the car "just in case," but hasn't needed it.

We've continued making regular trips to the church office the last few weeks. We've been at the Escalon Youth Center multiple times as well (loooooooove it!!!!!). It's nice to have some normal routine back until his therapy appointments steal our time again. Hopefully we can get those scheduled for early mornings (after we get the kids to school), so we can have somewhat-normal days after his appointments.

Each day continues to be run, run, run. I'm quite sure I need to install a revolving door at home. I can't even begin to count the number of times I leave and return home each day to keep up with work, taking the kids to school and picking them up, running errands, and managing the evening schedules for the kids. I'm glad we have a smaller car with better gas mileage now. That's a big plus! Jim keeps telling me, "I can't keep up with you." I tell him he doesn't have to keep up with me right now. Just having his help in managing a few more things around the house and with the kids is a HUGE blessing to me for now. It's nice to let him manage afternoon homework schedules or rotating kids in and out of showers while I tend to other things. This may not make sense to you if you haven't experienced the loss of them in the way we've experienced, but I assure you the littlest things that return to normal are a huge relief in the burden that has been carried for over a year. I wish I could explain it more adequately, but words fail me.

Tonight we had a scrumptious dinner provided for us by some special friends in our community. I didn't have to cook! Double blessing!!! We are so grateful for their thoughtfulness.

The picture I've added to this post is of a heart Jim colored with markers and cut out WITH HIS RIGHT HAND. Again, you may not think it's a very big deal, but it really is. For the last year he has struggled to even spread his fingers apart or hold items with his hand. The fact that he used markers and a pair of regular scissors is great improvement. . . . And, yes, I had his permission to share this pic. I would never want to embarrass him.

I can't thank you enough for your continued prayers and encouragement. These "better days" don't mean the challenge is completely over, but they sure boost our spirits. We thank God for how far He has brought Jim. "He alone is [our] rock and [our] salvation, [our] fortress where [we] will never be shaken." (Psalms 62:2 NLT). . . . And when we ARE shaken we know we just have to refocus on HIM, not our surroundings.

Expecting a miracle! ANY day will do!!!
♥ *Jim and Brenda*

Friday, September 2, 2016 – PM Update:
Another kidney stone baby has been born! Jim was in quite a bit of pain most of the day, but was finally able to pass a kidney stone tonight. That's #7 out of

the remaining 20, by our count. This one is at least double the size of the other ones. No wonder it hurt him so much today.

I feel rather creepy bagging these things in snack bags to take to UCSF for his next urology appointment. The urologist wants to do pathology on them and asked us to save them until then. Yaaaay us! We're creating quite the amazing collection. (Weirrrrrrrrrd!!!!!)

Sunday, September 4, 2016 – Afternoon Update:
Another kidney stone baby made its appearance this morning. Only a tiny one this time. Welcome #8 of 20ish!

Excerpts from Thursday, September 8, 2016
Happy Thursday!!!

We're off and running today! We dropped the kids off at school and thought we'd kill a little time at Starbucks jotting down some notes together for Jim before we went to the church office . . . buuuuut SURPRISE, it's Coffee with a Cop day. So we sat down and visited a bit with our local police officers. The longer we sat, the more people we ran into that we know! It was so nice!!! What an unexpected treat today.

We've been to the church office already and are now at Jim's 1st day of physical therapy to strengthen his legs. He's pretty excited about getting this going, but nervous about how he's going to feel after therapy.

It was such a relief to have some time off from his regular therapy schedule the last 2ish weeks. Buuuuut, now we're back to 5 therapy appointments a week again: speech once a week, PT (legs) twice a week, and OT (right hand) twice a week. Like I said before, OT and PT can't be scheduled on the same days or insurance won't cover them. So that pretty much leaves us with a minimum of 4 days of therapy a week; most weeks will be 5 days.

Oops!!! I almost forgot to share our "good news!" You may find it strange that I label it as good news, but whatever. (Yes, I just said, "Whatever!") Our whole life is strange now, so we're just gonna celebrate the small victories. Fair enough? . . . We have slept in our warm, cozy bed for 3 nights in a row now!!!! You may not find this very significant until I tell you that Jim has slept in his recliner and I have slept on the couch since last November! That's almost 10 months, with the exception of sleeping in hospital beds and chair-beds during his hospitalizations over the last year. We've tried from time to time to transition back to the bed, but he had so much pain in his right shoulder, or had difficulty rolling over with the use of only one hand, that we would get a few hours into the night and have to move back to the family room.

Although we are celebrating this small victory, I also have to say that IT'S ANOTHER ADJUSTMENT. (You know how much I've loved this over the last 16 months. Ughhhh!!!!) Thankfully it's an adjustment for the good this time, but nonetheless it is still change. The first night we barely slept, but decided to tough it out. The second night was a mix of toughing it out and resting peacefully. And last night was even better. And so, WOOHOO! for progress!!!

Jim continues to look really good. He feels good, too. Of the comments from family and friends over the last few weeks, this is the number one comment: "You look soooo good!!!!" Other comments include kind compliments that people feel his speech is getting much better. He struggles to receive these compliments because he compares his speech to how it was before his diagnosis. He still faces the challenge of getting his words out quickly and effectively, and so he has a hard time seeing that he really HAS improved. It continues to be his most sensitive challenge. He longs for the day he can preach again and speak with ease.

We know God is continuing to work in our lives, and He is strengthening Jim daily. I don't know what we'd do without our Jesus. We're in such capable hands! It makes us so much more dependent on Him than we have ever been. I believe this is growing us and strengthening us spiritually. And I believe He is enlarging our boundaries in our faith in Him, in our ministry, and in what we thought we were capable of handling in life. There must be a purpose in all of this. I don't know what it is. It still seems so foreign. I guess it's a good thing that we put God in the driver's seat to direct us to where we need to go next!

Expecting a complete miracle! ANY day will do!!!
♥ *Jim and Brenda*

Excerpts from Saturday, September 10, 2016 – AM Update:

We made it to the 9/11 service at the Escalon Fire Department yesterday morning. Jim was able to say the prayer for the ceremony and did a great job.

Hand therapy was next on the list and Jim tried many new exercises. I was impressed to see how well he did with them. He shows improvement almost every time we go. He was in great spirits and had the assistants and therapists cracking up at his funny antics. I told them I brought their Friday entertainment for them. That guy makes me laugh so much. I love to see his sense of humor taking over again.

We had a few Aha! moments yesterday:

- The first was not a good aha. The receptionist at Jim's OT broke the news to us that not only does he have to schedule his OT and PT days on different days, but the insurance company sent word to them that his speech therapy can't be scheduled on the same days, either. What does this mean? It means 5 days of therapy a week, unless we cancel one of his therapy sessions, which kinda stinks because OT and speech therapy are 2 blocks away from each other.
- The second aha moment happened on the way to OT yesterday, when Jim finally realized how to make the "th" sound. It finally clicked and he was so happy. He kept saying, "That. This. There. . . . " You don't

realize the relief of an Aha! moment until you've struggled with something for so long.
- His final Aha! moment yesterday was during OT. He has had a horrible struggle with his arm shaking uncontrollably when he does anything with fine motor skills. Yesterday the therapist tried a wrist brace to see if it would help and VOILA! the shaking stopped and he could actually focus on his fine motor skills without knocking over the item he was working with. Ahaaaaa!!!!!!

We finished up the day at the youth center monitoring kids, and we enjoyed watching them having fun. It was packed yesterday! Probably the fullest I've seen it yet.

We're at soccer games this morning. Gotta go! Time to switch kids out at the snack bar!

Excerpts from Thursday, September 15, 2016 – PM Update:

Well, hello!!! It's Thursday night already and the week has zipped right past us. It's been an extremely busy week with therapy appointments daily; working at the office in the afternoons; taking work with me to appointments; volunteering at the youth center; and covering the kids' stuff daily.

Jim is having another good week. He's very sore from his PT (legs). His therapists have been challenging him a lot and he's doing great. He even rode his stationary bike at home for 10 minutes straight the other day, and on Sunday he walked up the steps on the church stage! He's seeing a lot of improvement, but the therapy is making his legs stiff and sore. His body still heals slower than usual, so the tenderness lasts longer. Eventually this will probably subside more quickly.

He passed 2 more tiny kidney stones late this morning. Welcome kidney stone babies numbers 9 and 10 . . . of 20ish. (I think that's the right count. Idk.)

Jim continues to show much more improvement in other areas as well. He's helping as much as he can with dinners and cleaning up after we eat. He has been more available (because he feels good) to help the kids rotate between homework, chores, reading, and practicing their instruments while I'm finishing work or running laundry. He is using his right hand as much as possible for whatever task he is working on. He can pick up items off the floor easier now - it used to be hard for him to lean over like that because he would lose his balance easily. . . . Annnnnd, he has been teasing me like crazy lately. The fact that his sense of humor is present on a regular basis sure encourages me. That's my Jim! He loves to laugh and enjoy life. And it's so good to hear him laugh.

To me, it seems like Jim's speech is improving. He doesn't always agree with me about that. Other people have commented on it over the last couple of weeks, saying he sounds so much better. We're still praying for complete restoration of this VERY important aspect of his life.

I'm still trying to find balance in letting go where I need to and being available when Jim needs help. We had to drop our car keys off with Courtney to get our Expedition fixed earlier this week, so I asked Jim if he wanted to walk them in. He did. So, what did I do? I found myself sitting in the car watching his each and every step into the shop and back out again. I think I held my breath the whole time! Letting go is difficult!!! Seriously! I just don't want him to hurt himself and have something new to deal with in his therapy schedule. The poor guy has enough already.

We are so thankful for all of Jim's progress lately. It's not without a lot of prayer and a lot of hard work on his part. I'm very proud of my guy! And I'm very proud to say it's only possible because of God.

Expecting a complete miracle! ANY day will do!!!
♥ *Jim and Brenda*

Tuesday, September 27, 2016

Happy 50th birthday to the love of my life, Jim Davis!!!

Somehow it feels like words fail me this morning when I come to this momentous occasion. I guess partly because my heart is flooded with soooo many emotions over it.

Many times we have wondered if Jim would live to see this day: first in 2006, and then again with his brain cancer diagnosis last year. To be quite honest, just days ago I ran across our funeral planning notes in Jim's doctor/therapy notebook I keep for him for every appointment and hospitalization he has. We had jotted down these funeral notes last summer (2015), weeks after his diagnosis. I purposely put them at the back of the notebook because I didn't want to lose them, but didn't want to see them every day. I cannot even begin to describe the raw, piercing pain in our hearts as we jotted down his wishes for his service so I would know how to honor him best. We couldn't even get through the planning in one session because it was so heart-wrenching and our emotions overtook us quickly. We knew (as we know now) that God was in control, but the pain still came in great floods during those moments.

We have walked these last 17 months in faith, trusting God to see us through each day. Some days have been agonizing pain. Others have been filled with victories and laughter. But God has been there EVERY day. He has carried us.

From day one of his diagnosis we have trusted God for a miracle. And let me tell you, we've seen a lot of them on this journey. The fact that Jim is doing extremely well right now is evidence of God's mighty hand on his life. I can't stress enough how much this is NOT the norm for his diagnosis. We serve a mighty God and give Him all of the credit!

"You have decided the length of our lives. You know how many months we will live, and we are not given a minute longer."

This verse brings me so much comfort. I'm grateful that God decides the length of our lives. There is nothing that can shorten God's count - not even brain cancer. Jim is in capable hands and he will complete the number of days

God has designed for him from the beginning of time. Right now he's at 18,263 days . . . and counting.

Soooooo, happy birthday Mr. Davis! You are my sunshine and I love living life by your side. I wouldn't have it any other way.

We are EXPECTING A MIRACLE!!! Any day will do. ♥

Sunday, October 2, 2016 – Afternoon Update:

Christopher went to hang out with a friend this afternoon, and Hanna and Americis were invited to my mom and dad's house for the afternoon. I'm really supposed to be relaxing and taking a nap, as per the orders given to me, buuuuuut I can't pass up the opportunity to shout it from the rooftops . . . GOD IS AMAZING!!!!!!!

Jim had a full day of visiting with friends and family at his birthday party yesterday. He was supposed to sit down and visit with people as they came to talk to him, but he didn't follow orders very well. He was up, walking around and chatting with everyone. He kept finding his way to wherever I was standing and visiting with friends, checking to be sure I was doing ok. When he got home last night he was exhausted and was ready for bed pretty early.

We knew today would be another busy day because of a pastor appreciation lunch our church had prepared to honor us and the 2 other couples who serve alongside us. And there were parts of the service this morning that Jim had already planned to be part of today. . . . Let me just say right now what a fabulous day it was!!!! Today marks a huge milestone.

Here are the highlights:

- Jim did all of the communion service this morning - speaking and reading scripture.
- He stepped up the stairs onto the stage a couple of times and down again (with me "spotting him," of course!)
- He and our friend Arney Corbin both spoke during a special "passing of the mantel" ceremony to acknowledge our "new" youth director.
- He prayed and dismissed service.
- Then he walked down 10 stairs, from the sanctuary to the parking lot, all by himself. (First time for that in about a year or so!) Annnd, of course, I "spotted him" again and told him I'd break his fall if he fell down the stairs. Super glad it didn't come to that!
- We had the specially-prepared pastor appreciation lunch after service. Jim ate, then walked around by himself and visited with people.
- And, as if that wasn't enough with all of the other great things on this spectacular milestone day, he came to tell me he needed my help to go get plates of spaghetti for a new family in our church who didn't get their plates yet (an extra pot of spaghetti had to be cooked midway through serving). He made sure to personally serve them their plates because he was worried that they didn't get to eat.

Was Jim's speech perfect today? No. But it was pretty good! He made sure to take his words nice and slow. He got tripped up from time to time, but stopped to take a breath, reset himself, and continue on. I told him what a fabulous job he did today, and his reply was, "I can do better!" . . . I can't even believe this guy's determination to continue moving forward no matter how difficult it is for him. His biggest goal is to get back to preaching every Sunday. He misses it and still feels strongly called to it.

Amazing milestones, friends! Such amazing milestones. My heart is doing a continuous happy dance this afternoon.

I am grateful for God's hand on Jim. And, ya know, I'm humbled by and grateful for a wonderful church congregation and board who have not given up on us as their pastors. They have had multiple opportunities to move on and select a new pastor who was capable of ministering to their every need, but they have chosen time and time again to stand by our side in prayer, with encouragement, with love and support, and most importantly IN FAITH. We are blessed! We are flooded with blessings from these beautiful people God has put in our lives.

And now, I will try to nap with a happy heart that is overflowing with joy and praise. It might be difficult, but I'll try.

Thanks, friends, for rejoicing in these milestones with us. We are in the capable hands of our Savior. No better place to be!

Expecting a complete miracle! It's coming for sure. Any day will do!!!
❤ *Jim and Brenda*

21

CONTINUED PROGRESS

THERE'S SOMETHING TO be said for improvement and continued progress. It brings hope to the soul that normal will be restored. At some level, all of us crave the normal, routine things in life. It stabilizes us and helps us regain our bearings. Whether it's our normal, everyday routine or a special tradition/routine we have for specific days, it gives us solid footing and fortifies us in some way.

I had guarded myself against this hope for normal for quite some time. In the past year, life had changed so much that every time I had just settled into a new routine, our circumstances would change on a dime, and I'd be forced into another new routine. It was disheartening. It seemed like life was playing a cruel joke on me – this person who loves the predictable, routine things of life, the person who is comforted by them.

Nonetheless, this "hope" started to blossom again. July showed some promising improvements. August revealed a few more. September proved itself to be even better. So, as we wandered into October and November of 2016, it felt comfortable to finally BELIEVE that life might just be returning to normal, one step at a time. It was ok to hope for that again.

It was alright to breathe a sigh of relief and rest/relax a bit. Just maybe! It was a huge relief for this tired, weary soul to come to that conclusion.

October and November continued with the same steady progress we had seen in August and September.

Jim's OT therapist (for his right hand) did another assessment on Jim's hand at his therapy appointment on October 10th. Every time he was at the end of a set of authorized sessions, Jolene had to do an assessment so she could submit a request for reauthorization. All of his measurements of his hand function on that day showed good improvement. A few of them were very close to, or in, normal range. He had been working extremely hard for this, so it was great to see the fruit of his determination and hard work.

On October 11, 2016, we made another trip to UCSF. This time it was for a urology appointment with Dr. S. We ran into tons of traffic that morning, so it took 3 hours to get there. The appointment went really well. His urologist decided he wanted Jim to do a 24-hour urine test, so I would need to make some phone calls to get that set up. We were able to submit some of Jim's kidney stone babies for DNA testing (AKA pathology – LOL). I was so happy to hand those things over, after collecting them for months. It felt a little creepy bagging them in snack-sized Ziploc bags and setting them aside for this appointment. I was worried that I'd forget to take them with us and we'd be left with them forever.

Everything looked stable at this urology appointment, so Dr. S decided that he wanted Jim to come back in one year. He encouraged Jim to call if he had any complications with passing kidney stones before the one-year check-up appointment.

So, we headed home from UCSF, planning to return in 11 more days for Jim's next neuro-oncology appointment with Dr. B. Anytime we were within that timeframe of the next MRI appointment, our nerves were usually on edge. Our human nature took over and we would get worried and anxious, despite our attempts to fix our eyes on God and comfort ourselves with the fact that He was in control.

Excerpts from Monday, October 17, 2016 – PM Update:
This weekend was packed with soccer game/snack bar stuff, completing office work (from home, then at work to print), and then participating in the final events of our church's missions emphasis week. It was a fun, but super busy weekend.

Jim's working on passing another kidney stone, has felt pretty crummy all day, and has been in pain off and on. He "birthed" one small kidney stone baby on Saturday afternoon, but feels like another one is working its way out. So, he rested most of the day at home while I worked at the office. He doesn't seem like his chipper self tonight, and that makes me sad. Your prayers are appreciated for him.

This Saturday is Jim's next neuro-oncology appointment at UCSF. To be perfectly honest, I'm expecting the "WOW! Report" this time around . . . the "We don't know how to explain this" report . . . the "this is not typical" report. . . . In fact, if we have the opposite report - one that shows new growth in the brain cancer - I don't think I'll know quite how to handle it. I haven't prepared myself for that report. I haven't braced myself for it. I don't know that I care to.

Am I oblivious to the fact that we could receive a bad report? No. Listen. I KNOW that it's a possibility. I understand that much more than you would ever want to believe. I've heard the doctors' prognosis. I've seen the reports on Glioblastoma. I know more than I ever wanted to know about it. And some of it I've purposely chosen not to research. I'm choosing to continue to have faith that God has this in control. Call it blind faith, if you will. Call it stupid. Call it whatever you want, I really don't care. I just chose to trust that God has numbered Jim's days and nothing will interfere with God's will.

Do I have fear? Do I worry? Why, yes, of course I do at times. I'm human! Come on now, I'd be a robot if I didn't experience these very real emotions. I have to make a conscious effort not to focus on those worries and not to stay there for long. . . . Easy? No. Staying busy does help, though. It makes for very little time to focus on the "what ifs." And it sure is helpful to be exhausted at the end of the day so I don't lie awake in the quiet hours of the night to worry and fret. . . . Besides these helpful tips, I try very hard to stop my wandering thoughts from going places I don't want them to be. And then I pray when they do start to wander out of control. That's what keeps me in "perfect peace."

"You will keep in perfect peace all who trust in you, all whose thoughts are fixed on you!"

And so, we wait once again. We count down to this Saturday, anxious to celebrate more of what God is doing in Jim's life, hoping and praying for the "WOW! Report," and trying to keep our thoughts focused on our very capable Savior.

Friends, WE ARE EXPECTING A MIRACLE! Truly expecting. And ANY day will do, but we'd like to see more of the "evidence of things unseen" this Saturday. Thank you for continuing to pray and believe with us! We love you!!!
Blessings,
♥ *Jim and Brenda*

Excerpts from Thursday, October 20, 2016 – PM Update:
Jim passed another kidney stone just before noon yesterday. That's the second one this week, annnnnd he feels like still another might be working its way out. If it arrives before Saturday, we'll have a "triplet week!" Oh the joy these kidney stone babies bring him. Not!

On Saturday, October 22nd, we headed back to UCSF. Arney and Dana decided to come along with us to encourage us and continue walking the journey with us. They drove their Suburban, so I didn't have to drive. It was a huge blessing to be able to sit back and relax in the back seat while someone else was behind the wheel. That had become a luxury at that point in life.

Courtney was going to meet up with us at UCSF.

We arrived just before lunch, and first things first, we headed for the restroom. Jim and Arney headed to the men's restroom, on the right. Dana and I went to the women's restroom, on the left. Within a few minutes of entering the restroom, Dana and I heard a loud yell from the other restroom. Once outside again, we asked about it and were told that Jim had just passed another kidney stone. Welcome, kidney stone baby #3 of his set of triplets for the week. Needless to say, it was a painful one. He said he thought it was at least the same size as the largest one he had passed that we submitted for pathology, maybe bigger. I jokingly said that we needed to call the three he had passed that week the 3 Stooges.

That day also marked the 10-month anniversary since Jim's brain surgery.

We stopped for lunch inside the restaurant area across from the UCSF hospital on Parnassus. I chose to eat the same exact lunch I had on the day of Jim's surgery . . . well, what I could stomach that day while we waited for Jim's surgery – Panda Express' Orange Chicken with Chow Mein.

After we finished lunch, we headed to Jim's MRI appointment. Jim's appointment with Dr. B, his neuro-oncologist, was next on the list, so we made our way to his office to get the results of the MRI. It was so amazing to be able to get his results immediately. I always hated waiting a week for the results from Jim's local oncologist. It messed us up emotionally for days on end.

Saturday, October 22, 2016:
We just finished Jim's neuro-oncology appointment about 45 minutes ago. Here are the results we've all been waiting for . . .

- NO NEW GROWTH!!!!
- Everything looks stable.
- No chemo needed at this time.
- He can start driving short distances, and increasing it as he feels comfortable and can tolerate it.
- The doctor agreed that these are not normal results, considering that his last round of chemo was 11 months ago (November 2015). Typically they would see some growth by now with this kind of aggressive cancer.
- His next appointment will be sometime in January.
- The doctor was very pleased about how Jim looks, and told him to keep doing whatever he's doing. This was the first UCSF neuro-oncology appointment that he didn't use the wheelchair to get to!

We are so excited! PRAISE GOD FOR ANOTHER GREAT REPORT!!!

Expecting a miracle! TODAY'S A GOOD DAY!!!
♥ *Jim and Brenda*

With results like that, we were ready to celebrate. Arney, Dana, and Courtney went with us to Rain Forest Café on Fisherman's Wharf to have an early dinner. We snapped some celebratory pictures in the waiting area of the restaurant before we were seated. We enjoyed a wonderful meal at this restaurant chain we had grown to love together. We usually ate here in Disneyland with both of our families, and ordered volcanoes for dessert. So, of course, dinner wasn't complete without a volcano. We finished up, then decided it was time to start heading back home.

Excerpts from Tuesday, October 25, 2016:

- Jim has been in pain and feeling a little nauseated all day. He's passing another kidney stone. Poor guy!!! He said he feels like judging from its location it will pass very soon. That would be the 4th one in a week and a half! Goodness!!! Lots of kidney stone babies.
- My chauffeur, Jim, drove me to Target before his speech therapy yesterday morning. This is taking some getting used to after having to drive EVERYWHERE for the last year and a half!!! It seriously is another adjustment! By the way, he did great. We're just playing it safe and making sure he's only driving for short trips, without much traffic, and without the kids in the car. As he feels more comfortable we'll continue increasing his distance and time driving. For now, we're celebrating this milestone. It's pretty cool!!!!

That's it for now. Have a great night!

Expecting a miracle!!! Any day will do!!! We're thankful for all the ones we've seen so far.
❤*Jim and Brenda*

Sunday, October 30, 2016 – PM Update:

Well, it's almost been a week since my last update post. I guess it's time to sum up the last 5 days and let you know how we're doing.

We're doing well. . . . There. All done! Goodbye. . . . Ok. I guessss I'll give you a bit more.

Jim's pesky kidney stone last week seemed like it would be a large one. It made him nauseous, kept causing him pain, and seemed to be taking its own sweet time to be born. It finally arrived on Thursday morning, without much fanfare. Surprisingly, Jim said it was a small one. I dunno how it caused that much havoc for him, but it did. After its arrival, Jim was feeling more like himself immediately. . . . So, if you've been following my updates recently, that makes 4 kidney stones in 2 weeks! Without going back to my old posts, I've lost count of the total he's passed since the end of July. I think that makes 14, leaving around 6 more in his kidneys . . . provided he's not still producing stones.

This week was a huge blessing to us. Jim had speech therapy on Monday, but was waiting for new OT (hand) and PT (legs) authorization. PT came through, but he elected to take the week off and start next week. He really wanted a break. He needed it! We're still waiting on OT. So, this week wasn't packed with PT/OT appointments. Woohooooo!!!

Although I had some office work that needed to be completed and some appointments for Jim and the girls (and, of course, LAUNDRY!!!), I had promised Jim I would do my best to take advantage of the week and rest as much as I could. Annnnd I kept my promise! (Even though it's hard to do nothing.) As 1,000,001 thoughts of things that needed to be done rolled around in my little brain, I did my best to rest, relax, and do nothing during the times nothing was scheduled/pressing. At his request, I even skipped doing the church bulletin. ("Oh nooooo!!!! Not the church bulletin! How will we ever function?!?!?" . . . Yes, I know. My thoughts exactly.) As silly as it sounds, skipping my usual duties feels like I've signed off on failure. Yes, I'm hard on myself. I know. But I DO understand the importance of taking time to rest when I can. I'm not Wonder Woman, ya know. (Surprise!!! You thought I was.) And I'm not getting any younger! Sooooo, this week I took advantage of every opportunity I was given to take it easy. Twice I sat by the fire in our living room and just dozed off and on. TWICE!!!

Since passing his kidney stone on Thursday, Jim is feeling more like himself. I know I've said this so often in the last month or so, but I'll say it again: HE JUST LOOKS SOOOOO GOOD LATELY!!! He has his sense of humor back. He is getting around so much easier. And he has driven the car a few times this week. (That made him so happy!) The transition between not functioning to functioning is still rough. We are trying to discern DAILY how much is enough, too much, or not enough for allowing Jim to step back into his previous abilities/responsibilities. I definitely don't want to hold him back, but I fear letting go too soon on something and reaping the consequences of it because I should've been there to help. And so we continue assessing, reassessing, balancing, and stepping out (with a little fear and trembling). Your prayers in this area are appreciated. We need wisdom with each new step.

As I think over the last year and a half, and all we have been through, I can just barely believe it. I feel numb, seriously numb. I feel intense pain. I feel shattered to the core. . . . I probably feel every emotion under the sun. . . . I don't know how we've made it this far, except for by the grace of God. There is no way we could have endured this far without our faith in Jesus. Our Comfort. Our Hope. Our Peace. Our Anchor. Our Provider. Our Healer. This is where our hope remains. This is where we anchor ourselves. This is the One we look to to complete the miracle He has started in Jim. God is faithful. We are grateful that we're in such capable hands.

Thanks, friends, for your unending prayers and lice (ummm, that's supposed to be "love," but it's just too funny to correct. I'll let you have a good laugh, like I did). . . . Ahemmmm. Thanks for your love. (Better that time. Haha.) You are witnessing this miracle day-by-day, right along with us! Don't blink. He's working right in our midst. He's showing Himself strong.

Expecting a miracle! ANY day will do!!!
♥ *Jim and Brenda*

Sunday, November 6, 2016 – PM Update:
Today marked another milestone for Jim. God is so good! Last month he facilitated communion and did most of a passing-of-the-mantle ceremony for our youth director. This month . . . Communion and sermon!!!!

Here's the scoop from my perspective (the perspective of his head cheerleader):

I wasn't leading worship, nor was I on the worship team this morning, so I was able to stand next to Jim during worship. As we got closer to the end of worship, he looked at me and said, "I'll let you hand out the communion trays to the servers this morning." Although I don't usually do this, I agreed to help. A few minutes later, he turned to me and said, "Ummm, go ahead and play the piano during communion. I'll pass the element trays out." I double checked with him a couple times and he said he was fine with it.

Why would I take time to confirm he was ok with it? Because although he's using his right hand more and more, it's still difficult for him to grip/hold certain items. I knew that holding a stack of 2 trays filled with cups of grape juice and handing them off 1 by 1 to the church board might be nerve-wracking.

As I sat playing music for our communion time, I had just enough space to peek around the music stand to see him, so I could watch him as he handed out the trays. (I do admit that I hit a few sour notes occasionally from being so distracted by this milestone. Oops!) But SCORE, he handled it like a boss!!! No spills. No mishaps.

He continued to read scriptures and lead us through communion. Some of it was rough speech-wise, but he continued on until he finished. As he concluded, I beamed inside. Just beamed.

But then it was time for his sermon. He had been working on it all week. Friday afternoon he walked around his church office, practicing his sermon to help him with his speech while I worked in my office. He started his sermon with prayer, then opened his eyes and gave me the look like, "Can I do this?" I nodded and smiled from my seat, assuring him he had this. (Most of the other times he has talked recently he had me stand by his side to give him the assurance he needed. Today was a BIG day for him to "go it alone," just him and God!)

His sermon wasn't long, but it didn't need to be. He spoke on the difference between joy and happiness. Happiness being something that changes constantly depending on our circumstances. Joy being something that comes from God in spite of our circumstances – no matter how stinky they might be. He shared from his heart about how God's Word encourages him on the darkest of days.

On the speech level, he started off a little rough while reading the scripture he started with. From there on, it just got smoother and smoother. He took it slow, but was steady with each word. He walked around the stage a bit as he spoke, looking quite comfortable, sharing straight from his heart. He was easy to understand and did such an incredible job!!!!

Many people shared later that they, once again, cried through most of service, thanking God for the miracle-in-the-making. I admit I had to wipe some tears myself. I wanted to just jump up and root him on (yes, pom poms and all!) because I knew what a huge accomplishment this was for him. I knew what excruciating effort went behind each word. I know his daily struggle with this.

Let me make this perfectly clear: we give ALL praise to God for this new milestone/victory! Jim did his part for sure, but it's only possible because of what God is doing in his life.

Jim still tires very easily. After church he was exhausted. It took a lot out of him. But YAAAAAAAAAAY!!! Woohoo!!! Woot woot!!! I gave him the pep talk and assured him of how great he did. . . . I know when I speak at church, the enemy likes to steal my joy afterwards by making me feel stupid. I was not about to let that creep in today (creep = action annnd creep = person).

So there you go. My account of another fabulous day! I know. I know. I'll try to put my pom poms back in my purse now. It's soooo difficult with my determined guy! Most days I juuuust get my pom poms stored safely away and have to pull them out again because he has accomplished another goal. But I don't mind. Honestly. I don't. I'll pull those pom poms out as often as I need to for my sweet LoverBoy.

Expecting a complete miracle! Any day will do! We are so thankful to see it bit by bit. We're sure not "there" yet, but God is showing Himself so strong.
♥ *Jim and Brenda*

Excerpts from Wednesday, November 16, 2016 – PM Update:
Jim passed another small kidney stone last Wednesday night. By my count I think that makes 15 since July 27th. (If we're counting since the beginning of March, that would put him at 25 kidney stone babies "birthed.") His last ultrasound was at the end of July. At that time, he had 20 stones. If he's not producing any more stones, we think he has about 5 left. If he's still producing them, wellll then we have no idea how many he's harboring.

Jim is enjoying being able to drive. He doesn't do it every day. He really is content with just knowing he can drive when he wants to. For now, since he is usually extremely sore from his therapy sessions, he is happy to let me drive most days. It sure is handy to have a second driver in the house, though. We've needed it a few times in the last week.

Jim is doing so much more than he has in the past year. He is moving around much easier (except on days his body is suffering from the backlash of his therapy sessions). He showers and dries himself without help - I stay close by to be sure he is safe getting in and out. He still struggles with buttons and zippers (because of limited use of his right hand), but he CAN manage them if he has enough time and energy to tackle them. He can open jars and bottles with both hands now. Lots and lots of areas of improvement! I'm sure I'm forgetting tons of things.

We are so thankful for all God is doing in our lives. We know He is working on our behalf all the time. A friend reminded me tonight that Jim and I don't even see ALL of the progress like everyone else does. We are too close to it every day to recognize every detail. It's kinda like a growing child. If you're with them day in and day out, you probably don't notice how much they've grown. If you haven't seen the child in a while, you notice the growth more quickly. Sooo, I'm sure that's true for Jim's progress. Everyone else sees the change more than we do.

Although one might look at our lives right now and assume that everything is "back to normal" . . . "There's so much progress!" . . . "There's so much improvement!" . . . I assure you that to us things do not seem "normal" quite yet. Far from it! We still feel the strain of not having full closure on many levels. Jim still struggles daily with pain in all of his joints. He still struggles with his speech (I'd say it's his number one challenge) every single day. He works extremely hard to get his right hand to function normally throughout the day. He still has to manage his energy each day to make sure he doesn't overdo it. When he does, he pays for it for a day or two. Annnd, for now, our schedule is nothing close to normal. We look forward to working back into a semi-normal work week with minimal therapy and doctor appointments very soon. Even that will take some adjustment.

All of these areas don't even begin to touch the surface of the emotional trauma we (and our families) have faced the last year and a half. Some wounds will take the rest of our lives to heal. Some things will take time for us to reorganize and regroup into the "new us" as we continue navigating life. We are definitely changed. No one can go through experiences like this and remain the same. We are redefined. Some areas are good. Others not so much. Our comfort? Knowing God can use these things for His glory no matter how ugly they appear to us now.

Our biggest thorn? Not knowing. . . . Not knowing WHEN this difficult cancer journey ends. Not knowing HOW it will end. Not knowing what tomorrow holds. Not knowing what the next 5 years hold, or even beyond that. . . . We are well aware that Jim's progress and medical report this far is not the norm for GBM patients. We know that going a year with no chemo and having no new tumor growth is only by God's mercy.

As I stop to reflect, I realize NO ONE knows what tomorrow holds. No one knows where they will be in 5 years. So, we can only live in the present. In today. We can impact our world with each day we are given, one day at a time. We can show God's love and grace to those around us every day. We can be held every day in the very capable hands of our Maker. Annnnd so that's where Jim and I have to place ourselves each day, in those capable hands. Knowing we are held. Knowing we are safe. Knowing He is in control, and reminding ourselves that we are not. It's comforting and peaceful, but at the same time it's a very vulnerable feeling. And that's where TRUST and FAITH come into play. That's where the rubber meets the road. It can only be comforting and peaceful WHEN WE LET GO. . . . Difficult? Oh, yes! But oh, so worth it.

These last years have been a trial by fire to bring us to the place where we HAVE to trust, where we have to rely on our faith in God. When I've had nothing else solid to grip, I had to rely on God's unchanging character the way I always told others they should in their time of need. It's the lesson I've always needed, but never wanted to truly experience because it brings excruciating pain and uncertainty. Buuuuut, it also brings the comforting "I've got this" squeeze from my Savior's hand to mine each time I grasp for something to cling to. Oh, to master this faith and trust completely!!! But the truth is I've only touched the surface. The truth is I still struggle with letting go of EVERY area of my life. The truth is I'm human.

Tonight, I reach out to grasp my Savior's hand and trust He will take us where we need to go from here. I'm trying to have complete faith and "laugh at the future," knowing God is in complete control. So, here I go . . . .

What wonderful miracles we have witnessed! We continue waiting for a complete miracle. Any day will do!!!
♥ *Jim and Brenda*

Tuesday, November 22, 2016 – PM Update:

Progress! Progress! Progress! Jim is seeing it every day and I love being right by his side to witness it firsthand. It's exciting!

This morning, as we drove through Starbucks on our way to his PT appointment (legs), he looked at me and said, "I feel good! I think I'm going to feel good for Thanksgiving and Christmas this year." Those words bring comfort to my heart and a smile to my face.

Jim passed another tiny kidney stone on Sunday night. He says he thinks another one is working its way out. Once it passes, that will account for kidney stone babies #16 and #17 (of the 20 they saw in July). He's so ready to be done with those crazy things.

Yesterday he had speech therapy. Jim asked his therapist about his progress and what other tools he needs to continue improving his speech. As they discussed it, he and his therapist decided that now is a good time for him to stop speech therapy. He has the tools he needs. Now it's just a matter of continuing to use them in daily life and giving his brain and body a chance to heal. His therapist said Jim can call at any time and come back in for any needs he has. This man has been an incredible help to us over this last year. What a huge blessing his knowledge, compassionate nature, and patient listening skills have been for Jim! I can't say enough great things about the quality of therapy Jim has received from him. Jim Sparkman at The Speech Path has blessed us on this difficult journey. . . . Soooo, we can subtract 1 speech therapy appointment every other week from our schedule!

PT (legs) was today. Jim still has his assessment for therapy next Tuesday. We weren't sure if they would ask for authorization for more PT or not. While talking to his therapist today, we got good news that he is extremely pleased with Jim's progress and doesn't see the need for additional PT for his legs. He had Jim do his regular exercises today. He also had him get down on the floor and back up again a few times to be sure he was steady and able to do it alone. As we got ready to leave today, he recapped all of Jim's progress all the way back to his shoulder PT and you could just see a sparkle in his eye about how far Jim has come. He was very impressed. Very. . . . And soooo, 2 more therapy sessions a week are coming off our schedule! Woohoo!!! (Well, after next Tuesday. He still has his assessment appointment. I think I'm getting ahead of myself.)

We are going from 5 therapy sessions a week (1 speech, 2 PT, and 2 OT) to only 1 OT appointment per week for his hand. . . . I. Can't. Even. Believe. It. . . . Life is returning! We can go to work! We can plan normal things and not try to schedule around therapy appointments. And, while we're at it, let's just be real here: Jim hasn't been hospitalized since March and hasn't been to ER since June! THAT, my friends, feels so good!!!

Tonight we helped decorate the church sanctuary. Jim assisted here and there as he was able and did such a great job. We enjoyed setting everything up and preparing for Christmas. Once we finished, they served refreshments downstairs. Jim walked downstairs and back up! It doesn't sound like a very big deal until you know that he hasn't been in the church's basement for almost a year and a half because stairs have been too difficult for him to navigate. Yaaay for taking the stairs like a champ! (Yes. I'm pulling out my pom poms again. Watch out!!!)

Tomorrow he has hand therapy in the morning, then we're free for the rest of the week to enjoy time with family and celebrate Thanksgiving. We have so much to be thankful for. Soooo much!!! God continues to show Himself faithful and strong in our lives. Every day seems to reveal new areas of progress in Jim physically. We are so grateful.

Well, friends, that's it for tonight. I just had to share Jim's new milestones. God is good!!!

Expecting a complete miracle! (We're getting there step by step.) Any day will do!!!
♥ *Jim and Brenda*

22

KIDNEY STONE HAVOC AND THE HECTIC HOLIDAYS

TAKE A LITTLE walk down memory lane with me. If you remember correctly, back in chapter 3 of this book: "The Rollercoaster" – I likened our story to one of a rollercoaster, with a lot of ups and downs, twists and turns, and upside-down loops. Then, at the end of chapter 9: "Whatever You Do, Don't Fall" (from January 2016) – I gave you a strong warning and referenced <u>A Series of Unfortunate Events</u>.

Here. I'll just copy and paste that second one for you, to help refresh your memory:

"Once again, we thought we were back on track to a somewhat normal life. We had a brief chance to breathe . . . or, in reality, at least to take half a breath before the next emergency. We falsely believed that things were finally settling down and we could attempt a normal routine.

And here, I almost feel like Lemony Snicket in <u>A Series of Unfortunate Events</u> cautioning his readers to stop reading if they were looking for a happy, uplifting story with a beautifully resolved storyline. I feel compelled to share the first paragraph of his book "The Bad Beginning" because it is so appropriate for the long saga of unfortunate events I'm recording:

> "If you are interested in stories with happy endings, you would be better off reading some other book. In this book, not only is there no happy ending, there is no happy beginning, and very few happy things in the middle. This is because not many happy things happened in the lives of the three Baudelaire youngsters. Violet, Klaus, and Sunny Baudelaire were intelligent children, and they were charming, and resourceful, and had pleasant facial features, but they were extremely unlucky, and most everything that happened to them was rife with misfortune, misery, and despair. I'm sorry to tell you this, but that is how the story goes."

We, like the Baudelaire children, had many more battles coming our way. We just didn't know it yet."

You may have laughed at the warning and thought to yourself, "Ehhh, that sounds a bit over the top!" I don't blame you. Truthfully, I would have thought the same if I hadn't been forced on the battlefield myself. I'm sure by now you can clearly see that the warning I gave you was fully warranted . . . and we still have a much longer journey to travel together, my friend.

As I sit here and try my best to pen these chapters, I still can't believe that this was our life . . . MY life. . . . It's so surreal. It doesn't seem possible that it all went down like it did. I still can't believe that I haven't had to be institutionalized from the insane events we trudged through, from crumbling under the immense pressure of every hospitalization, doctor appointment, therapy appointment; every bit of crushing news or even good news; and the day-to-day chaos our life had become. I don't know how we survived those days. I don't know how *I* survived.

August, September, October, and November of 2016 all seemed to be a steady climb to the top of the rollercoaster. I had just begun allowing myself to hope for some sort of normal in life. . . . Allowing. . . . Giving myself permission. . . . Talking myself into the fact that it was ok to embrace this new change and I could "jump on in." It took a while to convince myself that I wasn't just naively hoping that life would return to normal; I was actually seeing a normal routine again . . . to some degree. The mental and emotional battle of these thoughts I'm expressing is almost impossible to express adequately. After so many grueling battles, it took A LOT of convincing myself that normal – or some sort of semblance of it – had routed back around to our house again.

Then, December arrived, and the rollercoaster caught me off guard with some subtle unexpected dips, twists, and turns. They started on the very first day of the month:

Thursday, December 1, 2016 - PM Update:
We've got good news, ehhh news, and yucky news. Don't worry. It's nothing earth-shattering.

First, for the good news: Jim finished physical therapy for his legs on Tuesday morning. He did his usual routine, the therapist assessed him, and without much fanfare we left the building for the last time. Everyone there has been so nice to Jim. They were excited for his progress and congratulated him on how far he has come. . . . He is now officially down to only hand therapy (OT) - one time a week!

The ehhhh news: It's castle project time for 7th graders . . . and we have 2 of them!!! . . . Yes, I know everyone has a difference of opinion on this. Some are delighted to coordinate these school projects after school. But, let me just say how I loathe large projects that have to be completed at home. Life seems upside-down enough, without adding 2 castle projects that are due quicker than I'd like. Annnd, they require a partner, so it requires a bit more schedule coordinating than I want. Sooooo, ughhhh!!!! (Don't burn me at the stake, you fabulous parents who live for at-home projects. Everyone has their weaknesses.)

The yucky news: Jim doesn't feel good tonight. That pesky kidney stone that he thought was working its way out last week decided to take a little vacation until last night, but it came back with a vengeance. He's dealing with nausea off and on today and has been in a lot of pain in his left side. Please pray that it passes quickly. He's just getting back to the point where he can go into the office each day for a few hours. This kinda stuff sets him back not only because of the pain, but it drains his energy quickly, too.

Sooooo, there ya have it! 5 steps forward. 2 steps back. But there is still progress, so we'll continue moving forward as much as we can. Right? Right!!!

Expecting a miracle! ANY day will do!!!
♥ *Jim and Brenda*

By December 2nd, Jim was still in a great amount of pain from his kidney stone. He had gone to sleep right after dinner the night before, and then moved to the bed later. He even slept in, which was very rare for him, and laid low after he got up. The pain remained high, even after taking his daily back pain meds.

I called Jim's urologist's office at UCSF early in the afternoon to ask about what we could do to help him. They said to go to our local hospital if the pain continued, since UCSF was a couple of hours away from our home. They knew about the previous issues we had encountered with "Dr. One-In-Five-Urologists-In-An-Area-Where-There-Should-Be-Twelve," so they said they would be in contact with the staff at our local hospital to help us.

After debating it for hours, Jim finally reluctantly decided to go to ER at our local hospital. He asked me to call our neighbor Mike, from Escalon Community Ambulance, to see if he could assist Jim by transporting him to the hospital via ambulance. He was in so much pain, he didn't think he could endure having me take him in our vehicle, and he also knew that if we just walked into ER it was very possible that he would be waiting HOURS to be seen, like his previous visit. He was a strong guy, and could tolerate quite a bit while still keeping his cool and trying to remain pleasant, but he didn't think he could tolerate the pain for much longer.

I began packing a few things, knowing it was possible that they would keep Jim overnight. I thought I was experienced enough that I could do these things without Cara and Courtney, but I proved myself wrong. After getting to the hospital, I realized that I left my phone charger at home. That used to be one of the first things I put in my bag on our way out the door to the hospital, but now that we had experienced many months without emergency trips to the hospital, I was out of practice. I quickly updated friends and family, and added a humorous quote from the movie Finding Nemo: "You think you can do these things on your own, Nemo, but you can't!"

Once Jim arrived in ER and I was allowed to go back and advocate for him, the staff was very pleasant and helpful. They did a CT scan, and it revealed multiple stones in his kidneys – at least 8! Sigh! Thankfully, there were no blockages. They said he had a urinary tract infection that was probably caused by the kidney stones. The scan also showed that the lining in his bladder was thickened and inflamed – called cystitis. They believed that was caused by the number of stones he had passed since March, or it was possibly from the infection.

They gave him some IV pain meds to help him get the pain under control, then sent him home with prescriptions for antibiotics and a stronger oral pain med to get him past the painful symptoms.

We headed home very early in the morning on Saturday, December 3rd, and we were extremely tired.

Saturday, December 3rd – Mid-morning Update:
When you feel like you've been run over by a truck, but you have to get up and get ready to go get prescriptions. You brush your teeth and then realize halfway through that this is NOT your toothbrush. It's your husband's extra toothbrush. It's a good thing he loves me!

By Sunday evening, December 4th, we were back at the hospital. Jim wasn't able to manage his pain very well at home with the prescriptions he was given at the hospital. He barely slept on Saturday night and decided to stay home from church that morning (which was super rare for him). We tried to manage everything at home to prevent another trip to ER, but his hospital discharge paperwork said to go back in if he had blood in his urine . . . and he did . . . so, off to the hospital we went again.

When we got there, they took Jim back to a different unit than we were usually in. It was the last room at the end of the hall, and it barely had anything in it other than space for 3-4 hospital beds. There wasn't a nurses' station per se, only a rolling cart with a computer on it sitting in the right corner of the room. We could watch them clearly from across the room, at Jim's station in the first bay.

As we went through the hoopla of bringing the physician's assistant up to speed on Jim's recent symptoms, she decided that it would probably be necessary to irrigate his bladder. Jim asked how that procedure would be done, but once she explained that it required a catheter and pumping water into his bladder he tried to strike a bargain with her very quickly. He decided that if she gave him a little more time, he would urinate (and he was sure there wouldn't be any more blood in his urine), then the physician's assistant would realize that he didn't need to have his bladder irrigated. She didn't really like the idea of giving him more time, but she could tell by his chart that he had been through a lot and she wanted to spare him any extra pain and loss of dignity. A deal was made!

They gave him a little more time before they realized it was still necessary to irrigate his bladder. Before long, much to his dismay, the nurses inserted a catheter and began the irrigation. He continued to have blood in his urine, paired with a lot of pain, so at 1:30 AM they decided to admit him to the hospital and find a room for him. I grabbed my bags from the car and toted them to his room, ran through the check list of questions with his new nurse, and tried desperately to get some sleep on my chair-bed.

By Monday morning, we received word that Jim's mom was on her way to a different local hospital, after already being seen and released one day before. It was concerning.

Monday proved to be a very frustrating day, but by evening we finally had a game plan. The urologist assigned to Jim (thankfully not "Dr. One-In-Five-Urologists-In-An-Area-Where-There-Should-Be-Twelve") said he wanted to try to remove the catheter on Tuesday morning. He wanted to see how Jim did with that before he evaluated him further. Jim was still having a lot of pain in his bladder and at his flank. They decided to work with him to manage his pain effectively, and if they were successful they would be able to discharge him. The hospitalist also noted that the tests from his Friday visit showed that he didn't have a urinary tract infection as they suspected. The debris in his urine was more likely from the stones and cystitis because the cultures hadn't grown anything.

Tuesday, December 6th – Afternoon Update:
(Yes, I had to double-check what day it is! Haha!!!)
  Here's the latest update. Sorry in advance for info that sounds too personal. I don't know how to share this stuff tactfully.

- Jim's catheter was removed this morning at 6:30.
- He was able to urinate, but had a lot of pain. No blood, so that's good.
- The hospitalist was good to discharge him, but wanted to be thorough. (We soooo appreciate that!) At our request, she ordered another CT scan, just to be sure everything is ok. (They didn't do a new one when he came back in on Sunday night with blood in his urine. The last one was on Friday night.)
- This afternoon they found 2 oral meds that are helping with pain and the bladder inflammation. He feels much better with having better pain relief for a longer time. The hospitalist will send him home with these prescriptions.
- CT scan is complete. They see 2 stones (one on each side) that are in the ureter and are trying to pass. That explains the pain and the blood. That answers so many of our questions that seemed to be lingering out there. I'm glad we asked for the repeat CT scan. The stones aren't very big, so they think he can pass them at home. He is good with that.
- Jim should be discharged soon. If he has more blood, or pain that can't be tolerated at home, they said he should come back in.
- He will follow up with his UCSF urologist in a couple of weeks.

THANKS FOR YOUR PRAYERS!!! We love you all so much.
  Please continue praying for Jim's mom. An appointment with her surgeon today revealed the need for an additional surgery next week. . . . As a matter of fact, just cover the ENTIRE DAVIS FAMILY in prayer, please. We can't get a break!

Expecting a miracle . . . on so many levels! ANY day will do for a breakthrough. We continue to have expectant hearts. (Discouraged at times, to be honest, but still expectant!)
♥*Jim and Brenda*

We happily spent Wednesday and Thursday at home together. But, by Friday, Jim's mom was back at the hospital. She had been to ER multiple times, but they kept sending her home. Since Jim and I hadn't pulled our weight in helping to care for her (due to our own circumstances), we agreed to stay at the hospital to try to advocate for her. Jim couldn't speak well, so I ended up having to pull the doctor off to the side to ask for a minute with him.

He reluctantly agreed to meet with me in another room. I entered the room and sat down in the chair that he motioned to me was acceptable to sit in for our conversation. I calmly explained to him that we felt Becky's situation was urgent and they needed to stop sending her home. Then I pretty much told him that if it took me yelling and screaming that Becky needed care, I could oblige him. I expressed that I didn't think it should be necessary to lose my integrity and start yelling in order for him to hear the urgency of our request, but I could definitely step over that line if that's what it took. He politely explained that he would have to get clearance from the hospitalist to have her admitted. I acknowledged that I understood what he was saying.

About 30-45 minutes later, he returned and asked for me to go talk with him again. This time we entered another room set up with a small couch on each side, facing each other. He explained that the hospitalist denied the request to admit Becky to the hospital, to which I begged him to please try again, adding that I COULD yell and scream if that's what it took. He said he would try again, but he couldn't guarantee it would work. I thanked him, then asked him if the hospitalist was hesitant, to ask if he would be willing to come talk to me in person.

We waited another 30-45 minutes before we saw the doctor again. We had been standing in the hallway next to Becky's bed, because the room she had been in had water damage to the ceiling. The doctor motioned "come over here" with his head and took a few steps around the corner from where Becky was. He reported that he was successful in getting the hospitalist to admit Becky, then stated that a few specialists would be coming by for an assessment before they moved her to another unit.

I thanked him repeatedly for helping us, then he left and I never saw him again.

We updated Jim's family about the change in status, waited for Becky to be moved to another unit, then said our goodbyes so we could go home and get some much-needed sleep. We had missed the Christmas party with our church that night, but we felt that it was much more important that we stay with Becky that evening.

Monday, December 12, 2016 – PM Update:
Although there are a lot of chaotic situations happening in life right now, I'd like to share a tiny, joyful milestone:

Jim got a FOR-REALS haircut today! He's super excited about it. First real haircut since Summer 2015. We've been buzzing it with clippers at home since his chemo and radiation started last year and made his hair evacuate the premises. It started growing back quite some time ago, but it was growing in patches. It's filling in better now. . . . And today, a for reals haircut!!! Woohoo!!!!!

I'll try to type up a more complete update on him later tonight, if I have time.

Expecting a miracle! ANY day will do!
♥ *Jim and Brenda*

Jim's mom had surgery on Thursday, December 15th. Even though the surgery was considered high risk, they were able to use general anesthesia and the surgery was successful.

Excerpts from Sunday, December 18, 2016:
I promised an update on Jim a few days back (possibly a week ago by now). Oops! Sorry. So much has happened this last week and the days keep flying by. I can't even keep up. I've had Christmas cards to mail out for 2 weeks now, but here they sit on the table next to me.

First of all, Jim is doing pretty good. He's still dealing with challenges from kidney stones. He says he felt the 2 stones that were seen at the hospital slowly make their way down, and he stopped having the flank pain he was experiencing. He never saw evidence of the stones, though. In talking to our primary care physician, apparently they can drop into the bladder and stay there for a while. Who knew?

This week Jim started having right side flank pain again, so we assume another stone is wreaking havoc. He has a urology appointment at UCSF tomorrow. Hopefully we'll get some more info then.

Jim's hand therapy (OT) continues to go well. He has such a great team of therapists and assistants that work with him. He always has them laughing with him about something humorous during his therapy sessions. (I love his sense of humor. I live for his silly antics.) Last Wednesday, his lead therapist did new measurements to record his progress. Are you ready for this??? . . . His grip strength improved from 9 lbs. to 18 lbs. IT DOUBLED!!! And his pinch strength improved from 5 lbs. to 9 lbs.! Almost doubled. I told him I needed to pull my pom poms out of my purse to celebrate his small victory.

The use of Jim's hand has improved dramatically, from no use to pretty good use of it. It still is a major challenge for him daily. He longs for the day it will have normal function again. I pray for restoration of it every time I pray for him . . . along with full restoration of everything else he has challenges with. The shaking/tremoring he experiences when he uses it has decreased quite a bit, but still rears its ugly head when his hand gets tired. I have no idea how my guy pushes through every day with a smile on his face (most days) and with bold determination to overcome these obstacles.

Soooo, have you met my handsome new chauffeur? My Love has been driving me almost every place we've gone in the last week. My cozy little passenger seat feels beyond amazing with this sweet guy by my side. How I've missed being HIS co-pilot, instead of vice versa. This week I've relaxed, texted, made phone calls, read office emails, and everything in between, while he transported me around. It's such a simple luxury, but oh, how I've missed it incredibly. There are SO MANY little details that have changed in our daily routine over the last year and a half, that I don't dare take these things for granted again once they return to normal.

Marcus and Cara get to come visit next week! Eeeeeeeek!!!! We haven't seen them since the first week of August when they moved to Washington to start their new adventures together. We're looking forward to an "uneventful" week of family fun and lots of laughter. (God knows how much I need laughter right now.)

I've had my share of pity parties over the last couple of weeks. Like I said, things have been very crazy. I don't pretend that I'm always on top of the world. I try not to make a big deal of it, but the struggle does exist. I only share this to be open and honest. I'd never want to come across as being fake, or make someone else who is struggling to falsely believe that I've got it all together so they should, too. Struggle is real, and it's a part of life. Enough said. Let's move along now.

We appreciate your continued encouragement and prayers. We love and appreciate each of you immensely. God has blessed us with an army of friends and family.

Expecting a complete miracle! ANY day will do!!!
♥ *Jim and Brenda*

Monday, December 19, 2016:
Back home after a 12-hour day to San Francisco. I wish we could say we roamed around and had fun, but basically we waited for the doctor for hours because he got stuck in surgery later than planned. Then we got stuck in horrible traffic on the way home, taking us almost 3 hours to get from UCSF to Dublin - where we all jumped out of the car with glee to eat and take a much-needed break. We did play the ABC game in the car multiple times to pass the time and to keep me from road rage.

We didn't get a lot of info this trip. As always, the urologist was very kind and sympathetic to Jim. We really like him. He said the 24-hour urinalysis Jim did last month didn't reveal much. Basically, he said for him to watch his sodium intake (moderation) and drink a glass of milk with dinner or eat some yogurt because his calcium levels looked a little low. Other than that, he basically conceded (finally) that these kidney stones were probably caused by the chemo and radiation therapies last year. [Noting in hindsight, to clarify: That was the discovery we were waiting for. We always thought chemo and radiation caused the kidney stone cycle to start, but everyone wanted to argue with us that it just wasn't possible.] It makes sense, since he didn't have this problem before then. The tests don't reveal anything else, so that's good. The urologist wants to spare Jim another surgery, so unless he sees an urgent need for it he is taking a more low-key plan of care. Since Jim has already passed around 25 kidney stones, it's safe to say most of the ones left will be fine for him to pass at home. If he has complications, we can contact UCSF or go to our local hospital at any time.

He wants Jim to come back next month and do an ultrasound. He's scheduled to do that, then see the doctor immediately afterwards. Hopefully that trip doesn't get drawn out like today's did.

Our kids all ditched us when we got home tonight. They each had plans with friends. Considering today was pretty boring, they probably can use some fun.

Off to work tomorrow . . . .

Still expecting a miracle! ANY day will do!!!
♥ *Jim and Brenda*

Christmas Eve - December 24, 2016:
We've finished out the night and just sent the kids off to bed. Tonight was nothing like we expected or planned for when entering December. Things just have a way of changing and you have to roll with them, disappointments and all.

We typically spend Christmas Eve with Jim's family. Jim and I arrive early for our unsaid duties of helping his mom open the last jars and cans, preparing the celery with cheese spread, and making the family salad dressing recipe. This is followed by the arrival of the rest of the family, bearing parts of the meal. After dinner, Jim and I duck out for a bit to do a Christmas communion service at church. When we return to his parents' house, the kids are giddy to open gifts. Group pics of the kids. Then the wrapping paper flies and the kids are quickly done, enjoying their gifts from gramma and papa. Once everyone has finished, they pack up and head home for the night, knowing that his mom has been preparing food and gifts for days and now needs rest.

Tonight? Well, tonight was much different. His mom is still in the nursing facility. His dad is home, but is facing his own challenges. It just isn't the same. No celebration together. No homemade spaghetti or stuffed Italian squash. In fact, Jim has been fighting a chest cold and didn't want to get his mom or dad sick, so he couldn't visit either one of them today.

Last minute, this afternoon, we were invited to join the Corbin/Jenkins celebration, complete with a white elephant gift exchange and yummy finger foods. We were able to enjoy ourselves for a couple of hours before running off to set up for communion service tonight. What a blessing this family is to us!!!

Last year we sat in Jim's hospital room at UCSF on Christmas Eve. Jim was recovering from his brain surgery 2 days earlier. We FaceTimed his family and wished them a merry Christmas, longing to be with them. The only other comfort for the night was a group of carolers in the hospital halls, who stopped to offer us a pan cookie and say merry Christmas. It was seriously the highlight of our Christmas. It was the only moment of Christmas joy delivered to Jim's room.

This experience has opened our eyes to the loneliness one can feel on these holidays. It's a very depressing thing. Our hearts go out to those who are going through this this year (or at any other time). If you've never experienced this, I pray you never do.

To be home with our family tonight and tomorrow is the best gift we could ever have. We are blessed with great friends and family. We have been blessed with an entire year since last year's sad Christmas. An entire year to spend with friends and family. An entire year for Jim to have more challenges, but to grow stronger and for healing to continue. An entire year to see the miracle of no growth in brain cancer that is deemed to be highly aggressive. An entire year of tears, celebrations, sadness, joy, and walking in faith. Faith, navigating the seen and still believing for the unseen.

Uncertainty and fear marked last Christmas: How effective would this surgery be? How long does Jim still have with us? Is this sad Christmas to be our last together? What will this coming year hold? (And ohhh, the craziness we didn't see coming!)

This year we still face many of these uncertainties, but we face them after a year of seeing God's hand on Jim's life day, by day, by day. We face them with faith that has had a full year of growth. We continue to face them holding our Savior's hand.

Tonight we wish you all a merry Christmas! May you enjoy EVERY friend and family member you have the pleasure of enjoying Christmas with. Hug them all tight. Tell them how much you love them. They deserve it!

We love you all!

Expecting a complete miracle! ANY day will do!
♥ *Jim and Brenda*

Cara and Marcus arrived for a visit late on Tuesday, December 26th. They drove from their home in Washington to spend about a week with us for the holidays.

We had a Christmas celebration planned at my parents' house the next evening. That proved to be a lively occasion. Just as we stepped into my parents' house, we heard Cara yelling for her dog. I turned and saw her sprinting to catch her dog and Courtney's dog, who had captured Christopher's chicken. (My parents let him keep some chickens at their house, because they live out in the country.) Then Marcus ran by. Then Courtney (who had been running a high fever all night/day) ran by. I took off to look out the front window and saw both dogs being restrained. Christopher's chicken was laying on the walkway in front of my parents' front porch. It was on its back, playing dead. After checking on the chicken multiple times that night, she seemed to be ok. We were very thankful for that, because starting Christmas with a dead pet chicken just kills the holiday spirit. This is my account of "The Chicken Incident of 2016." You're welcome!

We did our best to enjoy the evening with my family at my mom and dad's house, but truthfully, I had been fighting a chest cold for a few days. Courtney was in even worse shape than I was. She needed someone to drive her to Kaiser to pick up her prescription for antibiotics while everyone else had dinner. I offered to take her. The trip was a VERY quiet one because she felt so horrible. When we returned, Court went out to her house and went to bed. Sweet Cara had made a plate for me while I was gone, so I didn't miss out on the meal they had. Later, I was able to curl up in a cozy chair near the table my kids, nieces, nephews, and brother were sitting at. I closed my eyes and listened as they played a hilarious new game. In spite of the fact that I didn't feel well, it was wonderful to be able to celebrate with my family that year. I treasured that gift!

Sunday, January 1, 2017:
We started the year off by adding to our family!!! Kidney stone babies #5,674,531 and #5,674,532 arrived tonight. (I might be exaggerating on those counts just a little, but it sure seems never ending - especially to Jim.)
So, back to the babies . . . New Year's twins!!! One is enormous. The other is small.

Jim was considering going to the doctor tomorrow because he thought he had a UTI. Thankfully the "babies" arrived tonight. He's feeling sooooo much better. Poor guy!!!

Dad and babies are doing fine. Lol!
Happy New Year!

Wednesday, January 11, 2017:
The last few weeks have been packed for sure. I haven't updated you here for a few reasons:

1. No time. 2. When there was time, I was exhausted. 3. Sometimes my emotions have to be sorted through before I can adequately express what is happening (or how I feel about said events). Annnd 4. I just haven't felt very well. Not horrible, just dragging from a chest cold that keeps hanging on. My energy is taking a while to return.

First of all, Jim is doing pretty well. He is drained from the same chest cold I had, but has been plugging along every day. He was in the office half days for 3 days last week and made it to the youth center 3 times. He is frustrated because it takes so much out of him, but he truly enjoys being back at work. Many afternoons he tries to take it easy and rest up for the next day.

Jim is still going to hand therapy once a week. Marcus and Cara went with him the week that they were here, because I was sick. We continue to see progress with his hand, but it's such a slow process. It wears on him to constantly have this challenge, among others. Being his number one cheerleader, I can say I'm thankful that I got to witness two small things this week: 1. He signed a church check request with his right hand. Not perfect, but he did it!!! 2. I caught him sweeping up crumbs and such at the youth center with a broom and long-handled dust pan USING BOTH HANDS! Again, it may not sound like much to you, but this progress is coming from a man who used to have trouble drying off after a shower or dressing himself. Big progress when you look at it from that point of view. (No, I'm not putting these pom poms away. Woot woot!!!)

He has a urology appointment at UCSF next week. They'll do an ultrasound before his appointment to see how many kidney stones babies he's still harboring. We are praying they don't find any more.

The following week is the BIG appointment: Brain MRI and an appointment with his neuro-oncologist at UCSF. I have a love-hate relationship with these appointments. I try really hard to look at things from a positive perspective and have faith for a good report, but I definitely have moments when the "what-ifs" grip me. The waiting is really the hardest part. We count down to these appointments every 3 months to get a good report, only to start all over again. It's great to get wonderful reports of no new growth, but it's maddening to not have full closure. What can we do? There's nothing that we are capable of doing to change the journey we are faced with, so we just keep living life the best we can. Each day we put one foot in front of the other and continue pushing forward.

So, I've updated you on Jim. Now for me . . . I've been struggling a lot the last month. I'm sure many of you have caught on to that from my post last week. I'm ok, but I'm struggling. Life has thrown me many curveballs the last 2 years. Because of these curveballs, I am not the same person I've always been. I'm changed. I'm different. I'm stronger. I'm weaker. I'm exhausted.

Exhausted is a word I feel like I've worn out these last 2 years. I'm tired of using it! It's getting really old. In assessing my situation, I've come to the conclusion that my body has been on massive overload this whole time. Sure, I may look like everything is together, but that's not always the case. When it IS together, it's because I've killed myself to get it to that point. And it's not without consequences. Recently I've had issues with feeling like my adrenaline is kicking in when I'm trying to rest. It only takes one small thing to set me off, then I'm on 100% and can't go back to sleep for a few hours. Other times it's that worked up feeling in the middle of the day, when it makes no sense to be amped up like that. It's like being in emergency mode at all times. It has been necessary for our survival on this journey - advocating for Jim; hospital visits; caring for him and staying alert to his needs at all hours of the day/night; and probably much more than I even realize - but it is catching up to me. I'm trying to find new boundaries for myself to preserve my own health and aid in my exhaustion challenge. My chest cold didn't help this at all.

As for these healthy boundaries, I'm working hard to reorganize my life and take things off my plate that were never my responsibility. I'm taking off hats that aren't mine to wear. One of these hats is the church's bookkeeping job- which was Jim's mom's. I took this job on in May, in hopes of preserving it for her short-term so she could heal from her surgery. Month after month has rolled by, and she hasn't been healthy enough to return. Many have said I should've handed this job over months ago, but I wasn't able to for multiple reasons. The top reason was that it would have taken more time than I had to train someone to take over. Remember, it wasn't until about a month ago that we went from 4-5 therapy appointments each week down to only 1 per week.

I started training someone last week and I'm excited about taking this hat off. I CAN'T WAIT!!! I'm confident she'll do a great job.

Slowly, but surely I've been releasing some of the responsibilities I've covered for Jim's job back to him, assisting where needed but trying not to hover over him or interfere with how he feels led to do his job. It's another balancing act. I want to give him freedom, but I don't want to dump too much on him all at once.

This last week I actually cleaned off the top of my desk at work. I still have a few items straggling that need to be completed, but it's looking much better than it has for the last year and a half. It brings me some much-needed peace to start seeing a little organization again. Once I get a chance, I'll start reorganizing the drawers and files so I can have a clean start. I've been at work almost every weekday for the last 2 weeks, too. I guess that's a good start to a reorganized life; start with my schedule! Haha. (Hey! I'd take a few weeks in the Bahamas to start it off good, but I guess this will do.)

On the home front there are many areas that need reorganization to save time in everyday life. I'm tired of surviving. I want my life streamlined and efficient again. I NEED it. I'm taking on tiny clean-up tasks as time allows and as I am physically able. It's slow progress, but I'll take what I can get at this point.

Along with these challenges, I've been dealing with filing fraudulent charges for Jim's bank card; re-parenting teenagers who need help to reset habits that will not serve them well in life; and still working through the emotions of my husband having brain cancer. Although I know that God is bringing healing to that horrible diagnosis, merely typing that last sentence chokes me up. It's hard to even say it because it makes it more real. This journey is the most difficult thing we've ever encountered in life. We know God will use it for His good, but the pain we have experienced along the way is deep and searing. It is life-changing, to say the least.

I've started this year off with resolve to take all things to God in prayer immediately. Need someone to fill a ministry at church = stop talking about it and pray right there. Looking for specific paperwork that eludes me = stop and pray. Lacking wisdom for parenting = stop and pray for God to give the wisdom and direction I need. I'm not one for New Year's resolutions, but I'm setting this as my new goal. It has worked well so far. I'm so thankful for my faithful Heavenly Father.

If you've read my post to this point, you probably deserve a trip to Disneyland or some other fabulous prize. Unfortunately, I can't provide that for each of you, so I'll just say thanks for caring enough to read every word. This venue gives me a way to work through my feelings. It also helps me feel like I'm not alone. I appreciate each of you for sticking with us, posting encouraging words, and continually praying for us. God is carrying us through. He is faithful.

Expecting a miracle! Any day will do!!!
♥ *Jim and Brenda*

Wednesday, January 18, 2017:
Only have time for a quick update, so I'll copy and paste what I sent to family. We just got home. It was quite a day for traveling. High winds and lots of rain. We narrowly escaped the attack of 2 large tumbleweeds on the way home. We're safe and glad to be out of the storm.

Jim's appointment went well. They did a urinalysis and will call with any results they get that requires antibiotics or other care. He thinks the blood in his urine is because the stones have decided to shift around again. (I hadn't posted about this yet because it started last night. Thankfully, he already had the appointment today.)

The ultrasound shows 5-6 small stones still left, but they look stable. The largest one they saw on the CT from December is gone now. It was close to 7 mm! He thinks that's one of the ones Jim passed on 1/1.

The doctor wants him to come back in a year, unless something comes up before then and we need him.

. . . One last thing: on a humorous note: when I asked the urologist how many stones were left, he said, "It depends on how you count them." When Jim and I got in the car we decided he must use common core math or some new method.

If only kidney stones and hectic holidays were our only challenges to worry about, that would've been somewhat do-able. Sadly, more battles were waiting around the corner. . . .

www.ingramcontent.com/pod-product-compliance
Lightning Source LLC
Chambersburg PA
CBHW071807080526
44589CB00012B/724